BEALE STREET DYNASTY

BEALE STREET DYNASTY

*Sex, Song, and
the Struggle for the
Soul of Memphis*

PRESTON LAUTERBACH

W. W. NORTON & COMPANY
NEW YORK   LONDON

Manufacturing by Courier Westford
Book design by Lovedog Studio
Production managers: Devon Zahn and Ruth Toda
Map treatment by Michael Truncale

ISBN 978-0-393-08257-9

W. W. Norton & Company, Inc., 500 Fifth Avenue, New York, N.Y. 10110
www.wwnorton.com

W. W. Norton & Company Ltd., Castle House, 75/76 Wells Street,
London W1T 3QT

1 2 3 4 5 6 7 8 9 0

To Elise

CONTENTS

PART III
BIRTH OF THE BLUES, 1901–1918

PART IV
THE LID, 1918–1940

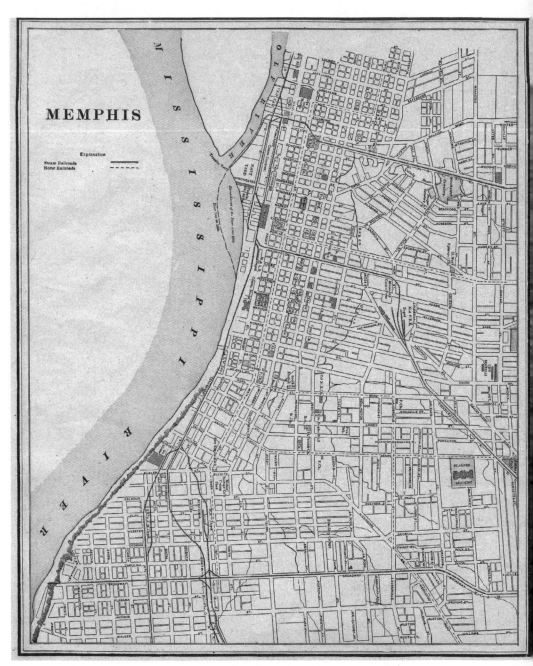

Memphis in 1901.

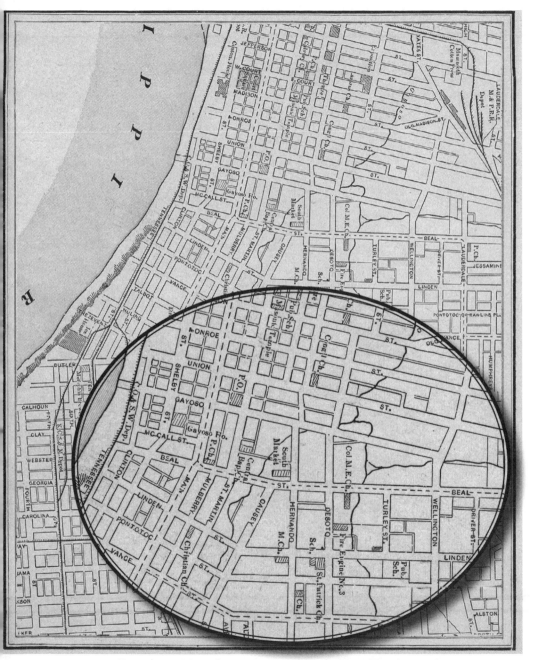

Downtown Memphis, 1901. Inset: Beale Street District.

BEALE STREET DYNASTY

PROLOGUE

JUNE 6, 1862,

DAWN ON THE MISSISSIPPI RIVER

AT MEMPHIS, TENNESSEE

Artillery thunder ricocheted over the river, jolting the crew of the *Victoria*. She was an eight-hundred-ton paddle-wheel steamer, at the moment employed for the cause of the Confederacy as a blockade-runner, shuttling supplies between her home port of Memphis and New Orleans.

Captain and crew gathered on deck to watch the five Yankee gunboats and two ironclad "rams" meet a rebel fleet of eight river steamboats armored haphazardly with scrap metal.

One of the *Victoria*'s cabin boys bore the captain's name and likeness. Robert Church was twenty-three years old. He belonged to his father not only as a son but as a slave. Captain took care of him, though, and Robert had enjoyed as adventurous and free an upbringing as was available to anyone, much less a Negro, in nineteenth-century America. Capt. Charles Church had instilled in his son a degree of personal pride, telling him, "Don't let anyone call you nigger."[1]

River life gave an outlet to Robert's courage and wit and provided him an education unlike anything most slaves could comprehend. He had survived disaster, like the fiery sinking of his father's steamboat the *Bulletin No. 2* in 1855. He studied rich white planters and black-leg gamblers at leisure. He procured their whiskey, attended their card games, and learned their thirsts.

The Mississippi cultivated some of the elite black men of the nineteenth century, and Robert Church came of age with Blanche K. Bruce, a future U.S. senator from Mississippi, and P.B.S. Pinchback, who would become the nation's first African-American governor, serving Louisiana. These leaders grew familiar with the feeling of cash and coin in their pockets, and they would be noted for their craftiness and flash.

Now the gunboats flying Old Glory overtook the rebel ironclads—and presented Robert a dilemma. He could either stay with the *Victoria* and await Federal capture—and possible liberation from slavery—or risk his life swimming to the Confederate shore.

As the story goes—*splash!*[2]

Sloshing through the water, he couldn't have known that he'd safely make it ashore, much less that he would grow there into something the world had never seen, that he would reach a yet-incomprehensible status: the South's first black millionaire.

Even more improbable is *how* he would do it. Like many a great and wealthy man, Robert Church was also compromised. He courageously built a fortune through taking unbelievable personal risks, for while black men across the South were being hanged and burned alive for committing alleged and unproven offenses against white women, Church became the wealthiest black man in the South due in large part to his whorehouses that employed white women.

He built not only a fortune but a civilization around himself.

This is the story of how a slave became an emperor and of the dynasty Robert Church created. Though he founded it on debauchery, he ran his kingdom with sensitivity to virtue. He helped support both Ida B. Wells, as she developed into a radical civil rights journalist, and

W. C. Handy, as he laid the foundation of American popular music. The Church dynasty evolved from a red-light real estate empire into the most powerful black political organization of the early twentieth century.

Beale Street ranks as the dynasty's crowning achievement. Thanks in large part to Robert Church's audacity, vision, and acumen, Beale became the Main Street of Black America, a site of monumental innovations, thrilling promise, and devastating tragedy that wrote the headlines, played the soundtrack, and forged the secret history of an era, unmatched in prowess by any three-block stretch in the land.

Beale was both of America and exceptional. Entertainer Rufus Thomas, a Memphis mainstay from the 1930s to his death in 2001, said, "I told a white fellow . . . If you were black for one Saturday night on Beale Street, you would never want to be white anymore."[3] Sam Phillips, the white record producer who launched the careers of Elvis Presley and Jerry Lee Lewis, first visited the street in the 1930s, when he was sixteen, early in the morning during a pouring rain. "My eyes had to be very big, because I saw everything, from winos to people dressed up fit to kill, young, old, city slickers, and people straight out of the cotton fields, somehow or another you could tell: every damn one of them was glad to be there."[4]

In a climactic struggle, Beale Street also fueled the powers that would destroy Robert Church's legacy. But before Church could build a dynasty, he had to make himself.

PART I

BIRTH OF
A KINGPIN,

1866–1885

*I wonder why they gave it
such a name of old renown;
This dreary, dismal, muddy,
melancholy town.*

—W. H. RUSSELL

Chapter 1

THERE IS
NO YANKEE DOODLE
IN MEMPHIS

A *lone mule* pulled the streetcar down Main. People on foot, on horseback, or in buggies, and hacks and drays of cotton and lumber wore the cobblestones slippery and black. The street shot southward toward the fort. Five solid blocks of brick buildings had lately grown up here, some as high as five stories.

Past Beale Street, Main's cobbles turned to dust, and brick buildings shrank to whitewashed log shanties. The change and its suddenness, in the half-dozen blocks from the heart of town down to South Street, felt like a jump from eastern metropolis to western frontier.

The trouble started down this way.

Blue-coated Negro soldiers from Fort Pickering congregated in the rough-built groceries and makeshift cabins, drinking and firing their pistols on Grady's Hill.

At the last stop before unyielding darkness stood a large rambling frame structure, set on a huge yard with a few small sheds and dwellings scattered around. Here a white woman named Mary Grady ran a Negro dance hall and served drinks—"wine, soda water, brandy peaches, and such as you would find in any little shebang," she would say.[1] Here the disturbances grew louder every night of April 1866. As Gen. George Stoneman, commanding officer at Fort Pickering, the garrison at Memphis, later explained, "These soldiers, inflamed with liquor, coming and going from this house, were in the habit of firing their pistols promiscuously, in all directions, endangering the safety of my command."

Though Memphis had emerged from the Civil War physically intact, forces were converging to make the city a key battleground in the next phase of national conflict. Just over a year after Gen. Lee's surrender, Memphis told the country that reconciliation would be even more vicious and bloody than anyone had feared.

Memphis had sprouted from one of the few sites along the Mississippi River that could accommodate a metropolis. With the Chickasaw Bluffs protecting it from annual flooding—and providing Memphis's distinctive moniker, the Bluff City—its location on the river guaranteed prominence in the national flow of goods to market, as did its proximity to potentially millions of acres of cotton. In 1857 the Memphis-Charleston Railroad had opened the first route from the Mississippi River to the Atlantic Ocean across the South, establishing a route between a large East Coast slave market and the envisioned inland cotton empire. A Confederate triumph might have made Memphis one of the more prominent cities on the continent.

After the war, the city ranked among the three or four largest populations in the former Confederacy. It had fallen into Union control June 6, 1862, following a brief naval conflict on the river. While Federal forces bombarded Richmond and burned Atlanta, Northerners had moved to

Memphis, and by 1866 they were ministering churches, running businesses, practicing law, publishing newspapers, and teaching Negroes, all to the disgust of a local citizenry that had overwhelmingly supported the cause of Southern independence.

Memphis's local conflict mirrored national news. Despite the military triumph of the Union, the president and Congress fought over control of Reconstruction, the controversial government plan to return Confederate states to the United States. The president, a moderate Tennessean named Andrew Johnson, favored leniency toward rebels, while Congress, packed with a "Radical" element of the Republican Party, wanted to keep the South under heavy federal military supervision.

At the heart of the struggle, the two sides grappled over black voting rights. Johnson bitterly opposed Negro suffrage, while Congress vehemently supported it. And wrapped around the Negro suffrage question was that of Negro legal status—*civil rights*, as the issue had come to be known. The fight over these issues came to life on the streets of Memphis in the spring of 1866.

Maj. Gen. George Stoneman, the tall, heavy-eyed West Point graduate who commanded Fort Pickering, had led both infantry and cavalry during the Civil War, though Union commander Joseph Hooker scapegoated him after the spectacular Confederate victory at Chancellorsville. Hooker relieved Stoneman of his duty and sent him to Washington, D.C., reportedly to recover from chronic hemorrhoids. Back in the field with William T. Sherman in Georgia in 1864, Stoneman had been captured and became the highest-ranking Union prisoner of war, completing his peculiarly decorated service. An appointment in June 1865 made Stoneman commander of Tennessee, and he established his headquarters at Memphis. There he presided over fifteen hundred soldiers, both colored troops and white "regulars."

In this sharply divided city, Unionists characterized themselves as "loyal" and believed former rebels—called secesh, short for "secessionist"—guilty of treason. Former rebels generally despised Republicans and anyone who dealt in any helpful way with the black population, had Northern heritage, had served in the Federal army, or professed true loyalty to the Union, referring to them as "abolitionists" or "radicals." Some advocated killing them, destroying their property, and running them out of town. The *Daily Memphis Avalanche*, the city's leading morning newspaper, struck a paranoid and resentful tone, typical of the secesh point of view, in April 1866: "Look at the conduct of the Radicals in Memphis. Most of them are strangers. They come among us and propose to exercise rights which they deny us. They are for negro suffrage . . . for the Civil Rights Bill . . . in a word, for every thing that humiliates and degrades the South."[2]

Tension simmered as patrols of the Negro soldiers from Fort Pickering, aggravated citizens and the local government, all of whom took great offense at armed black men, many of them former slaves from the city, telling them what to do.

While Union commander Stoneman presided over Fort Pickering, a Confederate hero returned home. Before his rise to national notoriety as a rebel cavalry commander, Nathan Bedford Forrest had made his mark on Memphis, helping guide the growing city's destiny. A flesh trader, railroad investor, and politician, Forrest lived the life of a gentleman in a hell-roaring river town, hunting fugitive slaves, seconding a friend in a duel, and pooling his resources with other prominent citizens to relieve the city government of its valuable stock in the Memphis-Charleston Railroad.[3]

In matters of governance, Alderman Forrest flashed the unconventional wit that his battlefield admirers would recognize—on the question of loose dogs, he suggested he knew a Mexican who would lasso the beasts for a dime apiece.[4] On another occasion, he fought to make it easier for slave dealers to do business. He served as mayor pro tem in summer 1859, and citizens turned out en masse for the free ice water and spicy repartee served at council meetings during his tenure.[5]

For all Forrest's accomplishments at war, an atrocity tainted his legacy. On April 12, 1864, his cavalry had attacked Fort Pillow, forty miles north of Memphis. With a typically courageous charge, the rebels had taken the fort, spilling over the walls and through portholes. But as the defeated Union soldiers dropped their weapons and offered surrender,

Forrest's men kept killing. More than one witness would say the rebels shot the defenseless like dogs.

Fort Pillow's Union garrison contained 262 colored troops from the Memphis Battery Light Artillery and the Sixth U.S. Colored Heavy Artillery, all of whom had organized at Fort Pickering in Memphis. Some of the colored troops may have earlier crossed Forrest's auction block in chains. Two hundred colored soldiers were believed to have been killed at Fort Pillow, with the remainder captured. A federal officer who arrived to bury the Union dead observed "bodies with gaping wounds, some bayoneted through the eyes, some with skulls beaten through, others with hideous wounds, as if their bowels had been ripped open with Bowie knives."[6]

After the war Gen. Forrest commented but little on political matters, publicly supporting North-South reconciliation when asked, and he would deny the charge he'd perpetrated a massacre at Fort Pillow. But the truth behind these matters carried far less power than what people believed. To a superstitious, fearful Negro populace, Forrest was the ultimate rebel talisman. The memory of his cavalry struck terror into the hearts of Memphis's ex-slaves. Forrest moved into Gayoso House, the city's finest hotel, near the Freedmen's Bureau, the federal agency charged with protecting the new citizens that he had once bought and sold.[7]

While Forrest himself remained fairly quiet, the Confederate spirit prospered. The June 1865 mayoral election kept Hon. John Park in the office he'd won before the war. Prewar, Park had belonged to the exclusive Democratic Political Association along with Forrest. With his stringy mop of white hair, Park resembled either a frontiersman or a lightning-struck prophet, and his public speaking bore the charm and subtlety of either. His incompetence was never in doubt, for both Confederate and Union commanders had replaced his administration with martial law during their respective wartime occupations of Memphis. Memphians had elected Park, in 1861 and again in 1865, on the stridence of his opposition to Northern culture, especially "Republicanism, abolitionism, free-loveism, atheism, [and] every other abominable ism that strikes at the organization of free society or constitutional govern-ment," as he had put it in his 1861 inaugural address.

Among Mayor Park's first acts, upon reelection on July 12, 1865, was the mass appointment of sixty-eight new policemen, to make a force of 180, all but seventeen of whom had been born in Ireland. Many had served together already in the rebel Second Tennessee Infantry, bet-ter known as the Irish Brigade. Two days after being appointed, Police Chief Ben Garrett warned his new charges against performing their duties while intoxicated. The next day the former Irish Brigade raided one of the first racially integrated businesses in Memphis, perhaps in the whole South: a whorehouse located on Front Street, where they apprehended women and patrons of all shades.

The Memphis police and Negro troops made for two sets of armed, angry men in blue patrolling the streets.

Mayor Park bristled at the federal occupation, declaring time and again that the city could take care of its own affairs and needed no help from the government.

Union General Stoneman observed Old Glory waving in only three places in the city—over his fort, at the Freedmen's Bureau, and outside the office of a Radical Republican newspaper. One of the old Unionists of the town remarked, "Everybody residing in Memphis knows that the flag of our country is not respected here, and the national airs would be hissed in a minute . . . but strike up 'Dixie' and there is a shout, always a shout, and play it for the twentieth time and every time there is a shout. There is no 'Yankee Doodle' . . . in Memphis."[8]

The sum of all secesh nightmares appeared in one tidy piece of leg-islation then being volleyed around Washington, and no words short of *General Grant* sent greater terror through rebel circles than *Civil Rights Bill*. The bill conferred citizenship on anyone except Indians born in the United States, guaranteeing their equal rights, without regard to race, to enjoy protection of the laws, to bring suit, and to make contracts, and it forbade any state law to deny these rights. Its magnitude was lost on no one. The bill, according to the historian Eric Foner, "represented the first attempt to give meaning to the Thirteenth

Amendment [which abolished slavery], to define in legislative terms the essence of freedom."[9]

In early April news came down that President Andrew Johnson had vetoed the Civil Rights Bill. At the same time, word trickled in that Gen. Forrest, off seeing to business on his plantation, had killed a Negro worker, fracturing the man's skull with an ax. Defiance was in the air. A week later, for only the second time in American history to that point, the House and Senate overrode a presidential veto, passing the Civil Rights Bill on April 9, 1866. A local editor opined, "It is like the victories of Pyrhus over the Roman armies—more disastrous to the conqueror than the conquered."[10] Memphis secesh stood poised to make prophecy of his opinion.

Chapter 2

A PROMISCUOUS
RUNNING FIGHT

The day's political ideas mattered little in the street, where concepts such as civil rights had long gone feral.

Negroes from the surrounding country were settling the low land along Bayou Gayoso, a sometimes sluggish, sometimes roaring creek that snaked its way throughout the city, breeding mosquitoes and drowning drunks and children in the dark. The marsh bore settlements called Happy Valley, Rotten Row, and Satan's Promenade, "where the most reckless, dissolute, and depraved characters—male and female—sought abodes of infamy and crime."[1]

In Happy Valley, *civil rights* distilled into its most frightening form—miscegenation. Politicians could squabble endlessly about who got to vote, but in Happy Valley social equality had already taken root.

A Memphis policeman named Dave Roach took up the fight against interracial sex. He picked up little bits of talk on the Happy Valley beat. During the dark hours of the morning on April 17, he learned that a dark-skinned character known as Sweet Charles had holed up in a certain shanty, where, in the delicate phrase of the news, "the doctrine of miscegenation was being practically illustrated."

Roach pushed open the door and found Sweet Charles knotted up in "elegant breakfast trio" with a pair of white women. Sweet Charles slipped away in the ensuing turmoil, but Roach paraded the women to the station house.[2] This episode accounted for but a single incident in a one-man crusade, as Roach smashed brothels and invaded homes where rumor had black men with white women.

As much as Dave Roach became identified with the dreaded *miscegenation*, another man in town had made his name synonymous with the hated Civil Rights Bill.

Since swimming from the Mississippi River to the Memphis shore on the morning of June 6, 1862, Robert Church had plotted to do on dry land as he'd done on the river. As Gen. Robert E. Lee surrendered at Appomattox, young Bob Church had set up shop in Memphis. He intended to open a billiard hall and applied to the county clerk for the appropriate permit, but the clerk refused. Church set up his tables anyway.

In summer 1865 the police visited Memphis's first black-owned pool hall. Arrested and bound over to criminal court, Church went to trial in mid-April 1866. Recent events made the simple case one of heightened legal prominence, a litmus test of the times. Church's attorney howled that the license had been denied Church due to the color of his skin. Under the freshly minted Civil Rights Bill, no law could bar Church from obtaining the license. Whatever reason had prevented the county clerk from granting a Negro a billiard license was out. The rules had changed.[3]

The Church decision represents the earliest documented enforcement of the hated Civil Rights Bill in Tennessee and perhaps anywhere. The dashing young black scion of a prominent Memphis family walked free April 17, 1866, a few hours after Dave Roach rousted Sweet Charles in Happy Valley. The news reached as far as Charleston.[4] Church had taken his first stand for equality, not to access the ballot box or the classroom but to freely promote vice. He would make a life of such brilliant plot twists.

Already a nuisance to the secessionist element, Church now sported a bull's-eye. An editorial in the *Avalanche* the day after his victory read, "The *Avalanche* is the friend of the negro . . . and for his sake we hope he will deport himself in the future in such a way as to retain the sympathy of the community in which he lives . . . but he must be prudent, VERY PRUDENT, or the war of the races commences and the negro is doomed."[5]

On the last day of April, as if in response to the growing tension, Gen. Stoneman called off the unpopular Negro troop patrols. He mustered out scores of black troops, leaving a force of 150 to guard the fort. On Stoneman's part, there was at least some calculation to give Mayor Park, the police, and the city an opportunity to back up their talk of keeping order without federal assistance. Their insistence had grown obnoxious to the general, and perhaps he hoped to give them enough rope with which to hang themselves.

Stoneman followed the discharged troops into the streets outside the fort, where they'd been in the habit of socializing. He heard reports of their boisterousness and investigated. "On the evening of the 30th of April," he later said, "I went about through that locality and discovered the cause (of pistol firing) to be drunken soldiers who attended a dance-house kept by one Mrs. Grady, on Grady's Hill, South Memphis."

On May 1, just over a year after the end of the war, crowds of the recently discharged black soldiers congregated in the warm afternoon sun on South Street, the main thoroughfare of the town's raggedy frontier section. Their pockets full of pay, they tipped into the grog shops and shebangs and wobbled back to the dirt street, singing, cheering Abe Lincoln, and firing their pistols.

A merchant summoned the police, and several officers lingered nearby. Capt. A. W. Allyn came from the fort to see about the fuss but left unimpressed. "Disturbances had been going on perhaps for a week, more or less," he said, "pistol firing and carousing. I discovered it was a disturbance made by the negroes at a dance-house."

At about five that evening, four Memphis police, uniformed in blue with their copper stars plain to see, arrested two colored soldiers on

South Street, toward Main. Witnesses more or less agree that the colored soldiers were drunk, obnoxious, and confrontational, and the police appear to have been well within their rights to break up the festivities. As the police began marching the soldiers east, a throng of colored soldiers and citizens, perhaps as many as a hundred, gathered behind the police, shouting for the officers to halt. The officers proceeded, and reaching the bayou, they shoved the two soldiers across the creaking bridge. The colored citizen and soldier band fired warning shots over the policemen's heads. The cops, still on the bridge, swung around and fired into the crowd. The colored people returned fire—a policeman named Stephens took a shot in the thigh and fell halfway through the bridge.

Though the fracas was near the fort, officers had grown inured to the behavior outside Mary Grady's dance hall. "I heard several shots," Capt. Allyn said, "but I thought the Negroes were, as usual, discharging their pistols in the air."[6] He opted not to send help from Fort Pickering.

Dust clouded, gunpowder burned. One witness described the eruption of "a promiscuous running fight." The two sides locked into hand-to-hand combat. Soldiers smashed policemen with sticks, and a cop landed a severe blow to the back of a Negro's head with a brick.[7] A policeman broke his pistol over a soldier's head, and in trying to detain as many brawlers as possible, cops shouted, "If you move we'll put daylight through you."[8] Blood ran from the Negroes' nostrils and heads. At least three Negroes fell dead during this initial violent outburst, though many others received beatings and bullet wounds.

During an investigation of these events, Memphis police chief Ben Garrett was interviewed about the force. He testified that the mayor appointed the officers without seeking his input. He had to work with whomever the mayor gave him.

The interviewer asked Chief Garrett, "What are the qualifications required to fit a man for policeman?"

"He must be steady, sober, discreet, and an energetic man. He should always know how to read and write," Garrett replied.

"Did a majority of the police of Memphis appointed previous to these riots come up to the requirements which you have mentioned?"

"In every respect they have not."

"Were a majority of the police sober men?"

"They were sober sometimes."[9]

The police scattered, carrying their wounded man to safety. They returned to the corner of South and Causey with reinforcements. Two hundred strong, this posse found the streets empty. What followed looked like all the recent hateful newspaper rhetoric in action, the commencement of the war between the races, the Negro's doom.

A colored lady named Ellen Dilts lived on Causey Street, near the site of the clash between police and soldiers. She had witnessed a few fights in the war years. She and her husband, a Federal soldier, had lived in Vicksburg, Mississippi, which fell under siege in one of the war's bitterest chapters. She knew something was wrong with all the commotion outside. Hundreds of police and colored people filled the neighborhood, hurrying by her door. All the ruddy white men looked to her like devils. "They looked like they were Irish, with kind of red faces," she said. "Some of them, though, appeared delicate." After a storm of gunfire, Negroes she'd never seen took shelter in her home. Asked if she too was scared, she would calmly reply in war-hardened fashion, "No. Nothing ever frightens me. I have been fired at too many times by rebs."[10]

Reports of the fracas echoed through the densely packed little city—its population had doubled during the war and stood at about 50,000—and chaos spread as fast as flame in dry kindling. Malicious misinformation and psychological manipulation would figure significantly into subsequent phases of the disturbance.

Rumor had the colored soldiers forming a battle line outside Fort Pickering. Truthfully, the final black act of aggression had already transpired, and most of the colored troops had returned to the safety of Fort Pickering's walls. Less than an hour after the clash on the bayou bridge, City Recorder John C. Creighton pulled up in his hack at Causey and

Vance (midway between Beale and South streets) and delivered orders: "Kill the last damned one of the nigger race, and burn up the cradle, God damn them. They are very free indeed, but God damn them, we will kill and drive every last one of them from the city."

The crowd erupted in cheers.

With the Negro troop force dispersed, the police mob scattered, fanning out by groups of two to four to eight or ten, mixing officers and citizens. They turned their aggression on whoever was unlucky enough to be black and in their way.

A colored drayman named Jackson Goodell was tending to his sick wife, unaware of the violence. He was carrying a pan to a store on Beale where he wanted to buy some cornmeal for their supper, when two police appeared, revolvers brandished. Goodell didn't like the looks of them and tried to get out of the way; he slipped into a store and out another door, heading away from the cops. They shouted that he was a damned rascal and leaped on him, beating him with their guns, landing fifteen or twenty blows about his head. "Any one of the blows would have killed me," a white onlooker named C. M. Cooley thought. "They knocked him down in the gutter, when someone shot him twice."[11]

A neighbor who attended church with the Goodells hurried to tell Jackson's wife the news. "Sister Lavinia," the woman shrieked, "Jackson is killed."

Lavinia Goodell found her husband in the ditch that served as a gutter between the wood-block pavement and the plank sidewalk on Beale. He groaned, and she hoped there was life enough left in him to save him. She placed her palm against his chest and spoke his name. She held his head and called to her neighbors to help her carry him inside, as three more police entered the street. "Here is a damned nigger," one said. "If he is not dead we will finish him." This frightened her away.

A policeman on horseback arrived, shouting, "Kill them altogether; the God damned niggers ought to be killed, no matter whether the big or the small ones." And so Mrs. Goodell took cover indoors.[12]

Storm clouds crowded out the sun. Panic-stricken black men and women locked up their doors and clasped their shutters as the thunder of gunfire and drunken bellowing approached. It must have sounded, to good biblically minded colored folk, as if the demons of Hell had torn loose.

Meanwhile a group of men broke open the door at Lucy Taylor's house just off South Street. Taylor, having seen the police beat and kill soldiers, had already told her brother, a soldier, to flee. This left her alone taking care of two children, without any protection.

Four whites, at least one in police garb, smashed into her house. She watched, shocked, as they broke through the door and dived through a window. "They done a very bad act," she would say. As two of them searched the house for valuables, one man held a knife to her throat. "I had just had to give up to them," she said. "They said they would kill me if I did not. They put me on the bed and the other men were plundering the house while this man was carrying on." Her two small children slept nearby as her ordeal continued. Finally one of the pillagers put a stop to the rape. "She's not in any situation to be doing that."

When asked what the man had meant, she explained that she was over five months pregnant—"I have been in the family way ever since Christmas."[13]

Gangs raped through the side streets off South. As a lady helplessly watched, a posse descended upon a young married woman next door. "There were as many as three or four men at a time had connexion with her," she would say. "She was laying there by herself. They all had connexion with her in turn around, and then one of them tried to use her mouth."[14] Upon learning this, the victim's husband left her.

In the vicinity of Happy Valley, Officer Dave Roach and three other men ransacked a colored home, and as he led his mob back into the street, he announced, "It is white man's day now."[15]

Sounds and reports of the riot reached Gen. Stoneman at Fort Pickering. His point had been illustrated vividly in blood and fire—Memphis could not protect its people from themselves. Still appropriately deferential to local authority, he sent word to Mayor Park, offering the use of Union soldiers to stifle this disturbance. His messenger, however, found The Honorable "too drunk to talk."

◆ ◆ ◆ ◆

Overnight a spontaneous underground railroad started up among sympathetic white people who risked their lives to conceal their black neighbors. Unionists infiltrated rebel conclaves to intercept plans for the next assault and spread word to the targets to get out. Negro soldiers and Northern preachers and merchants received knocks on the door late at night.[16]

Jackson Goodell's body disappeared during the night. The bodies of dead colored soldiers, though, were left out in full view.[17]

Wednesday morning, May 2, dawned. A physician arrived at his office near the riot epicenter on South Street. "It was just as quiet as on a Sunday," he'd say.[18]

But hope for peace soon died.

Policemen and rabble read the daily papers. "Life has been taken—the result of the incendiary impression of the Radicals upon the feeble and too willing intellect of the negro," bellowed an *Avalanche* editorial. "The Police deserve the very highest credit for the gallant conduct they exhibited in enforcing the majesty of the law when the messengers of death were hurled at them on all sides."

The *Daily Argus* published "The Reign of Bloodshed": "Again the irrespressible [*sic*] conflict of races has broken out in our midst, and again our streets are stained with blood. And this time there can be no mistake about it. The whole blame of this most tragical and bloody riot lies, as usual, with the poor ignorant deluded blacks."

The county sheriff—not to be confused with the city police—sent word during the night for all *good* men to meet him at Henry Fulsom's ironworks to arm up and quell any disturbance. Trouble was, as the sheriff would say, none of *them* showed up. He unwittingly armed a band of rascals and drunks.

By nine o'clock, a massive crowd had gathered, up to a thousand strong, around the corner of Main and South streets. One man said, "I met John Park, the mayor, making an ass of himself and drunk. [He claimed] he was going to straighten out the whole thing, but he did not make any effort to do it." A policeman, drunk, holding high a drawn revolver, passed; "his star shone out very conspicuously" to one observer.[19]

The previous night's wild orgy gave way to a more organized, systematic one. A long line of police and white citizens filed up South Street from Main, two by two over the bayou bridge, and moved toward the colored shanties at the east end of the street.

In hostile array, two men invaded Harriet Armour's house. "This outrage was attended with circumstances of too disgusting and shocking a character to be mentioned except by the most distant allusion," according to one official.[20]

But Armour put it more bluntly. "They came into my room," she said. "Mr. Dunn and another gentleman." They barred her door behind them. "Mr. Dunn had to do with me twice," she said, "and the other gentleman once. And then Mr. Dunn tried to make me suck him. I cried. He asked me what I was crying about, and tried to make me suck it."[21]

As during the night before, the violence spread over an area at least six blocks wide. Some of the attackers had smeared their faces black with soot from the previous night's burnings. Other bands moved about the streets with almost military precision. A constable named O'Hearn, a veteran of the CSA Second Tennessee Infantry, commanded a force of fifteen men. From horseback, he called out, "Number ones, fall in," as if on the march. This group's mission entailed torching "every nigger building, every nigger church, every God damn son of a bitch that taught a nigger."

They wanted Joe Clouston, a mulatto barber who had been the first property owner of color on Beale Street. The horde vowed to get its hands on the editor of the Republican *Memphis Post* and "put him in the middle of the fire." They burned Lincoln Chapel, a newly constructed South Memphis church named for the Negroes' martyr.

A grocer watched a policeman whip a Negro down Beale Street with a riding crop.[22]

Gen. Stoneman and Mayor Park, the two men who might have restored order, instead engaged in a frivolous correspondence, rife with posturing and politics. After nearly a year of marching troops through

the Memphis streets, ostensibly to keep peace, Stoneman suddenly
wanted the city to protect its own citizens. Park, of course, insisted that
he could keep order in his city.

The general, with troops and guns at his disposal, had the power to
stop the riot at any time. He certainly had a front-row seat to the fight.
He had not previously consulted Mayor Park about when and where
to send soldiers on patrol, and he had no legal obligation to Park. The
general had full authority over his command and could have at least
endeavored to control the situation exploding in the streets.

His motive for inaction became clear in the riot aftermath when
he wrote, "I do not believe the perpetrators of the outrages during the
Memphis riots will ever be punished unless the strong arm of the federal government is made use of for that purpose."[23]

A congressional committee that would travel to Memphis and investigate the riot arrived at a similar conclusion: "The riots and massacres
of Memphis are only a specimen of what would take place throughout
the entire South, should the government fail to afford adequate military
protection."

For the Radical cause, Memphis provided the perfect test case of
an unsupervised South. Plenty of other motives figured into Radical
outcry for a federal occupation of Dixie. Gen. Stoneman had substantial
reason—a postwar military downsizing, already under way—to believe
his job depended on Radical Reconstruction. Radical congressmen's
political careers certainly depended on it. Memphis could prove to
the country that the South *needed* Radical Reconstruction to prevent
bloody anarchy.

A conspiracy among enemies kept the riot going. Mayor Park allowed
his police to punish Negroes and Yankees, while Gen. Stoneman was
seemingly willing to sacrifice lives and property to prove the need for
Federal occupation of the former Confederacy.

Officer David Roach was heard again declaring, "This is white man's
day!" As the night and the rain fell, he and his group beat and burned
along De Soto Street, past Beale Street to Gayoso Avenue. They found
Bob Church, victor of the recent civil rights case, at his saloon.

Church had dark straight hair, bear-greased and parted, intense brown eyes, and beige skin. Nothing about him betrayed African heritage. Roach ordered Church to go inside, and as Church closed up his saloon, a dozen shots roared. A hot pain burned into his neck like a hornet sting. He felt the sensation of a stone crashing into his head, and his sight went dark.

The policemen headed straight for the barrels. They gulped Church's whiskey, and when they were through, they ran the rest out onto the floor. They dismantled his controversial billiard tables. They went for the cigar counter and the till. They emptied the till and puffed cigars as they left Church to bleed away.

They put the torch to Church's saloon, as a neighbor named Mary Jordan looked on. "I was very much alarmed," she said, "as it was so near. My husband was just dead and buried and I had a sick child in my arms, and they had begun shooting at the colored people."

She gathered her family in their house. "There was my little babe, seven months old, my little girl, eight years old, and my eldest daughter, about sixteen. We were all in there when it was set on fire. They would not let us out until the house was all in flames. . . . I told my children to follow me. My daughter said, 'mother you will be shot.' I said, 'better shot than burned.' . . . I took up my shoes, but I was so scared I could not put them on."

Barefoot, she fled. "When I was running away with my babe a man put a pistol to my breast, and, said he, 'What are you doing?' I said, 'Trying to save my babe.' 'Sit down,' said he, and I sat down and they did not trouble me anymore."

Rain fell, "and my babe got wet," said Mary Jordan, "and it afterwards died."[24]

Mobs tore the delicate social fabric of black Memphis. Back over off South Street, a band of at least a dozen men, citizens and cops, set a colored schoolhouse on fire. Next door stood the home of an industrious old colored man named Adam Lock, who'd hand-built a number of homes in the neighborhood—"snug little buildings there, about 12x13," said Lock. With fire eight or ten feet away, he struggled to save his house. "I had to knock off that side of my house," he said, "and the women drew water and turned on it till the fire got too hot for them to stand it." His son and some white neighbors climbed the roof to douse the threatening flames while he moved his belongings into the yard. "There were four men on top of my house," he said. "The roof was burnt pretty well but I saved my house that night." Still, he kept his things tied in blankets in case he needed to evacuate.[25]

As the inferno spread, a bright sixteen-year-old named Rachel Hatcher rushed to the burning home of a neighbor to help. She emerged from the fiery shanty to see a mob of white men surrounding her with revolvers pointed. She begged them to let her leave, but a neighborhood grocer, visibly intoxicated and enraged, said, "No, if you don't go back I will blow your damned brains out." Rachel made her break, and the whole crowd fired their pistols.

Her mother had been side by side with Rachel, trying to help save the neighborhood. One second they were together; the next, Rachel's mother saw her child lying dead. In shock, Rachel's mother fled. Their neighbor Adam Lock watched Rachel in horror. "The fire," he said, "first caught a white handkerchief she had round her face, then her clothes caught on fire, but she never moved."[26]

One of Rachel's killers masqueraded about in her hoopskirt.[27]

"She was about the best scholar they had in the school," Rachel's classmate remarked.[28]

A newspaper report circulating up north would describe "the carnival of blood and fire continued the whole night. The sky was continually lit up, sometimes by one, and again by four or five fires in different parts of the city at a time. Crowds of armed rioters were moving up and down the streets, firing, shooting, and threatening negroes and Union men."[29]

One such crowd reached the little shebang on Grady's Hill, where drunken Negro soldiers had lately enlivened the nights with pistol fire. The house stood on Hernando Street, off South. Mary Grady and her husband associated freely with Negroes, renting out rooms to colored boarders, in addition to running the dance hall and refreshment stand that catered to freedmen.

Mary was resting in a front room late that night, when she heard a knock and a rummaging and saw a crowd of men break down her door. They pointed guns and commanded, "Halt!"

"I was lying down," she would recall, "and said, 'I am halted.'"

A member of the posse coming through the door said, "Here is that nigger resort." Another said to Mary, "You keep a nigger ballroom and I am going to kill you."

Instead they searched the house, finding her cash stored in a trunk and a black woman in a bed. "They felt of her and wanted to get in bed with her," Mary would explain. "She told them they would have to kill her before they got into bed with her."

And so the rampage petered out right where some folks had placed the start of the trouble. As Thursday, May 3, dawned, a memo from Gen. Stoneman circulated among the city leadership: "Gentlemen: Circumstances compel the undersigned to interfere with civil affairs in the city of Memphis. It is forbidden for any person, without the authority from these headquarters, to assemble together any posse, armed or unarmed, white or colored."[30]

With that, the general sent his regulars into the street and snuffed out the Memphis riot.

In the days after riot, an anonymous communiqué reached several teachers of colored students: "You will please to notice that we have determined to rid our community of negro fanatics and philanthropic teachers of our former slaves. You are one of that number, and it will be well for you if you are absent from the city by the 1st of June. Consult your safety."[31]

Though the riot had begun out of a long-simmering dispute between the police and colored soldiers, it quickly devolved into a widespread attack on all colored citizens, resembling an attempt to destroy everything black residents had built in their first year of freedom. Negroes had proven industrious and, by their accounts, had toiled at blacksmithing, carpentry, shoemaking, brewing, and dray driving—good, honest trades—to save up hundreds in paper dollars and silver money. "We lost a wardrobe, a bureau, and a trunk of clothes, a washstand, a carpet on my floor, and a great deal of clothing," Mary Wardlaw testified. She and her husband had been left without a way to earn their acquisitions back: "They even burned up the old man's ploughing gear and harness."[32]

A man who lost a pair of two-hundred-pound hogs, twenty chickens, and "right smart of garden stuff" was asked if he'd ever taken aid from the Freedmen's Bureau. "No . . . I always depended on myself," he replied. He said he hadn't had any difficulty with anyone else—"Never, since I have been a man."[33] Austin Cotton, who'd been beaten on Beale Street, declared, "If you can bring a colored man or a white man that will say that I have spoken a cross word in eight years, you may take me out and hang me today."[34]

The riot victims had built roughhewn cabins, like true American frontiersmen, made friends with their neighbors, joined newly organized churches, and sent their children to the newly constructed schools.

Police and mobs killed forty-six colored people, and two white men perished during the rioting. Five rapes and a hundred robberies were reported, while ninety-one houses and sixteen schools and churches were burned.

Three U.S. congressmen—Radicals Elihu Washburn and J. M. Broomall and conservative George S. Shanklin—arrived on May 22, three weeks after the riot, to conduct an investigation. They interviewed hundreds of witnesses, some black victims, some white political and business leaders, men with Union sympathy and some rebels, who filed into a suite at the Gayoso House.

After a week of interviews, an unusual-looking fellow approached the investigators. He could have been an Indian or a German for all anyone could see. Washburn, the committee chair, asked him, "How much of a colored man are you?"

Bob Church said, "I do not know—very little. My father is a white man. My mother is as white as I am. Captain Church is my father. . . . My father owned my mother."

Washburn asked, "Were you a slave?"

"Yes sir, but my father always gave me everything I wanted, although he does not openly recognize me."[35]

Church had provoked the mob's hatred with his invocation of the Civil Rights Bill but had survived its worst. Though the rioters had failed to kill him, their marks would stay with him. For the rest of his life, he would suffer debilitating headaches from a bullet hole in his skull. Whatever sense of equality he had won in court two weeks earlier only carried so far.

For many former slaves, the riot killed faith in the army, in the Freedmen's Bureau, and in the federal government. But it also led to a rebirth. Since much of what they had built around Fort Pickering burned, they abandoned it. They circled their wagons, tightening their geography and concentrating their homes and institutions close together. They would build communities around themselves rather than in anyone else's protection. They would gravitate to their own prominent citizens. They would gravitate to Bob Church.

Chapter 3

A FRIGHTFUL STATE OF MORAL DARKNESS

Bob Church had the money, the looks, and the motive to leave Memphis, but he stayed anyway. He could have slipped into the white world, where his name and face were unknown. But leaving would have run against the nature of a man whose daughter would claim, "If it ever has been true of a human being that he knew no fear, it can be said of Robert Reed Church."[1] The riot had seared into Church a deep sense of determination. He stayed in business right where Officer Dave Roach had shot him on the evening of May 2, 1866, in his saloon on De Soto Street. There, "between Union and Beal," a reporter noted a few months after the riot, "may be well termed the negro portion of our city."

Gen. Stoneman's reluctant use of federal troops from Fort Pickering to stop the riot, to protect the black citizens under fire, had cut the cord between burgeoning black Memphis and the fort and relocated the "negro portion of our city" six blocks north and straight up Bayou Gayoso to the area around Beale (then Beal) Street. The neighborhood mimicked Church's defiant posture.

"The colored population seem to consider that part of town their own," the reporter noted, "where they can do and say what they please."

And there they were said to engage in dangerous behavior: "On Sundays particularly, they strut around that locality in such an offensive manner that white ladies are compelled to make a detour to avoid being insulted by the groups of idlers who throng the sidewalks, and loaf on the corners."[2]

On a Sunday evening, February 3, 1867, Officer J. W. Sheffield of the metropolitan police patrolled down the plank sidewalk of cold, rutted De Soto Street and encountered just such a group of loafers at the corner of Gayoso, congregating around the city's most visible colored citizen. They refused the officer's order to disperse, not so much defiantly as indifferently.

The policeman grabbed Bob Church. As the story went, Church cursed Sheffield, pulled his derringer, and fired a warning shot over the cop. Sheffield pulled his own pistol and smashed the handle down on Church's head, then dragged a stunned Church to the station house.

Newspapers outside Memphis picked up the story and ran with it. They sensationalized it, even up north, describing Church as a "notorious negro."[3] In one version, his warning shot became a wounded policeman. Never mind that when Church went to trial, facing a charge of assault with intent to kill, the jury acquitted him, and the judge charged the policeman with perjury. Another paper wrote of the incident:

We have frequently written of the annoyance to peaceably disposed citizens of the various negro beer gardens in the heart of the city, where the worst passions of the freedmen are excited, and they riot in disgusting debauchery. At one of these places kept by Bob Church, near the corner of Desoto and Gayoso streets, an affray took place . . . which will probably have a tragic termination. . . . We hope the police will break up all these places in the city. We have no objection to the negroes dancing and making as much noise as possible, and even having a little fight among themselves, providing it is outside of town, where decent people will not be annoyed and kept awake half the night.[4]

A police reporter later noted, of Church's appearance on the witness stand to face a gambling charge, "Bob has been before the courts so often that he knows pretty well how to evade the dangerous points."[5]

◆   ◆   ◆   ◆

Less than twenty years later, Church had undergone a complete transformation—at least as far as the public could see. Upon the news of his second marriage, on January 1, 1885, the *Avalanche*, a publication that had fanned the riotous flames of 1866, noted, "The groom is the wealthiest of our colored citizens and has always given liberally to any enterprise for the benefit of the city. In business his word has ever been as good as his bond."

The *Memphis Daily Appeal* called him "honest and punctilious in the observance of his obligations. By energy and prompt attention to business he has shown to his race what possibilities are in store for them, as he has accumulated a fortune of nearly $100,000, and lives in luxurious ease, respected by all."

What brought about such a change of sentiment? The answer is tangled up with the story of Church's fortune, how he built it, protected it, and used it. He was inextricably a man of his city. What shaped Memphis, after the war and the riot, shaped Church. He distilled all the odd, disparate ingredients that made the city, and together they grew.

Every Sunday, Church and his daughter Mollie, born in 1863, climbed into a carriage to go visit her grandfather, a white magnate now retired from the river and enmeshed in local matters of the steepest political and economic consequence. "Captain Church always welcomed me cordially to his beautiful home," she recalled, "would pat me on the head affectionately, and usually filled my little arms with fruit and flowers when I left."[6]

As Mollie grew up, her father used these carriage rides to impart little pieces of personal history. Bob Church was a passionate man, and she wondered about his capacities for both tenderness and violence. He looked at her, gestured toward the captain's home, and said, "He taught me to defend myself, and urged me never to be a coward." Indeed, in troubled times, she heard the captain tell her father, "If anybody strikes you, hit him back, and I'll stand by you."[7]

Church's transformation from notorious Negro to race leader living in luxurious ease, respected by all, owed nothing to him knowing his proper place. His public persona was daring, flashy, and violent, qualities all on display in one memorable instance, when he rode a gaudily carved and gilded sleigh he'd purchased up north onto the streets of Memphis. His friends laughed at the idea of keeping such a vehicle where it seldom snowed. Then came one wintry day, as Mollie later recalled:

My father drove up and down Main Street in his beautiful sleigh several times. It was drawn by a horse that was a decidedly high stepper. People were enjoying the unusual fall of snow immensely and were throwing snowballs at each other in the street with great glee. As Father drove . . . a shower of snowballs struck him. At first he took it good-naturedly and laughed with the crowd, although they hurt him and frightened his horse. He soon discovered that the innocent-looking snowballs were stones and rocks covered with snow. . . . After he had been pelted with these missiles several times, a large rock was hurled at him and struck him in the face. Then he pulled out a revolver and shot into the crowd of men who had injured him.[8]

Bob Church's mother had died when he was a boy. According to family lore, she had been a Malaysian princess, though in reality she had lived as Capt. Church's slave and concubine. Not only did mores permit white men to bed black women, but white society justified these affairs for mixing white blood into the supposedly lazy, childlike colored disposition. White men were doing their part to uplift the Negro.

Bob Church represented the socially acceptable outcome of miscegenation, but another character prominent in the riot played it the wrong
way.

Back during the tumultuous months of 1866, Mary Grady, a white
woman, had run the enterprise—variously described as a shebang, a
dance house, "a nigger resort," and "a nigger ballroom"—that received
official blame for generating much gunfire and eliciting much acrimony
in the days leading up to the riot. She returned to public scrutiny two
years later in an affair that played on white fears about racial mingling.
On Wednesday, August 12, 1868, she shot a colored girl named Isabella
Walton in the head.

Mary Grady's husband, who installed pavement around the city,
reliably left home every morning. In his absence, a Negro hack driver
named Jim Rucker visited Mary. As a detective investigating the shooting would tell a reporter, these visits occurred frequently, until the
neighborhood opinion found the black man and the white woman guilty
of improper intimacy. "Suspicion became a certainty, the guilty couple,
indeed, taking no pains to conceal the infamous affair," the reporter
explained.

When Rucker suddenly ceased calling on Mary, she became curious
and dismayed and sought supernatural assistance. That August morning she went to an old African who lived in her neighborhood. This man
was "looked upon and reverenced by the negroes as a *Voudoo* or *Fetish*,"
noted the reporter, with a heavy dusting of italics. "He told her that the
negro girl Isabella Walton had *conjured* Rucker, and that the *conjure*
was too strong for him to break immediately; he, however, undertook
the job, and went to work to collect the material for the *hoodooing*." The
obi man gathered herbs for a *grigris* to break the spell on Rucker.

Meanwhile Mrs. Grady went after the girl. She armed herself with
a delicate Smith & Wesson cartridge pistol and ambushed Isabella. In
daylight on the street, she shot Isabella in the head. Isabella dropped to
the ground. Mary dropped the pistol and ran. [9]

Mary Grady disappeared for two days, until the police apprehended
her and took her before the judge. Grady's victim, young Isabella, sat at

the witness stand with her head wrapped. She unraveled the bandage to show the severity of her wounds and, to the delight of the courtroom, revealed that the bullet burned her hair down to the scalp in one conspicuous spot. No real harm to the victim meant no real punishment for the perpetrator. Even Rucker, the Othello figure, facing a charge of accessory to the shooting, had his case dismissed.[10]

The white fascination with voodoo revealed and recorded the presence of African Negroes in the city—"Congoes," as they were called. The increasing popularity of the practice became associated with a return to black roots. "Before the war," a reporter noted, "owners of slaves found it to their interest to counteract and put down the teachings of the 'obi-men'—using, frequently, severe measures to accomplish their end—but the removal of the master's restraint has been followed by a relapse into a barbarism of superstition." Voodoo implements became markers of stereotype: "every 'coon' in the land will have a 'hoodo-bag' strung around his neck, and will consult his 'Obi-man' before undertaking even the blacking of a pair of boots."[11]

The magical methods and modes circulated widely, as another reporter explained.

The practicers of the art, who are always native Africans, are called hoodoo men or women, and are held in great dread by the negroes, who apply to them for the cure of diseases, to obtain revenge for injuries, and to discover and punish their enemies. The mode of operations is to prepare a fetich, which being placed near or in the dwelling of the person to be worked upon (under the doorstep, or in any snug portion of the furniture) is supposed to produce the most dire and terrible effects upon the victim, both physically and mentally.

Among the materials used for the fetich are feathers of various colors, blood, dog's and cat's teeth, clay from graves, egg-shells, beads, and broken bits of glass. The clay is made into a ball with hair and rags, bound with twine, with feathers, human, alligators' or dogs' teeth, so arranged as to make the whole bear a resemblance to an animal of some sort.[12]

Depravity in Negroes manifested in a leather bag around the neck or a white woman in bed. Papers fixated on black man–white woman unions while expressing regret for having to devote its columns to such matters. Their descriptions of the female party often exceeded normal editorial constraint: "twenty years old, of good figure, sallow complected, but possessed of regular and rather pleasing features." This particular white girl had been orphaned, left to an impoverished aunt in Mississippi. Verging on starvation in 1865 (at age fifteen), she received the proposal from a Negro baker, "very black" in skin tone, and she accepted. Relocating to Memphis, the pair became first the object of gossip and next of a police raid; but when they showed the court a legal license of marriage, their case had to be discharged. "This, we believe," wrote an *Appeal* man in June 1870, "is the first time in a Memphis court that marriage between the races has been recognized. The story of the woman shows the frightful state of moral darkness and misery in which the war left a class of the white population of the South."[13]

◆ ◆ ◆ ◆

Bob Church mixed too, but he mixed smart. He left white women alone and befriended white men. He kept one foot in the drawing room of his rich white father's home, and one foot in Happy Valley. Others border-hopped between these worlds, but only Church had credibility in both.

The founders of Memphis, back in 1819, had included the adventurer James Winchester and the future president Andrew Jackson, along with a lawyer named John Overton. The latter, being more versed in legal legerdemain, had come out controlling much of the city proper. After the Civil War, John Overton Jr. still had much of his family's chunk of town.

Overton's grandfather and father had owned Memphis while scarcely setting foot in it. John Jr. would do things differently. During the war, he had ridden with Gen. Forrest and his rebels. He had been present at the Fort Pillow massacre, and he had surrendered with Forrest in May

1865. Overton relocated to Memphis after the war and took up the real estate business, leasing and selling pieces of his duchy. By 1870, not yet thirty, he was becoming the city's most powerful figure.

That year the Memphis police commissioners divined a steadily flowing revenue stream: they licensed houses of prostitution and gambling parlors. The city took one hundred dollars annually per whorehouse into the treasury and issued a document bearing the mayor's signature to each licensed operator. By spring, fifteen houses of ill fame were contributing to the city coffers. Prostitution had gained such legitimacy that numerous females stated their occupation as "bawd" in that year's census.

Some elected officials, however, like John Hallum, objected to the practice. "The city," said Hallum, in a meeting of aldermen and councilmen, "through the actions of its police board, participates in the wages of sin and crime, and thus becomes a *particeps crimins* to the deeds of the evildoer. The spirit of temperance and the voice of divine law unite in stating 'Lead us not into temptation.'"

The council president rebutted, "The gentleman says lead us not into temptation, but I never come downtown at night, and I never go into a drinking place. I do not visit the places he referred to, so that he does not require to say to me, Lead *us* not into temptation."[14]

The gallery roared with laughter, and at that moment one of the great, defining customs of Memphis, Tennessee, was born. The city would continue to sanction and regulate houses of prostitution until 1940.

Keno parlors paid five hundred dollars a year for their privilege.* Whorehouses interspersed themselves among polite residences, the disorderly living beside the orderly. Members of the latter group complained to the police commissioners, the board of aldermen, and the common council, but these bodies merely passed the complaints off to one another without ever ruling decisively.

---

*Keno was bingo for money. Players purchased number cards, and the first to record five numbers on his card in a row won the accumulated money from every card in the game, minus a percentage to the game's host.

Most brothels featured no more than five courtesans, but the renowned Mansion on Gayoso Street set the standard for luxurious hospitality. Second Street had a number of bawdy houses plus two music halls, the Parlor and the Metropolitan. The latter hosted the Memphis debut of the debauched dance known as the can-can, with the celebrated Aline Le Favre in the lead. "Several members of the moral police force appeared on the scene and captured the festive and versatile Aline and her attendant coryphées" upon her March 5, 1870, performance. The Metropolitan's proprietor obtained an injunction in municipal court to restrain police from interfering with his show.

So Gayoso and Second streets met at a prime cut of tenderloin real estate, parallel to Main, three blocks east of the river, three blocks south of the very heart of town. Two blocks north sat some of the more fashionable businesses and residences in the city. Beale Street, one block south, showed signs of becoming a Main Street for freedmen.

As merriment reigned, the handsome mulatto with the bullet hole in his head rented a two-story brick building on the corner, opening his new business in September 1870.

Doors on both streets led inside, and a discreet opening allowed entrance "without being seen by news or scandal mongers," an early visitor reported.[15] The first floor held an elegant bar supplied with choice wines, liquors, and cigars. The next room held a lavishly furnished billiard parlor. The *Appeal* noted, just as Church took lease of his new place, "It is the fashion now-a-days with newspaper reporters (and it has been accepted by most people as proper and right) to regard base ball as the 'National' game of the United States. We think billiards entitled to be so dubbed."[16] White Memphis's billiard palaces were some of the more wholesome resorts in the city, and now black Memphis had its version—with a second-floor oyster bar, no less.

A barbershop operated in a side room, with a door opening onto Gayoso Street. A hack stand was set up on the Second Street side, a hub for all colored taxi, delivery, and courier business. The hackmen rinsed off their wagons between runs and kept the sidewalk and street outside the saloon wet. Church employed a watermelon man to sell

fruit to passersby, and the slow call, sustained from thin to deafening, carried over the street din—"Waaaaaatermelon. Coooold, sweet,
Waaaaatermelon"—all to the chagrin of Church's many polite, white
neighbors.

The gold-leafed signs above the building's entries said, "R. R.
Church," but the deed displayed the name John Overton Jr.

Chapter 4

BIRTH OF A KINGPIN

Nathan Bedford Forrest, sitting in a train as it rolled through flat West Tennessee, cast his gray eye over abandoned farmlands. Asked where energetic laborers could be found to work these fallow fields, he said:

> Get them from Africa. If you put them in squads of ten, with one experienced leader in each squad, they will soon revive our country. I want Northern men to come in here, and would protect any man who comes to build up the country with my life, but they won't come. Europeans won't come. I say, let's get Africans. By pursuing a liberal policy to them we can benefit them and they us. The prisoners taken in war over there can all be turned over to us, and emigrate and be freedmen here.

He had already imported one such shipment. "They were very fond of grasshoppers and bugs, and I taught them to eat cooked meat, and they were as good niggers as ever I had."[1]

Behind his publicly professed "liberal policy" toward Negroes,

Gen. Forrest had joined a new clandestine organization that vowed to uphold the society of the Old South. This brotherhood, the Knights of the Ku Klux, wielded terror against freedmen. The Klux power of intimidation ran contiguous to the evil magic conjured in Negro minds by the term *Forrest's Cavalry*—apocalyptic knights on horseback. Forrest, Confederate talisman, was good for the hoodoo business.

Despite his more deliberate efforts, Forrest had established an important center of black freedom—in 1859, as Memphis's finance commissioner, he had located the city market on Beale Street at the corner of Hernando. The marketplace had immediately become the hub of black social life during slavery. Fiddlers drew crowds, calling out dance figures, and house servants on errands gossiped in the shade below the canvas tent's awnings. Those corners at Beale and Hernando would form a nexus of black culture and power for the ensuing century, a location unlike anyplace else in the world. Forrest had unwittingly placed the cornerstone for one of the outstanding black communities in the country.

That the foot of Beale Street soaked in the river determined its identity more than any other factor. In this town dominated by cotton, the free black population would provide the industry's labor just as slaves had in 1860—black hands picked cotton and drove drays that carried sacks laden with white gold from the cobblestone river landing inland to brokerage houses and gins.

The key figure in the new black Memphis economy was the roustabout. These muscular men carried thousand-pound bales of cotton, packed in enormous blocks or cylinders like hay, down steamboat gangplanks to the waiting drays and wagons. Steamboat lines paid rousters well. They were the most prosperous and yet least rooted black workers in the cotton economy. Living on riverboats, they seem not to have been real family men. Because they carried cash and spent it fast, Beale Street got accustomed to accepting black dollars. The roustabouts sauntered up from the cobblestone landing, their britches rolled to the knee and metal cotton hooks shining from their belts.

The growing city's culture and character followed the river. Every steamer unloaded immigrants. Colored people flocked up the muddy roads from Mississippi; some crossed over the river from Arkansas. In the Beale district, whites, mulattoes, and blacks lived side by side by side, sometimes within the same building. They mixed so quickly on and around the street, no one had time to make rules about who could go where or what they could do. Beale Street itself, while undoubtedly becoming the Negro hub of the city, was heavily white residential, running the gamut from the sailors' rooming house at number one Beale to the fine homes of the Topp and Phelan families some seven or so blocks up.

International variety was the only rule among white citizens interspersed between. They hailed not from ol' Virginia or South Carolina but from Poland, Hungary, Switzerland, Norway, Italy, France, and every German state—Bavaria, Hanover, Hessen, Prussia, and Württemberg. The British Isles sent numerous representatives, as did the West Indies and China. Whatever ideas about the Negro percolated on this street, they didn't come straight from the Old South slave powers. Europeans launched every type of business—blacksmiths, gunsmiths, cafés, confectioners, druggists, dry goods, grocers, saloons, seamstresses, milliners, shoemakers, tailors, and laundries. Beale Street's international flavor undoubtedly appealed to Negroes, who wouldn't have to patronize businesses of rebels or race rioters here.

By war's end, the street already had some black history, being home to the city's first property owner of color. Joe Clouston had bought a Beale parcel in 1857 and erected an impressive building that included his home, a grocery, and a barbershop. After the war, other important Negro institutions found homes in the neighborhood: the Freedmen's Bureau set up on Second between Beale and Gayoso, the Freedmen Bank was established on Beale right around the corner, and the mother church of Memphis Negroes, First Baptist, stood on Beale two blocks from the bureau. By the time of the 1866 riot, Beale had everything a freedman could need, from work to fashionable grooming and spiritual sustenance.

The Beale Street Baptist Church, in time, housed the largest colored congregation in the state. Its architectural splendor created pride among the humble strivers, who saw it as concrete testimony to the collective will and resources of a focused black community. Another two blocks east, the Le Moyne Normal Institute educated Beale children years before the public school system opened to Negroes. Though Beale Street still looked like an ill-developed country road, community cornerstones were laid by 1870.

The first notable musician in residence on Beale Street had arrived by 1869. He seems an unlikely, even ridiculous figure, a bespectacled Prussian named Herman Arnold. His reason for settling on Beale is unknown, and his rigid, martial approach to music seems incompatible with the Beale Street spirit. He might even appear counteractive to the street's history, an anomaly—*on* the street but not *of* the street. Yet he played a crucial role.[2]

Born in 1837, Arnold played cornet and led a brass band. By the time of his arrival on Beale Street, he had made an indelible mark on Southern music history. Back in 1861, while living in Montgomery, Alabama, he had served as musical director for Jefferson Davis's inauguration as president of the Confederate States of America. For the occasion, Arnold orchestrated and committed to paper, perhaps for the first time, the popular minstrel air that would serve as that ill-fated country's national anthem, "Dixie."

Herman Arnold taught music in his Beale Street offices. A few doors down a relative named Frank Arnold opened his studio. Frank taught violin by day and led the orchestra at an opera house by night.

The earliest prominent musician of color on Beale was Wesley Duke (aka West Dukes). Born in Mississippi around 1830, his master had taught him violin and transported him to entertain white plantation dances. Duke trafficked in reels, jigs, and breakdowns. Purportedly, he could read music before he could read or write his name. His audiences danced quadrilles and the Dan Tucker, as Duke's figure caller dictated. Duke lived within a few doors of the Prussian musicians and performed regularly for walk-up Negro crowds at Nathan Bedford Forrest's creation, the Beale Street Market House, which stood within a block. The cry of the violin and the romp of the cornet filled the air, giving Beale a sound of its own.

◆   ◆   ◆   ◆

Memphis became the region's hotbed of black political activism, even as the city's Confederate spirit grew. It was a strange but typically Memphis contrast. Ex-president Jefferson Davis arrived in 1869 to head an insurance company. He would call the city home for the next seven years, but he was a political nonentity. The same year President Davis relocated to the Bluff, a colored barkeep named Ed Shaw defeated a white contestant for county commissioner. Shaw belonged to a Radical Republican cadre stationed more or less officially at Bob Church's saloon. The *junta negra* helped elect Joe Clouston Jr., son of Beale Street's first black property owner, to the board of aldermen.

Church threw his weight into national politics as well. He helped his old friend from the riverboats, Blanche K. Bruce, become U.S. senator from Mississippi. A century before the civil rights movement brought activists who encouraged black Mississippians to vote, Ed Shaw courageously ventured below the state line to electioneer for Bruce's successful run. Black power, nineteenth-century style, convened at Bob Church's billiard hall.

Local papers remained strongly secessionist and riot-traumatized. They mocked and slandered colored riot standouts. In August 1876 the *Evening Ledger* went after Francis "Crutchy" Thompson, a crippled hoodoo woman who'd testified before Congress that she was raped during the riot—"The Medical Committee . . . after a thorough examination, reported that Francis Thompson was a man in every respect, and had about as much resemblance to a woman as the Egyptian Sphinx had to a mosquito." Bob Church's saloons saw political rows too numerous to catalog. If he completed any good deeds, they escaped wider notice. His reputation instead clung to violence, as he seemed constantly at the center of every Negro shooting affray, cutting incident, and brass knuckle assault from 1866 to 1876. The *Daily Appeal* reported of Friday night, September 17, 1869, "There was a grand ball at Bob Church's saloon . . . at which there were several tree fights, and which made the neighborhood howl for a while."[3]

He survived several attempts on his life, thanks to primitive firearms and impaired marksmen.

> Ed. Crawford . . . armed with a double-barreled shotgun, [appeared at Church's saloon] and while Bob's back was turned, raised the gun to annihilate him, but both caps snapped, and away went Crawford full tilt down Gayoso street. Crawford then went to prime the gun and while pricking the powder in the tubes the thing went off and so did Crawford—with a policeman for shooting in the corporation.[4]

Church and friends were mocked as *de 'siety*: "fancy negro gamblers, cappers, and thieves" impersonating refined white mannerism.

After a fatal shooting occurred August 2, 1876, in the vicinity of Church's saloon, the secessionist *Ledger* lumped Church and his place of business—"The Headquarters of the Infamous Gang"—in with the killer, a man named Sam Bizzell.

> On the southeast corner of Gayoso and Second streets a two story brick building can be seen bearing the sign, "Church's Billiard Hall." The building is used for a bar, billiard hall, gambling hell, barber shop, etc., and is kept by Bob Church, one of the swift witnesses of the Congressional Committee on the Memphis Riots. . . . This mulatto keeps a lively trap at the location above mentioned. Many a poor negro has been run through and robbed therein, as it is frequented by a crowd of negro loafers . . . the very sharpest and most expert negro gamblers and fancy negro hulks in the city, all of whom are Radicals of the deepest die. Church's establishment has been raided upon a few times, but so watchful are the boys of the police that while the gambling devices and cards were found on the tables, the players had left the ranch. A number of ugly scrapes which took place in this house called for police inter-

vention, but someway or other the boys always managed to escape legal punishment.[5]

Bob Church felt powerful enough to strike back. He grabbed the story and twisted it to suit himself. "I am too well-known in this community to ask for an endorsement of my conduct during my long residence in Memphis," he wrote in a letter published in the *Ledger*'s competitors. "I own my own place of business," he declared, but more important, "The Hon. John Overton, Jr., owns the premises occupied by Sam Bizzell, in whose shop the difficulty originated."[6]

In other words, if the press wanted to find someone guilty by association with Bizzell, then Overton was as likely a conspirator as Church. The *Ledger*'s exposure tactic backfired spectacularly. The *Ledger* typically trafficked in unabashed anti-Negro, anti-Republican, pro-Confederate invective, and in overpursuing a political opponent, it had ham-handedly dragged a city father and distinguished officer of the Lost Cause into the mess. Overton's prestige stood unmatched; his Confederate patriotism was unassailable. For Church, the Overton letter began a brilliant career in racial public relations, an indispensable element of his success.

◆   ◆   ◆   ◆

Interesting people in all times and places tend to do two things well—they straddle boundaries, and they bend public perception. Church did both, with increasing ease and skill. Yet it would take a trauma more drastic than the riot to change the way people viewed Bob Church.

Juggle the letters a little, and the word *whore* can become *hero*. Yellow fever had that effect in Memphis. Arriving in August 1878, the fever killed rampantly and graphically. People personified it as Yellow Jack and demonized it as the Black Vomit.

As soon as he heard reports of the first cases, Bob Church rushed home and packed his children's trunks. He hustled Thomas, eleven, and Mollie, fifteen, to the train station. Mollie later recalled the chilling scene at the depot.

> Those who were going were weeping, and those who could not go were crying as though their hearts would break. Every now and then a defiant voice would shout aloud, "You all are trying to run away from death. You are leaving us poor folks behind to die . . . but you had better look out. Death can find you where you are going just as easy as he can find us here with yellow fever."[7]

The children were bound for New York City, and their father rode with them as far as Cincinnati. They made the rest of the trip safely. Though Mollie fell sick in New York, she pulled through.

Every day in Memphis, the yellow fever sickened and killed scores. Mosquitoes were its vectors, spreading the disease from one infected person to the next. Fever epidemics struck and plundered Southern river towns periodically during the nineteenth century, arriving aboard boats in mosquito larvae. But its causes and behavior were poorly understood, which only heightened the terror among the living. The city went into quarantine. Volunteers sprinkled lime around the streets, while cannons fired to clear miasma from the air. According to the historian John Harkins,

> At its climax the virus attacked the body's internal organs, especially the liver, whose malfunctioning gave the skin a yellowish cast. If the disease did not kill the patient, the treatment might. . . . Some practitioners bled their patients and prescribed huge doses of purgatives and quinine. Others advocated ice water baths, hot foot baths, or hot plasters. These and other useless remedies and preventatives might be humorous if the situation had not been so ghastly.[8]

It was said that the bite of one mosquito did more damage to Memphis than the entire Civil War. By the end of August 1878, after deaths and evacuations, the city's population dropped from around 50,000 to below 20,000 and an estimated 14,000 of the remaining citizens were Negroes. Over two hundred deaths reportedly occurred on September 14 alone.[9]

As Memphis's death toll mounted, newspapers that had belittled the moral character of the Negro celebrated the valiant and dutiful McClellan Guard and the Zouaves, colored militia units that assumed law enforcement duty, protecting citizens from marauders who looted the bedridden and dying. Work exposed the McClellans and Zouaves to the virus, and many thus sacrificed their lives. Most of the three thousand nurses treating the sick were colored women. Harkins explained:

> Blacks numbered about 70 percent of the population that remained in the city, and they provided virtually the entire work force for the stricken community. They distributed the $700,000 worth of supplies which poured in from all over the nation. They collected and buried thousands of corpses. Unlike their white counterparts, who fled to safety, two black militia companies stayed and patrolled the streets to prevent looting. . . . Thereafter their presence ensured order.[10]

Negroes weren't the only pariahs to risk all for the greater good. Annie Cook, who operated the Mansion, the city's most famous brothel, at 34 Gayoso Street, freed her girls as the fever spread. Mansion girls could raise the dead, some said, and now Cook would comfort the sick. She opened her place as a hospital to the poor, and there the less fortunate convalesced, their flesh pressed to velvet, silk, and lace for the first and last time. Cook survived barely into September before succumbing to the fever herself. She was eulogized as the Memphis Magdalene.

From the Mansion window, you could see Church's Billiard Hall, where the proprietor remained open around the clock, providing a steady flow of the frontier's most trusted disinfectant—whiskey.

Though the first frost of 1878 brought relief, panic and sickness returned in 1879. The fever methodically infected every household on Shelby Street, heading toward Capt. Charles Church's. With his wife and daughter, Capt. Church left just in time. They relocated to a more wholesome climate in Blount Springs, Alabama, where the captain promptly suffered a brain aneurysm and died.

◆   ◆   ◆   ◆

The late 1870s brought as much change to Memphis as had three days of blood in May 1866. Besides Capt. Church, another pillar of the old city, Gen. Forrest, died, succumbing to chronic diarrhea in 1877.[11] Jeff Davis Jr. caught the fever and perished, and his daddy fled town for good. The Confederate spirit swooned. The Negroes stayed on and protected everything. Their commitment to Memphis had been nothing short of noble.

During the pestilent 1870s, while residents left the city by the thousands, Robert Church invested in real estate. He made two major property acquisitions during the fever years. On May 1, 1879, he purchased his saloon at Second and Gayoso from John Overton. And on May 2 he closed on a lot on Lauderdale Street, where he would build a magnificent home. He already owned at least five properties. He would acquire nine more over the next five years as Memphis stumbled along. He concentrated his holdings within the two-block vicinity of his saloon at Second and Gayoso.[12]

Just as Madame Annie Cook went from whore to hero, the fever transformed Bob Church. The riot had birthed the man, but the epidemic made him a king.

Secondary to the human losses, the fever brought Memphis a public relations disaster, as papers far and wide relayed the horrors that befell the city. Considering its dire prospects, some citizens advocated that the town be abandoned. Instead, it relinquished its city charter and adopted an emergency form of government. Memphis would now function as the Shelby County Taxing District. It abolished the office of mayor and its boards of aldermen and council in favor of a streamlined system of a single powerful executive, the taxing district president, and an eight-man bicameral legislature, made up of a board of police and fire commissioners and a board of public works. A series of bonds were issued to pay off the old city debt. It was here that the legend of Bob Church began. "Mr. Church showed his faith," an 1891 newspaper tribute would recall. "He holds Bond No. 1 of the first series. With this example before them, capitalists of the Caucasian race could not be shy, and the whole of the bonds was placed."[13]

This was how a violent, colored saloonkeeper of oft-questioned character grabbed the civic narrative, reshaping public opinion. In early 1882 the *Ledger*, a publication that six years earlier had accused Church of heading an "infamous gang" of thieves and gamblers, would describe him as "a quiet, courteous, businesslike man, who has accumulated quite a fortune . . . and is understood to be straightforward and reliable in all his business affairs."[14]

With a backdraft of goodwill, Church forayed into a dangerous scheme. In 1880 he purchased a property at 34 St. Martin Street, a few doors south of Beale Street in the heart of colored Happy Valley.[15] Only the tenant at 34 St. Martin, Miss Mary Eyrich, was not colored. Older lady, a widow, Eyrich used a dressmaker's shop as her front. That explained the scantily clad women: fittings. It also explained the male patrons: shopping for their sweethearts. Colored neighbors couldn't very well blow the whistle on a white businesswoman and her customers. The location protected patrons from detection, from their wives—no one inclined to know whorehouse visitors or care about their activities would be loafing around Happy Valley. Church understood every contour of the city's psychological topography and positioned his venture perfectly. There he reenacted on dry land what he'd learned on the river: serving white men's thirsts. Twisting the racial roles of the Southern sex trade, Church's houses enslaved *white* women.

With his prominent white friends, and the city indebted to him, Church became a titan in Memphis's new civic legend, a symbol to the world that any man, even a black man, could succeed in the rebuilding city.

The wealthiest of our colored citizens . . . has always given liberally
to any enterprise for the benefit of the city. . . . His word has ever
been as good as his bond. . . . By energy and prompt attention to
business he has shown his race what possibilities are in store for
them.

In the decades following the Civil War, black men were lynched for two
reasons down South: for daring to compete economically with white
men and for soiling the honor of white women. Bob Church was doing
both, with tacit license and open appreciation.

And with the dirt and dollars thus accrued, he "accumulated a fortune of nearly $100,000, and lives in luxurious ease, respected by all."

PART II

BIRTH OF BEALE,

1885–1892

*What benefit is a "leader"
if he does not devote his
time, talent, and wealth to
the alleviation of the poverty
and misery, and elevation
of his people?*

—IDA B. WELLS

Chapter 5

DIVIDING THE
WAGES OF SIN

He rode a mule-powered buckboard. From the ground up, four wagon wheels, flat planks with a bench atop—about the simplest wheeled transportation available.

This modest conveyance reflected David Park Hadden's vanity, for a more luxurious, private vehicle would have spoiled the effect of seeing him. He had thick reddish-brown hair and a gray-streaked beard that fell to his sternum. A gold-tipped ebony cane lay across the bench beside him, and a pearl stickpin adorned the shirt, but aside from these accessories, variety was the only rule. He wore seersuckers, gray pinstripes, and purple for Mardi Gras. He donned white riding gloves and sported more hats than a millinery.

He'd begun riding through town during the fever, behind a black mule named Hulda. She'd died, and now Napoleon Bonaparte pulled the buckboard. Pretty soon, Napoleon Bonaparte would die, and Hadden would swear to more serious matters, "on my late mule, Napoleon Bonaparte."

Now Hadden and Napoleon Bonaparte zigzagged through every alley, over every bridge, up and down each street, breathing in the silty river scent, fish dock fragrance, and coal smoke. Out in the open on Beale, his frontier bellow announced his approach, but he might just as well appear suddenly over an alley dice game. Hadden called every man by name, substituting "Colonel" for those he'd yet to learn. The people called *him* Pappy. Though he never stopped for long, whoever he set his blue eyes upon felt a moment of his jarringly complete attention.

Born in Elkton, Todd County, Kentucky, in 1840, Pappy Hadden came to Memphis in 1864 with the town under Federal occupation. He joined a cotton firm that eventually bore his name. He married well, successfully operated a plantation, and moved among the elite. At supper in Hadden's home, a servant stood behind each guest to fan away the flies.

Hadden founded the Secret Order of Memphi in 1872, comprised of gentlemen in his circle, who brought Mardi Gras to the city. Brightly liveried Negroes pulled floats through the streets, and the Memphi threw the grandest masked ball. Festivity mattered utmost to Pappy Hadden.

Hadden was elected to the taxing district's police and fire commission, and without the burdens of legal training or vested authority, he assumed the bench in police court. While riding with Napoleon Bonaparte, he scanned the jagged panorama for busted sidewalks, unkempt yards, standing water, or overflowing garbage. He'd send the police to round up whoever might be responsible and bring them to his courtroom. He soon was named taxing district president, the top public official, tantamount to city mayor, though without a strong legislative body to demand a share of power or offer checks and balances.

Hadden sought to restore the city of Memphis, to fix its streets, drain its sewage, and cleanse its water, to repopulate it and replenish its finances. Though many deemed the job impossible, unworthy of the required effort, he possessed just the sort of superhuman energy and dazzling personality that was needed.

Reporters alternately fawned over him and satirized him. They compared him to Gilbert and Sullivan's Mikado, and they analyzed his wardrobe almost daily. His lack of a Civil War record led to doubts about his bravery and suspicions that he might be soft on the Negro, but no one seems to have questioned his will. In addition to Pappy's agricultural activities and political power, he moved energetically in business circles, serving as vice president of Bluff City Insurance and president of the Manhattan Savings Bank, better known as ol' man Hadden's bank.

Among Hadden's allies, none stood more steadfastly than John Overton Jr. Hadden and Overton both belonged to the Democratic Party, the more socially conservative party of the day and the one to which most Southern white men belonged. But both were liberal on the race issue—Memphis's postepidemic reality required as much. In rebuilding the city, Hadden dealt fairly with black politicians and voters. That too had begun during the fever. On his rounds, he'd seen Beale Street's black militiamen, the McClellan Guards and the Zouaves, carry the city through crisis. He emerged from the fever with a sense of the city's unity—shared trauma had bridged some differences between white and black—and he did what he could to preserve that unity during recovery. Memphis's resurrection would need black participation.

◆　◆　◆　◆

Beale was a street of many layers, and Hadden traversed them as few others could.

As Napoleon Bonaparte nosed east on Beale from Main, his master cast his blue gaze over pawnshop row. He read the Hebrew names gold-leafed on plate glass, alchemists converting gabardine to gold. Hadden's alchemy transformed mud to pavement. He condemned shabby shacks and conjured brick facades with arched windows. He beheld the transformation, passing the Walnut Palace saloon, one of the street's fanciest, and Sartore the Tailor.

Across St. Martin, Goldsmith's Department Store and Hirsh and Schwab's Dry Goods had opened, increasing the cash flow and traffic on Beale, especially on Saturdays, when the hinterlands emptied into the street—black and white farmers and their families crowded into wagons and onto flatbeds and flooded Beale's plank sidewalks. A couple large wagonyards, the parking lots of the nineteenth century, were located on and adjacent to Beale, and cheap commerce followed. Grocers and grogs attracted Saturday crowds, which in turn pulled confectioners, hairdressers, and hog part cafés.

In 1884, in a sarcastic but fitting tribute, Memphis formally renamed a thoroughfare of whorehouses that crossed Beale as Hadden Avenue, and it would be known that way long after the city renamed it Third Street decades later. Rows of one-story frame brothels lined up neat as headstones down Pappy's namesake boulevard. One structure leaned belligerently in the background, a two-story brick front with a three-story frame addition called Noah's Ark, a grocery, Negro gambling dive, and site of regular knife fights.

For his part, Hadden took Beale Street's troubles seriously. Weary of the endless assaults and murders resulting from Negro dice scrapes, he sought to introduce a fair shake to craps and developed a device designed to prevent manipulation of the cubes. The thing was a leather funnel, with a system of wires inside that forced the dice to turn and tumble unpredictably. On the street they called it Hadden's Horn. It would remain in use in Beale Street's gaming houses until the mid-twentieth century.

The oldest profession prospered along Beale's cross streets—St. Martin, Hadden, Hernando, and De Soto—and though rebuilding Memphis demanded innovation and originality, Hadden recognized a worthwhile source of commerce and cheerfully carried forth the licensing of houses of ill fame, as well as those of hard luck.

The code remained unwritten, but openly disseminated, and one bright morning at police court, Judge Hadden spelled it out for a pair of beautiful blondes caught cruising the district on horseback while attired too seductively for moral purposes.

You girls are probably ignorant of our rules here but you won't be in a few minutes, for I'll state 'em:

You must stay in the house at night. In the day time you can go ridin' if you conduct yourself so people can't tell you're different from other ladies, but when you violate the rules you must suffer the penalty of iniquity and divide the wages of sin with the city. Ten apiece, please.[1]

Heading up the street, Hadden passed Charles Gallina, a Democrat chieftain who ran a saloon at 89 Beale. Gallina, as an elected magistrate, presided over a courtroom upstairs from the saloon. He served warrants in the district, convened the coroner's jury when floaters turned up, and was always good for a bail bond. Beale Streeters called him Squire Charlie. He had one attentive eye and one that looked where it pleased. The cheerful squire hosted political barbecues in the backyard and games of chance in his saloon below the courtroom, and this struck no one as contradictory. As he grew wealthy, Squire Charlie began running ponies in the races at Olympic Park. He named horses after his daughter, Mamie G, and his favorite lowdown louts from the saloon, Black George and Texas Bill.[2]

Most important, Gallina was acting Italian ambassador and consul on Beale Street, bringing scores of his countrymen to the town. He housed them while they found employment, usually in connection with the market house at Beale and Hernando. The affiliation—Gallina, the market house, the old country pipeline—enhanced the street's international flair and made the Italian faction a major power for years to come.

Riding on, Hadden took measure of the Beale Street Market House. Its weathered canvas awnings and fragrant stalls dominated a short block from Hadden to Hernando. Kerchief-headed Negro women kept pots of coffee brewing on camp stoves. Cheap, choice foods overflowed: homegrown peas a nickel a quart, a bunch of beets the same, strawberries at three quarts for a quarter, spring chickens up to sixty cents, smoked ham, bacon, lamb, Spanish mackerel, and Gulf pompano all to feed a family for under a dollar.

Across the street stood Englishman John Oakey's high-class saloon, its polished brass fittings and buffed mahogany glowing by gas lamp. Oakey called his place "Headquarters of the Elite" and fattened an upper-crust white-male clientele on roast pheasant, smoked calf's tongue, and oysters.

Respectable establishments like Oakey's and the Walnut Palace paid their property taxes, and joints like Noah's Ark and the brothels sent criminals before Judge Hadden to help fortify the exchequer or assist in the latest improvement project via the chain gang. Either way, the gravel and mud underfoot became brick or bluestone pavement as Beale Street rolled east toward Hernando Street. There Napoleon Bonaparte crossed paths with a less fortunate member of his breed, pulling the trolley along two thin lines of rust across a path of gravel and ill-fitting planks, a sheep bell on its neck ringing along.

The ringing bell signaled passage through a gateway, to an alternate reality. Beginning at the intersection of Beale and Hernando, rules governing the order of the world were suspended, twisted, or reversed.

On one corner stood the Zouave armory, a place laden with symbolic value and practical importance. The Zouaves had protected people's homes from plunderers during the plague, earning the respect of those whites who hadn't abandoned the city. As Reconstruction, and its promise for black Americans, collapsed throughout the South in 1877, white hate groups terrorized black businesspeople and intimidated black voters from the polls across the former Confederacy. But the black vote in Memphis remained strong.

No one appreciated the power of the black vote more than Pappy Hadden, who'd witnessed a surprising show of Negro political force. In 1882 he had allied with Ed Shaw, Beale Street's top black political organizer. They assembled a bipartisan, biracial group of candidates for the board of public works, running it as the People's ticket. An inclusive spirit embraced the election, with the *Public Ledger* noting, "As there seems to be a general understanding that all the substantial elements of the community are to be represented as far and as fairly as practicable, the name of Mr. Church has been agreed upon to carry forward this policy."[3] The candidates all were scheduled to speak at an election eve forum. Bob Church however, for reasons unknown, refused to participate. When a drayman and saloonocrat from the corner of Beale and Hernando named Lymus Wallace stepped to the podium, the crowd erupted in raucous laughter and derisive cheers at the sight of the little dark fellow tottering up to the dais. Wallace's verve stole the show, though, telling the audience, "There's a nigger on the People's ticket," meaning Church, "that you can't tell from a white man." He paused to let it sink in. "I am a black man."[4]

Lymus Wallace won the designated black seat on the public works board and would triumph in the next two local elections, serving until 1890. Wallace proved to be an effective leader for the street. He successfully petitioned for new electric lamps to be installed at the Beale Street Market House.

The streetlights shined on another Beale landmark, Battier's Drug Store. Owner George Battier was a second-generation Memphian who wore the halo of fever hero, having kept his pharmacy open constantly throughout the epidemic, disregarding his safety for the common welfare. His peers considered him a sensible businessman and knew him as a good Democrat and a good white man, which on the surface would make it seem all the more unlikely that he'd romance a woman of color—Mary Burton. Battier was in many respects just the sort of man to enjoy a kept Negress. But Battier and Burton lived openly together as man and wife in every respect but one. Battier repeatedly applied for a marriage license but was denied. Legend maintained that Battier once cut Burton's finger and drank her blood to mock the one-drop rule before a county clerk who refused to make them man and wife. The couple married legally across the Mississippi in Helena, Arkansas, returning home to a grand jury indictment on a miscegenation charge. They were found not guilty in criminal court July 27, 1885.

Pappy Hadden and Napoleon Bonaparte clambered onward, through saloon row. From Hernando to De Soto, Beale contained fourteen saloons on its north side and thirteen on the south side, three-stories, two-stories, and singles, mostly all brick with plate-glass windows; a few frame and dilapidated structures were mixed in like rotten teeth. Past saloon row, over De Soto Street, the key landmark was the imposing First Baptist Church, better known as Beale Street Baptist, with a golden statue of St. John gesturing heavenward. One half of a brick, two-story duplex next door housed the only colored-owned printing

press in town. There Hadden could find a tenacious warrior in a surprising package, a young black woman, barely five feet tall and twenty-three
years old, named Ida Wells.

Like Bob Church, Wells hailed from Holly Springs, Mississippi. And
the yellow fever had changed her destiny as it had Church's. Her parents
had perished in the epidemic that nearly leveled Memphis. She'd carried some of her surviving siblings to the city, to rebuild her life just as
Memphis began putting itself back together in the early 1880s. She took
a job teaching school in a rural hamlet in the county but took a room on
the south side of Memphis and inevitably found herself on Beale Street.

Unlike rural Holly Springs, Memphis glowed with prospects for Ida.
The city had its black public works commissioner, Lymus Wallace,
while two black attorneys from the neighborhood, Josiah T. Settle and
Thomas Cassels, served Shelby County as assistant attorneys general.
Ed Shaw remained a powerful leader, having served as wharfmaster,
the highest-paid local elected official, and county commissioner, while
recent memory included a black alderman still active in Beale Street
business, Joe Clouston Jr.

Not only did Memphis offer nearly unfathomable political opportunities, there was so much to do. Wells enjoyed going to the theater,
spent too much on clothes, attended church every Sunday, and strove
for membership in local black society, the ladies' teas, club banquets,
and select hops that revolved around the city's growing professional
class. She looked up to Bob Church's family.

Wells deliberated over the typical preoccupations of young ladyhood.
Petite, young, and brown-skinned, she was neither a dazzling beauty
nor without suitors. "With me, my affairs are always at one extreme
or the other," she confided to her diary. "I either have an abundance of
company or none at all. Just now there are three in the city who, with
the least encouragement, would make love to me; I have two correspondents in the same predicament."[5] Outwardly, nothing about her at this
time suggested the ferocity she would express in years to come.

Yet Ida had no intention of living as a second-class citizen. In September 1883 she purchased a first-class train fare from Memphis to

Woodstock, Tennessee, the location of her teaching job, and sat herself in the ladies' car for the ride. A conductor ordered her to go into the smoking car, and when she refused, he seized her by the arm and tried to force her. She balled up and sat-in right there, but the conductor pulled at her so that he tore her sleeve. She bit and scratched him, and the bleeding conductor and two passengers finally escorted her from the train entirely. While state law didn't exactly forbid such rough treatment, it did stipulate that a first-class fare entitled even a black purchaser to first-class accommodations. The smoking car didn't qualify. The Chesapeake & Ohio Railroad could have satisfied this requirement with separate first-class cars for black travelers but had failed to.

Ida sued.

On Christmas Eve 1884 a Memphis circuit court judge ruled in her favor, awarding her five hundred dollars in damages.[6] Her wildcat self-defense had been justified, for she appeared to the judge "lady-like . . . one who might be expected to object to traveling in the company of rough and boisterous men" in the smoker.[7] The victory indicated that justice applied to black women—yet another encouraging sign in Pappy Hadden's new city.

Bob Church, to keep current on racial matters, had begun voraciously reading and clipping Memphis's dailies as well as the colored weeklies. He held a blue grease pencil as he read and marked a line in the margin beside interesting stories. An item the *Avalanche*, published on the first day of 1885—his wedding day—captured his attention. His blue pencil slashed big X's around the headline:

X   CIVIL RIGHTS   X
A Negro Woman Gets a Verdict—Judge Pierce's Decision

It was the story of Wells's court victory over the C&O.

◆   ◆   ◆   ◆

Sundays came. Ida worshipped around, attending different churches throughout the district. Her heart, however, beat purely Baptist. It was a crucial part of her personality and a critical factor in her fate. Elites sought an intellectual, reserved worship experience—Bob Church went Episcopal. The Baptist Church, with its charisma and superstition, appealed to field hands. For a striver like Ida, being Baptist kept her in touch with the hard-working class that stood on the front line of race conflict, absorbing insults, violence, and a pittance in return for its labor. If working-class Baptists had the most grievances, they also developed the most productive outlet—Beale Street's fertile print culture flourished under Baptist auspices.

Ida's triumph in the railroad case made her an activist in the public eye, and she took that activism to print, finding her earliest audience through the pages of the *Living Way*, a Negro paper published by a colored printer on Beale.[8] Of her earliest journalistic efforts she would recall, "I had no training and no literary gifts. . . . [I] wrote in a plain common-sense way on the things which concerned our people. . . . I never used a word of two syllables where one would serve the purpose."[9] Her writing gained a national audience by the summer of 1885, reprinted in black papers like the *Washington Bee*, the *New York Freeman*, and the *Cleveland Gazette*. Ida discovered her gift for surgical social commentary: "It was through journalism that I found the real me."[10]

In her writing, Ida focused on her race's battle to elevate its social standing, what she saw as necessary internal improvements, rather than attacking white racism. She found plenty of black life that needed uplift, and while her critiques were nationally applicable, Beale Street provided the perfect microcosm. She criticized black fraternal societies, revealing groups' failure to benefit the larger community. Fraternal societies were integral parts of black communities, and Wells's critique boiled into a national controversy concerning the uplifting qualities of Negro secret clubs, the crux of her argument being "the history of an enormous amount paid into their treasuries with nothing to show for it in the way of real estate, parks, or even a multitude of widows and orphans cared for."[11]

She criticized the light-skinned elites who bought their way out of suffering without helping the many less fortunate of their race. She wondered, "what benefit is a 'leader' if he does not devote his time, talent, and wealth to the alleviation of the poverty and misery, and elevation of his people?"[12]

Did the voracious reader Bob Church receive the message?

◆　◆　◆　◆

In December 1884, as Ida Wells prepared for her court case against the C&O, a Negro named John McKeever sold a suit of clothes on pawnshop row that bore the monogram of a recently murdered white man. This did not look good—McKeever professed his innocence all the way to the gallows. He swung in the steamy morning of June 26, 1885.

That afternoon another suit of clothes found its way to pawnshop row. The stranger cashing them in wished to keep his identity secret. He had landed on Beale Street with pocket money and one spare suit. He had found a game at Bob Church's saloon and been promptly liberated of the contents of his pockets and the watch from his vest. There the stranger had heard all about poor John McKeever, who'd hung like the golden balls on the sign outside J. B. Gothelf's pawn brokerage. When Gothelf asked for the stranger's name to print on the pawn ticket, he said, "McKeever."

The stranger returned to Church's and lost the rest. He pleaded with the owner for a loan. Church said he might be able to help and asked the young man's name. Ed McKeever, the stranger said. McKeever was of tender age, Church could see, but hardened conscience. This was not the typical young man who gambled himself broke at Second and Gayoso. McKeever bore marks of fine pedigree.

Church took measure of this and asked McKeever where he had come from, asked about his family. McKeever called himself a colored man from St. Louis.

Church saw himself in McKeever—a white man professing dark heritage. He noted the difference. McKeever had nobody, no Capt. Church or Col. Overton to lean on. Church had no intention of bringing his children into the family business and liked the idea of acquiring a vigorous young apprentice.

Church dispatched McKeever, with a fat back pocket of house money, to shoot craps with the Negroes and keep the games moving at Church's two saloons.[13]

◆ ◆ ◆ ◆

At *nearly five o' clock* in the scorching evening of July 29, 1885, the sawmill half a block up Second from Bob Church's saloon began burning. Between the fire and Church's stood nothing but lumberyards. With the fire bells ringing, Church sent McKeever and some of the boys to the roof with a hose and buckets and organized a moving company among the pool shooters and drinkers.

The sawmill windows burst, and black smoke erupted up into the sky—hundreds of onlookers arrived within minutes. Piles of timber behind the mill ignited. The fire leaped down to Gayoso Street. Church calmly directed the removal of his furnishings, and the sidewalks filled with spectators, chairs, sofas, and beds. The heat melted telephone and telegraph wires, snapping the poles like matchsticks.

Flames charged through tinder Negro shacks to the double-brick tenement on the north side of Gayoso, numbers 80 and 82, a sporting house run by Mesdames Blanche McGee and Lou Sholes. A chorus of shrieks announced the fire, sending a few of the inmates naked onto Gayoso, while others flew from second-story windows down to the street. A few of the more collected residents passed their rose-hued cut-glass mirrors, regal purple sofas, Persian rugs, and tasseled pillows out their windows to safe hands below. All evacuated successfully and watched the flames engulf the brothel, later said to have been the most handsomely furnished in the city.

Flames licked fifteen stories of sky, and every available firefighter rushed to the blaze. Pappy Hadden materialized, shed his blue linen coat, led the volunteer bucket brigade, and ably manned a hose.

Concern turned to Church's hall, but the wind intervened, and firefighters extinguished the blaze at the foot of the colored billiard parlor, much to the relief of a singed and sweaty Ed McKeever up on the building's roof. Insurance on the structure had expired ten days before. It was a good thing, that wind shift. As the scene cooled, fire damage was tallied at $125,000, less than half insured. It cost Mesdames Sholes and McGee a combined $13,000 in furnishings alone, and their building burned to the ground. Most of the other destroyed structures had been cheap, uninsured shacks on the north side of Gayoso, east of Hernando Street. Many belonged to John Overton Jr.

Issuing an embarrassing revelation, the papers identified respectable businessman Dr. H. J. Shaw as owner of the handsomely furnished, ill-fated brothel lost in the blaze. Subsequently, the good Dr. Shaw would not be back on the sporting turf.[14]

The sawmill fire opened a huge opportunity to Bob Church. Dr. Shaw wanted out and Overton wished to avoid such publicity, and Church began gobbling up houses in the district.

Red lights flicked on everywhere Church amassed property—Short Third, Hernando, and scorched Gayoso. The birth of brotheldom on each street followed the same pattern Church had established on St. Martin in the early 1880s. One madam moved to the street and for a year or more perhaps gauged the amenability of the surroundings to the profession; within a few years a robust district had filled in around the first bawdy settler. Whorehouses would be hidden in the middle of colored neighborhoods to insulate them from polite white women. Before such a term ever held the slightest racial connotation, this sanctioned vice zone was called the "segregated district."

The back steps from Bob Church's saloon emptied right out onto Short Third Street, which ran for a single block, north and south, nestled perfectly for maximum protection between Beale and Gayoso streets. Short Third ended in the backyard of a Beale Street liquor store. Developed in 1884 and 1885, it had had one madam among its first residents in 1886, and by 1889 all ten houses on the block were sporting. Gayoso Street had long been associated with the profession thanks to the Mansion, of yellow fever fame, but only after Bob Church became involved did Gayoso flourish as the city's most notorious thoroughfare, concentrated in the block between Hernando and De Soto streets, one block parallel to Beale's saloon row.[15]

Church likely established his business model here: charge exorbitant rent and leave everything else to the tenant. It kept his hands just clean enough. He could claim, as he would in an 1893 legal scrap with Madame Biddie Sayers, that whatever his tenants did in his property was their business.[16]

Pappy Hadden emphasized festivity and cotton money in Memphis's recovery. All the city's power and most of its wealth lay in that one commodity. Cotton money trickled down, from lords and financiers to middlemen at firms to farmers, seasonal hands. The cotton business branched out to railroad expansion to transport the commodity, which branched into road and bridge construction. Pappy Hadden was a cotton broker and president of the cotton exchange, a local version of Wall Street's stock market.

Church grasped the Old South psychology prevalent among Memphis leadership. He knew how to feed the cotton king mentality, having grown up on the river around white planters and riverboat gamblers. He owed his existence to a wealthy white man who had kept a concubine. He would entertain Mississippi aristocrat planters and city capitalists in the manner to which they'd grown accustomed.

◆   ◆   ◆   ◆

New brothel construction provided but one gauge of the district's activity. A Negro named Cash Mosby organized train excursions that brought rural black visitors to Beale Street. They marveled at the brick-and-bluestone-paved streets and the electric lamp glow by night. They caught a glimpse of Beale Street's coal-black elected representative, saw two colored newspaper offices and the interracial family working the pharmacy, and had a white man serve them a beer. Quite a few excursionists became residents.

Robert Church may or may not have been financially involved in

Cash Mosby's successful venture, but he benefited from it, just as Cash made money on Church's big name. One of those pleasure cruisers recalled, "When I was quite a youngster, I used to ride excursions to Memphis and in those days it was the good name of Bob Church that drew people to Memphis from all over the South." That visitor was W. C. Handy, a figure who would have an enormous impact on Beale Street and its place in American culture.[17]

Throughout the 1880s, Church's reputation as a successful business-man and a respected gentleman, and his power as a beacon for his race, grew throughout the black South. The extent of public knowledge about his underworld life, however, remains a mystery. It appears to have been a secret, or perhaps it was well known but didn't matter. Church's busi-ness model merely reflected the Memphis way. The city's strategy for expanding after the war and rebuilding after the fever had been to fill the coffers with dirty money and launder those proceeds through inter-nal improvements. The strategy worked, both on the civic level and in Church's shadow city.

Moreover, Church acted within the quasi-law, as Memphis now had a time-honored system of vice licensing. Church scrambled potential criticism with his generosity and vision. He built not only whorehouses but residential properties. While white property owners overcharged black tenants for slum dwellings districtwide, Church endowed his single-story duplexes with cupolas and turrets, adding a touch of the fanciful to ordinary lives. He supported the colored papers with his advertising dollar and through them promoted a message of respectabil-ity, calling his saloon "The Only First-Class Hotel In the City," touting its modern improvements, choice eatables, and abundant artesian water.

Church's efforts dovetailed with those of the city itself. During the 1880s, thirty miles of innovatively designed modern sewers were tak-ing shape. Throughout its plague years, Memphis had sat, obliviously, upon the solution to its wretched water supply. Its efforts to clean up led to the discovery of an underground aquifer—billions of gallons of pure water. As the city recovered, its population expanded from 33,000 inhabitants in 1880 to 65,000 in 1890.[18]

As his city grew, Bob Church settled into the form of a wealthy Victorian man. His rich diet smoothed out his features, rounding his shoulders and face. In every other way, however, he remained a hard man. In early 1878 he had survived another gunshot wound to the head, this one courtesy of the sheriff of Lee County, Arkansas. A woman had been the source of dispute. Though he never drank heavily, he self-medicated—not an unusual practice in a time of rampant illness, when the opiate of the masses was still opium. The head wounds and morphine were hell on the eyes, and Church's stayed solid red.

At age forty-five, he began a second family, marrying twenty-nine-year-old Anna Wright the first day of 1885. She would bear him two children: Robert Jr. arrived in October 1885, followed by Annette in August 1887. To house his brood, Church designed and had built a palatial Queen Anne on a lot he obtained after the 1878 yellow fever epidemic, its dual gables ordained with ornately scalloped woodwork. It stood three stories tall on two acres, with stables and servant quarters out back. Inside were fourteen gracious rooms, splendidly decorated with crystal light fixtures and fresco walls. Over the mantel in the parlor hung a massive oil painting of the sinking of the steamboat *Bulletin No. 2*, an 1855 disaster that Church and his father had survived, there to remind guests of their host's courage.

The Church home was on Lauderdale Street, about three blocks from where it crossed the residential east end of Beale. Lauderdale was undeveloped in the early 1880s and pocked with vacant tracts. Lots there were affordable enough for black professionals other than Church to own, and several bought in. Despite its black residents, the Vance-Lauderdale area nevertheless became the fashionable neighborhood during the boom late 1880s. Empty lots sprouted mansions, and by 1890 the white elite had chosen to live side by side with its African counterpart—the races mixed on the picturesque boulevard, same as the Saturday crowd in from the farm on dusty Beale.

One never knew who might call at the Church home. Gawkers of all hues wanted to see the Negro mansion and regularly intruded upon

Mrs. Church's privacy. The white press humorously documented her customary handling of these situations.

> Recently there was a very handsome house built in a fashionable neighborhood by a swell negro, whose wife is considered a leader in the most exclusive colored circles of this city. Some of her white neighbors went over to . . . gratify their curiosity as to the inner appearances of the house. One of the callers told the mistress of the house that they had "just come over to see her new home." 'Then, madam, I shall do myself the graceful honor to send one of my employed servants to show you over the mansion," as the lady of color swept from the room, her long robe of blue silk trailing behind her.[19]

Church affected a reserved, cultured pose at home, displaying warm-heartedness and endearing quirks. His eldest daughter, Mollie, recalled him as "the very soul, the very quintessence of hospitality."[20] He had loved cooking since his youth in the steamboat galley and now delighted in serving visitors his specialty, broiled pompano. Once a steward who had to acquire supplies for each voyage, Church never dropped the habit of buying in bulk. The pantry overflowed with barrels of flour, buckets of lard, and bananas by the bunch. He took shipments of oranges and nuts in season and kept crates of live poultry cackling in the yard.

Church cultivated an air of greatness around his home, as the spirits from Church's cellar warmed the bellies and loosened the tongues of a who's who of the black intelligentsia. Old steamboat cronies, Governor Pinchback of Louisiana, and U.S. senator Blanche K. Bruce of Mississippi stayed over regularly, traveling between their homes and the nation's capital. Church's daughter Annette had a hard time minding her Victorian manners at the sight of the most renowned black man in the country standing hat in hand in the parlor.

> I was afraid of old people and as a child I used to show it, so my mother cautioned me that Frederick Douglass was coming and not to make any comments in his presence about his looks. . . . I ran

up and kissed him and then I told mother that he had large eyes
and commented on his looks after he left. He had this long white
hair and wore these suits with these long coats, long and white, and
he looked distinct from other men, and I was afraid of old people
always. I don't know why.[21]

Church protected his children from his life in the street, hoping
Frederick Douglass's grandeur, rather than his own saloon stench,
would rub off on them. Locally, Church avidly participated in the colored Whist Club, for polite games of cards, and the Live Oak Club,
for lavishly decorated banquets and purple oratory. He attended balls,
always with Mrs. Church on his arm, she draped in black silk and radi-
ant diamonds, he in tuxedo. He embodied everything Ida Wells aspired
to—and much of what she'd one day rail against.

It's difficult to determine who first influenced whom in the relationship between Ida Wells and Bob Church. Though he may have already
nurtured in his heart a fervent advocacy for his people and their affairs,
it hadn't shown through his action. He involved himself in politics, but
so did a lot of saloonkeepers. As much as the record shows, it appears
that Wells directed Church toward a new phase of his life.

◆　◆　◆　◆

In late 1885 Ida's public profile was on the rise. The editor of the
Washington Bee profiled her, crowning the twenty-three-year-old
"the brainiest of our female writers. . . . From a mere, insignificant
country-bred lass, she has developed into one of the foremost among
the female thinkers of the race."[22]

Being the brainiest black female writer paid nothing, however, and
combined with a teacher's salary, it equaled poverty. Ida nevertheless
looked and acted the part of the respectable professional throughout
her struggle, having her pompadour sculpted at Dogan's on Beale and
keeping up with ladies' fashion. She participated in a gathering known
as the Lyceum that met to promote intellectual and cultural nourish-

ment. Of one Lyceum gathering, the *Cleveland Gazette* had noted, "The crowning literary event of the evening was the Rival Queens, a scene between Mary Stuart and Elizabeth I impersonated respectively by Miss I. B. Wells and Mrs. V. E. Broughton. It was given en costume and both ladies acquitted themselves nicely."[23]

Early in 1886 Ida moved from one boardinghouse to the next. After her aunt and her two sisters, with whom she'd moved to Memphis from Holly Springs, decamped to California, she was of increasingly divided heart and mind. She worried about her brother A.J., who'd become a gambler. He hit her up for help routinely and just as routinely lost it in one of Church's joints or Noah's Ark. Ida wrote in her diary, on April 11, 1886, "It seems as if I should never be out of debt."[24]

She received a letter from her aunt Fannie, encouraging her to join the family in Visalia, California, adding that there might be a teaching job available. Ida had no desire to leave Memphis and her nationally significant, if poorly paying, work. But she felt she at least owed Fannie and her sisters a visit. She caught a train west in July 1886 and cabled dispatches to Beale Street from Kansas City, Denver, Salt Lake City, and San Francisco.

When she arrived in Visalia, Fannie persuaded Ida to get a refund on the return fare and take a teaching job there. "I regretted it almost as soon as I sold my ticket," Ida recalled.[25] She got the job and warily began a new life in the remote agricultural town with no more than twenty black families in residence. Ida had retreated from the front line of a momentous struggle to a place of irrelevance, and by the time she helped Aunt Fannie with living expenses, she had nothing left.

She wrestled with her feelings for weeks. Torn between her responsibilities to her family and to her race, she prayed to get back to Memphis. She had one desperate hope. In her diary, on August 26, she noted, "Wrote a letter to Mr. C asking the loan of one hundred dollars."[26] She had never met Mr. C but "told him that I wrote to him because he was the only man of my race . . . who could lend me that much money and wait for me to repay it."[27]

Ever since helping bail out Memphis from its postfever debt, Church

had remained sensitive to social responsibility. And he understood public relations. After the fire department halted the Gayoso Street blaze
of July 1885 at his door, he had donated one hundred dollars to the
department's general fund. But helping the outspoken little Ms. Wells
would garner him neither headlines nor favorable treatment.

She had pointedly asked her readers to ponder, What benefit is a
"leader" if he does not devote his time, talent, and wealth to the alleviation of his people's poverty and misery and to their elevation?

Perhaps this remark had unsettled his conscience.

Duality defined Church, a man equally capable of seemingly con-
flicting actions and stances: his violent temper and gracious hospitality,
his street brawls and loving fatherhood. He was black and white. He
closed like a pit bull on loans to lowlifes, seizing their bits of property and building his empire, low-balling pawned diamonds and stolen
watches; but a different ethic guided his transactions with wholesome
folk. As he built sex slavery plantations—yoking white women for their
labor and white men by their weakness—he devoted an increasing
amount of his attention and fortune to the shortfall Ida had exposed,
the needs of his community.

Ida set her diary down and returned to Visalia's makeshift one-room
colored school. On her way there, on the first Thursday of September
1886, she received an envelope: inside was a check from R. R. Church
for one hundred dollars. Mr. C had come through, and the Visalia colored school was out one teacher.

In Memphis again, Ida went to thank Mr. Church. She offered him
collateral and said she'd repay his loan with interest. He gazed upon
her with bloodshot eyes and said no. Toward the end of her long, useful
career, she recalled, "My gratitude for his kindly act and his trust in a girl
he knew only by reputation warms my heart today when I think of it."[28]

For Robert Church, this private act of generosity signaled the beginning of a new phase, the revelation of yet another facet of his complicated personality. Like his friend Pappy Hadden, Church had begun
dividing the wages of sin.

Chapter 6

CONTRIBUTIONS
FROM MALEFACTORS

The Beale district streets were theater for poor residents. Fans of the pugilistic, gladiatorial, and amorous arts delighted in the exploits of the Hot Dozen, a brick-throwing gang of colored orphans headquartered on the bayou, the knife fighters from Noah's Ark, the notorious Bad Blood chief among them, and streetwalkers like Callie Barker and Henrietta Woods—"two colored girls who hang about Beale and Gayoso streets to entice the unwary countryman to their room."[1]

Each morning the previous day's antics were relived before Judge David Park Hadden in the temple of justice. Hadden's chambers became not just center stage for rebuilding Memphis—they established the city's character, its style.

Here no star outshone Pappy Hadden himself.

Of the daily papers, only the *Public Ledger* rose to the level of Hadden's flamboyance. It brought critical verve to court reportage, recreating the melodrama commencing when,

At 9 o' clock the iron tongue of the old rookery bell that hangs in front of Police Court sounded its accustomed summons. Its vibrations disturbed the loose dust that clung to the cobwebs of the old ark and chilled the hearts of the poor devils whom it warned of their approaching fate. A motley crowd filed into court to watch the great man mount his throne and juggle justice according as his kaleidoscopic temper might be shaken up by each case.[2]

The Great Man wadded a few leaves into his cheek and passed the rest among the attorneys and reporters at the bench. He addressed reporters by the name of their paper. "Hello, *Ledger*," he said.

As the pleasantries drifted off and the tobacco juice began to flow, he rapped the gavel and announced, "The show is on."

He addressed tramps and vagrants as "Colonel." He fined a couple for fighting because the husband had broken a washboard in the melee. "Five dollars for wreckin' that utensil. I'll teach you people economy if I have to bankrupt you to do it."[3]

Whoever the police arrested could forfeit a certain amount of cash to bypass detention and trial. Forfeitures were tantamount to guilty rulings, for no one could expect Judge Hadden to return the money.

"I can't think what's got into the people," he confided to the *Ledger*. "They're gittin' so quiet an' law abidin' that there's no more real pleasure in life. Now just look at that docket—only twenty-five dollars in forfeitures up! We can't run the Taxin' District without contributions from malefactors, an' if this innocuous desuetude of original sin keeps on, our future will be gloomy indeed."[4]

Hadden's docket could run well past a hundred cases on a good day. He cleared them swiftly—imposing penalties of up to $50 a pair for fighting, while simple drunks went for $2, drunk and disorderly $5, and streetwalking $5. Disorderly conduct ranged anywhere from $5 to $25 according to the judge's humor. Charges of crooked dice were easily verified. If the first roll hit eleven—guilty!

The funds added up. "The books of the Police Department," noted the *Ledger* in September 1888, "reveal the fact that the money collected from those persons whom President Hadden interviews every secular day forms no inconsiderable portion of the city's cash." And Hadden's interviewees contributed more than cash: "The chain gang and the rock pile gang have been steadily at work and the value of their work upon streets and roadways cannot be justly estimated."[5]

Hadden seldom spent more than an hour on even the longest docket before moving on to another of his ventures.

The *Ledger* playfully admired Judge Hadden's methods, while understanding perfectly well what was going on. In the *Ledger*'s lines, Hadden didn't merely levy fines—he mulcted or taxed suspects. Gamblers paid for the privilege. Before the growth of the American police state and its attendant prison-industrial complex, Hadden made crime pay the city rather than making honest citizens pay for crime. Police court was the hub of rebuilding Memphis. Not only did Hadden's court raise funds and round up labor, his flamboyance, his eminence, spread like contagions through Memphis's civic personality. His flashy attire and verbal acuity, and his velvety violence, became central to Memphis's new identity. His actions in court, whether colorful, humorous, or brutal, would reverberate throughout the city's culture for years to come.

He sanctioned roundups to benefit the regional agriculture in which he—and the city—had a vested interest. "Any of our surplus population gone out to pick cotton?" he'd ask the bailiff at harvest time. The cops understood. During harvest time, smooth Negro hands provided convincing evidence for a vagrancy charge. Judge Hadden inspected suspects' palms for calluses and, finding none, sent them to work. He set his blue gaze on a muscular Negro on October 29, 1886. His Honor inquired, "Where are you from, Colonel?"

"St. Louis, sah," said the charged.

"Worst place in the world," Hadden said. "St. Louis people who enter this court leave hope behind. Fine you twenty-five dollars."

"Gimme one hour," the man pleaded, "and I'll leave town."

"Not any," said the judge. "Need such brawny visitors as you on the Second Street work."[6]

While the chain gang repaired bridges, chipped gravel, and paved streets, Judge Hadden banished more problematic figures to state court. Once convicted there, a man belonged to Tennessee penitentiary labor agent Joe Turney. Since at least 1882, as long as Hadden had been in power, Turney had traveled throughout the state rounding up prisoners to transport to the Walls in Nashville. Through this pretense, he operated a convict-for-hire program, placing lawbreakers on plantations or in mines throughout the state. He functioned as a convenient agent of political exile, or so it was said around Memphis, a link in the chain to days of old.

On Beale Street, no one conjured more fear. Joe Turney symbolized the Negro's powerlessness against the system. He seemed to materialize like a ghost, then vanish again, sometimes unseen, but with links of chain ringing behind him and somebody's husband, son, father, or brother mysteriously absent. To the poor and exploited on Beale Street, many a missing person's case was thusly explained, "Joe Turney's been here and gone." He was the modern-day slave trader, Nathan Bedford Forrest incarnate. His fearsome, spectral presence inspired the street's bards and balladeers, the now-forgotten men who sang the latest news, the words on the street.

◆   ◆   ◆   ◆

In early September 1886, as Ida Wells was returning to Memphis by train from California, vandals invaded the office of *Living Way*, the black Baptist paper she'd written for. It stood at the corner of Beale and De Soto, on the ground floor of a block of handsome two-story brick storefronts. They dismantled the printing press that had helped propel Ida to national prominence. They scattered some of the type—by far the most expensive aspect of the business—over the street and sank the rest into the bayou around back.

Her perspective, and that of *Living Way* editor R. N. Countee, had continued to focus on black self-improvement rather than white racism. They called their community to task and made foes out of neighbors. Countee "is about the best hated man in colored society," according to the *Ledger* of September 9, 1886, "and his enemies never let slip a chance to 'do him up.'"[7]

The demolition resolved any lingering questions Ida might have had about journalism. The young lady who'd come to Beale Street wanting both social acceptance and the ability to make social commentary found the two incompatible. Countee rebuilt *Living Way*, and Ida rejoined the fourth estate with her first salaried writing job—the *Weekly Baptist* hired her as a correspondent, augmenting her teaching salary by a dollar a week. Wielding the quill like a razor, she mocked the "community," noting that "there [has] not been a united action"—of blacks—"since the Haitian Revolution."[8]

Discord and dissolution hovered near the optimism and unity on Beale Street. For every solid element of black community, temptation beckoned nearby. The stained-glass windows of Avery Chapel, where Ida worshipped from time to time, obscured the fancy new brothels emerging just beyond the church's north wall on Gayoso. Her own brother was out there somewhere, rolling Hadden's Horn.

Her philosophy hardened. The avid theater-going girl aged into a combination of Susan B. Anthony and Carrie Nation. In print she scolded her people for spending their pocket money on tobacco, whiskey, and snuff instead of buying books and saving for homes.

She saw politics, once a great promise for the race, as providing a proliferation of dives and placing traps and snares for young black people. She concluded that without independent black society, the race would remain shackled to the white world, on Pappy Hadden's chain gang or rolling the dice with his horn. Building such society would require black philanthropy—"one wealthy man is worth more to us than 5000 politicians."[9]

Certainly her Memphis readers knew whom she had in mind.

◆　◆　◆　◆

Ida likely didn't count herself among the admirers of fiddle-playing Jim Turner, for just as she was protesting snuff, whiskey, the spendthrift segment of colored citizenry, and their "interminable picnics," he was entertaining the seemingly constant social gatherings around the district.

In 1887 Jim Turner was emerging as Beale Street's first star. He played violin, the lead solo instrument that attracted the most ambitious, flashy players, and got all the girls. Born blessed with magical hands in Arkansas in 1869, Turner had grown up in the Beale environment. As one admirer recalled, "He had unusually nimble fingers that allowed him to pick cotton, shoot dice, and handle the violin with equal dexterity." He knew the fiddle high and low—he learned lessons from Prof. John R. Love, who led a brassy ensemble on Beale, and from West Dukes, the breakdown fiddler who'd entertained around the market house since slavery.

Professor Love was a light-skinned letter carrier, plus organizer and leader of the Chickasaw Band. Of the early colored Beale musicians, no one held greater influence. In the words of George W. Lee, folk historian of the street, "He taught more men how to play music than has any other person of his race." He taught by ear, employing the same methods as Herman Arnold, Beale's earliest music instructor. Rudimentary lessons involved the professor whistling a melody and patting rhythm with his foot, encouraging his pupil to find proper accompaniment on a horn or violin. An advanced lesson included numerous band pieces following the same pattern with instruments. Love put a lead melody into their minds and set a tempo, repeating the rhythm until all the instruments joined. "These methods developed the pupils' ears so acutely that all they needed was to hear the leader strike a chord, and they would fill in," Lee wrote.[10]

The Chickasaws played big-stage pop. The overture from Gilbert and Sullivan's *The Mikado*—perhaps a tribute to Mr. Hadden—and a comic lullaby from *Erminie* graced their set, and Professor Love unleashed Jim Turner to delight the crowd. Turner fiddled rings around the down-home favorites "Billy in the Low Ground," "Old Hen Cackle," and "Shortnin' Bread." He mastered stage acrobatics and would jump from the bandstand to the dance floor and call dance figures, "Swing your partner," "All hands around," "Do-si-do," his voice booming above the band. "The more liquor he drank," a fan recalled, "the sweeter his violin became." Turner's mood swung, from infectious enthusiasm to brooding boredom. Too much *Erminie* made him grouchy. In these throes, he'd rap for silence in midnumber, banging his fiddle with the bow like a judge's gavel. "Then he would turn and improvise some melody that would make the dancers rave."[11]

Beale Street music in the 1880s: a rural-urban-high-low fusion, with a twist of improv.

Turner and the Chickasaw outfit established headquarters at a Beale tavern, second door from Hernando Street, across from Battier's Drug Store, at the welcome mat to saloon row.

Here one of Squire Charlie Gallina's Italian imports had set up shop. Vigelio Maffei had ridden the undercarriage of a freight train into town in the late 1870s. He survived the yellow fever epidemic tending bar at Gallina's, and by 1885 he had a residence and his own saloon. He moved into black politician Lymus Wallace's old establishment, a three-story brick building at 117 Beale Street. The muscle-bound Maffei stood maybe four and a half feet tall, but he never backed down from a challenge, be it a swim across the treacherous Mississippi or a $1,000 bet on a single tumble of the dice. He embraced his street name and loaned it to one of the iconic Beale establishments. Either his English spelling or comprehension of Negro argot needed work, though. The sign outside said "P. Wee."

Turner and the Chicks practiced, loafed, drank, and got messages at Pee Wee's. They fielded offers to perform and traveled to gigs in Arkansas, Mississippi, and Alabama. Just as Cash Mosby's train excursions spread Bob Church's fame throughout the hundreds of cotton-patch miles surrounding Memphis, the Chickasaw Band, particularly Jim Turner, spread the Beale Street mystique across the same territory.

One colored boy in little Florence, Alabama, a minister's son, had never imagined the likes of a moving picture or heard the sound of recorded music. His father told him the violin was the devil's toy and cautioned him away from conjured noise. But when the lad feasted his eyes and ears upon Jim Turner and the Chickasaws, his mind popped like fireworks. The minister's son had a word with the fiddler. Turner "talked about Beale Street . . . where life was a song from dawn to dawn. He described darktown dandies and high-brown belles. He recalled the glitter and finery of their latest fashions. Finally, he planted in my heart a seed of discontent, a yearning for Beale Street and the universe it typified."

The boy's name, W. C. Handy, would become synonymous with Beale Street.

◆　◆　◆　◆

Clamor in the streets—disorderly prostitutes, brawling madams, drunken whorehouse callers, darktown dandies, and high-brown belles—distracted public attention from the upper-level criminals. Madams moved from house to house, wenches were shown the road out of town, police court stayed busy, and the brothel owner remained safe.

Two parallel blocks, Beale and Gayoso, between Hernando and De Soto, framed a pungent little sector, bordered by lumberyards and the city railroad stables and its mule barns, the clean scent of fresh sliced oak battling acrid odors. Bayou Gayoso ran behind brothel row, a line of mostly small one-story houses separated from the nearby business section. Archaeologists have discovered heavy concentrations of oyster shells, perfume bottles, and clay pipes in the earth thereabouts.

Denizens cursed, threatened, leered, rushed the growler, and exposed their persons. In tones predicting pulp, the *Ledger* portrayed them to the good people—"Mag Maggins, who would be termed by an artistic alliterator 'a dusky dame of dissolute disposition,' was charged with drunk, disorderly, and vagrancy."[12] The policeman who brought her in said to Judge Hadden, "She was huggin' men in a tough saloon when I caught her." His Honor's lecture touched the finer points of degenerate decorum: "A little huggin' is very consolin' to a man when properly administered with appropriate adjuncts, but I don't like to see the practice threatened with relegation by makin' it common. Don't hug more'n one man at a time, young woman, an' don't do it where the police can see you." He noted, "She's one of a gang that makes it impossible for a white lady to walk along there without bein' insulted."[13]

It was a busy time for the girls at 170 Gayoso. Police arrested one female tenant, Willie Sullivan, "while on a hilarious jamboree, and [she] had to be carried to the station house on a dray. After being locked up Willie inaugurated a fistic entertainment with a fellow prisoner, and the turnkey had to turn the hose on her to quell her desire to fight."[14] Meanwhile "Maggie Woods and Lizzie Butler, a pair of handsome octoroons from 170 Gayoso, were fined $10 each on the testimony of a neighbor that they danced the cancan on the front porch of their abode in abbreviated costume from early morn to dewy eve."

Thanks to the cumulative powers of Mag Maggins, Lizzie Butler, Judge Hadden, and the *Ledger*, white ladies wanted no part of the district, and white men could venture just blocks from their homes and workplaces into a moral free zone that was invisible to their wives.

The police busted into a room off Beale to find Susie Brown and Hattie Jeffreys, colored prostitutes, lying on a bed, and Robert Clements, a white man, hiding under it, "to the scandal of the community," the *Ledger* sniffed.[15]

On the night of April 23, 1888, at 120 Gayoso, a small single-story house that Bob Church owned, "a tremendous row was going on inside and the police found two white men and a depraved white woman named Alice Gray dancing the cancan after the most approved style."[16] But while depraved legs kicked high, the state of Tennessee became curious about the use of funds and exercise of power in the Memphis taxing district.

Ultimately, the state attorney general filed a motion against President Hadden, alleging misappropriation of public dollars. The state sought the restoration of said money to the treasury and a perpetual injunction restraining Hadden from illegal exercise of power in office. He had already been indicted for malfeasance just months before. Though he had gotten off then, another charge brought greater scrutiny from higher powers and growing dissatisfaction from the public.

The state ruled against Hadden on May 2, 1888, adding that the law must be strictly construed as it is written. In other words, he and Memphis would have to comply with state laws that forbade gambling and prostitution. The whole scenario put President Hadden in a bit of a bind—his effectiveness as a leader, his successful methods of restoring Memphis, also presented the greatest challenge to his power. Under him,

Memphis's streets had solidified, electric trolleys had overtaken their mule-drawn ancestors, and clear artesian water bubbled into every home.

Hadden's success created other problems. The new city attracted new residents, which was a boon, and the new residents brought much-needed revenue. But that wasn't all—they also brought new attitudes. They came from Mississippi, Arkansas, and West Tennessee, bastions of white rule. And with them came a change in the city's moral climate. Many new arrivals didn't understand Pappy Hadden and his bipartisan, biracial politics. Back home, Negroes who got out of line ended up stretching rope; here they made decisions for white men. Opposition to Hadden blossomed in proportion to the influx. Hadden was accused of political miscegenation—"Hadden is not a Democrat and never was a Democrat. He is a hybrid, and the tide of his affections sets strongly with hybrids."[17] Hadden hatred manifested race hatred. It was said that Hadden drew support from "colored vagrants and outlaws, who live here on the sufferance of police who can use them, and several dozen purchasable Zulu warriors who are always to be found where the dollars are thickest."[18]

A concerned citizen wondered, "Mr. Hadden has, through his police, levied a monthly toll upon the gamblers. How this money is accounted for is another question."[19] Mounting suspicion forced the great man into a nakedly political act of contrition and reform. Suddenly—in the *Ledger*'s alliterative zing—David got down on dives. Of course, he didn't pursue the white reveler. May 5, 1888, saw a Saturday-night Negro roust, a favorite display of civic theatrics for years to come in Memphis. Police raided the Red Light Saloon at Beale and De Soto. They cleaned out the orchestra and dancers and emptied every bed from the rooms above. They hit 107 Gayoso next, and by the end of that raid, they had tied together a passel of Negroes and led them through the streets to the station house like a herd of scapegoats.

Monday morning the group stood under Judge Hadden's blue gaze. "Ten apiece, all 'round," he said, prior to hearing any evidence. "I want all these dens of iniquity raided. Raid 'em right now and make the habitués go to work."[20]

Chapter 7

FREE SPEECH,
HIGH REVELRY,
AND LOW SONG

Ida Wells read the *Memphis Daily Appeal* and the *Avalanche*.
She saw the stories. A matter of days in July 1889 saw "A Negro
Fiend Lynched—The Work of a Masked Mob At Iuka, Miss"
and "Swift Justice—A Negro Fiend Tried and Hanged by Judge
Lynch."[1] Mounting fears of physical violence mirrored a political
threat to black liberty—the Dortch Law, state legislation introduc-
ing a poll tax and other prohibitive measures against poor, unedu-
cated voters, passed in April 1889. Now new faces from Alabama,
Arkansas, and Mississippi—Judge Lynch's jurisdiction—were
filling Memphis. Wells sought sanctuary under golden John the
Baptist, who shined above pawnshops and saloons at Beale Street
Baptist Church.

Here she found the Rev. Taylor Nightingale preaching the
gospel of revolution. "No great race ever succeeded in the world
without wading through flame and flood," he said. When whites
accused him of provoking racial strife, he explained that Negroes

"must contend for their rights if they have to die in the ditch up to their necks in blood." He carried a pistol and hid a repeating rifle at his home behind the church, and in the church basement he honed a vastly more powerful weapon. There he reeled off the *Free Speech and Headlight.*

◆　◆　◆　◆

All the lynch talk revolved around sex. The white press described black men as "Negro fiends" and "Nigger beasts," overpowering white women. Whispers spread along Beale Street. Colored cop Townsend Jackson, a fixture on the street, got dismissed from the force for spending too much time visiting a married white gal on his beat. Reverend Nightingale contemplated the situation. Beale Street Baptist Church stood just a block south of Gayoso Street. Every day Nightingale saw white men pass below John the Baptist en route to debauchery. He understood the overwhelming reality of Southern miscegenation. But he could use lynch logic and lynch morals to make a larger point. With the city wilting in the summer heat and the lynch delirium gripping the countryside around Memphis, Reverend Nightingale and Republican leader Ed Shaw called a secret meeting at Beale Street Baptist for June 24, 1889.

A reporter with the *Avalanche* got wind of the gathering and interviewed Nightingale and Shaw. Shaw told him point-blank, "The purpose . . . is to form a society whose aim would be to prevent miscegenation." Shaw waved a piece of paper at the reporter, containing the names of fifty-one white men who were living sinfully with Negro women. "There are also seven houses kept by women with Negro blood, where the patronage is exclusively from the Caucasian race," he added. While everywhere else in the South claimed to be protecting its white women from Negro men, in Beale Street's alternate universe, black women needed protection from white men.

For colored politician Ed Shaw, gone were the days of alliance with Pappy Hadden. Now Shaw ripped at the very fabric of the Great Man's royal robe—prostitution had been a key ingredient in Hadden's revival of the dead city and a staple of his political power. The judge, though publicly chastened by a malfeasance indictment and the erosion of public trust, had refused to crack down on white-patronized brothels. He saw every criminal case in the city. If he couldn't license prostitution straightforwardly, he could punish it as he saw fit. Boss women at Bob Church's houses went before the judge periodically to pay fines for serving liquor without a license. Madame Lizzie Rial, Madame Etta Cooper, Madame Maggie Britton—they were never imprisoned, and the city filtered illegitimate money through legal channels while appearing to punish lawbreakers. Thus did President Hadden adapt his vice regulation to the confines of law.

Reverend Nightingale and Ed Shaw hoped to close the houses and shame the immoral white men, and Shaw promised to commence active operations without delay. Of course, they couldn't in any way go after white brothel keepers or white prostitutes, *white women*, but "woe unto the white man who dallies with the dark-eyed octoroon. He will be captured in the night and stretched across a log and punished as convicts are, as Negroes were before the war. His partner in sin will be driven out of town."

Nightingale grinned. "We wish to preserve the friendly relations between the negroes and whites," he told the reporter, "but the lines between them should be so deeply marked that they cannot be crossed."

That evening Shaw marched out of John the Baptist's shadow, crossed the bayou bridge, and continued up and along the stagnant water north a block to Gayoso. Standing on the brick sidewalk outside Birdie Golding's two-story brick house, he made himself heard. The women cursed him and launched bottles out the scalloped windows, and the whole street broke into an uproar, and madams went after Shaw as he hurried off.[2]

A thousand colored men convened at Beale Street Baptist Church the next night. They heard Reverend Nightingale read resolutions against the social evil and adopted a constitution and bylaws. Though they formally named themselves the Grand Union Fraternity, their street name—the Black Caps—called to mind those Caucasian protectors of feminine honor, the White Caps, better known as the Ku Klux Klan.[3]

In the morning, Shaw and Nightingale carried the Black Caps' resolution to criminal court judge Julius DuBose. Shaw read,

> Whereas . . . the evil of prostitution is on the increase, as is seen from the shameless practices every day occurring . . . and nearly one half of the illegitimate children born of colored mothers in this city betray the shameful fact that they are the children of white fathers, who by clandestine practices are backed and encouraged by certain colored women who keep these houses and inveigle the young and unsuspecting for the pleasure of white men . . . against these places of debauchery, against these dehumanizing practices, we respectfully ask your further interpolation, and on behalf of the good Negroes of our great city . . . offer an indignant protest against this open and notorious lewdness.[4]

One can see why the Black Caps didn't bring their decree to Judge Hadden.

◆   ◆   ◆   ◆

That night a white bartender named Warren McFadden and a few friends went to the brothel of Etta Cooper, a well-known madam and occasional tenant of Robert Church's. McFadden wanted to see his moll Daisy. The visitors initiated the standard social procedure, buying a round of drinks for the girls in the parlor. McFadden wanted to cut to the good part, to Daisy, and obnoxiously expressed it. This offended lady Cooper's decorum. His companions warned him, "She's a thumper from way back," and escorted him out to the sidewalk.

McFadden wiggled free and busted back through the whorehouse door. He smacked Madam Cooper in the eye with a clay beer bottle, turned, and ran the hell out onto St. Martin Street. Figuring he'd dusted her, he slowed and took a look behind—to see her charging after him holding her skirts in one hand and his bottle up in the strike position. He dove into a saloon, where she cornered him until a policeman intervened.

Next morning in police court, Judge Hadden told McFadden,

> Young man, I know Etta Cooper pretty well. She whipped out some sheriffs here once, and she has given the city some trouble. But when a man goes into places of this kind he takes his character, his reputation, and even his life in his own hands. It appears you went to Etta's house; that you were drunk; that you struck a woman and then ran away from the consequences. You ought to run before you hit any woman. Discretion in these cases is better than valor, and because you did these things I am going to fine you $50.[5]

Hadden discharged Madam Cooper, also there on drunk and disorderly, without punishment. Clearly, the Black Caps would be getting no help from Judge Hadden.

The Black Caps hit the whoring turf at night, patrolling Gayoso, Beale, St. Martin, Hadden, and Hernando. They rode the streetcars and harassed anyone who aroused their suspicions. Unlike Klansmen, they showed their faces. They carried unconcealed weapons. To some, they appeared no different from other Negro militiamen or drill organizations of the area. Though the Zouaves and McClellans of fever days had shrunk in prominence, the exclusively colored Tennessee Rifles, with their caps and fatigues, were a common sight.

Of course, the black sporting class cared not at all for the Caps, and members of the elite spoke against them too. "They're fools to waste their time trying to reform Negro women who prefer dishonor and degraded white men to respectability with a husband of their own race," said former county attorney general Thomas Cassells, a mentor of Ida Wells. "The law cannot stop the evil no matter how rigidly the authorities endeavor to enforce it . . . and if there is an effort to carry out the threat of whipping white men it will result in bloodshed."

◆ ◆ ◆ ◆

In the middle of all this, Reverend Nightingale made another decidedly bold move: he offered the editorship of his newspaper, the *Free Speech and Headlight*, to a woman.

Though Ida B. Wells ultimately accepted, she countered that she should become an owner of the paper as well, and so she purchased a one-third stake. And here on Beale Street, while Nightingale and the Black Caps fought for the honor of their women, she became the only female, black or white, in the country to own and edit a city newspaper. The paper immediately shortened its name to the punchy and poignant *Memphis Free Speech*.

Meanwhile the Black Caps bore down on white johns. Andrew Sanderlin, a colored magistrate, kept his courtroom at the corner of De Soto and Gayoso, sharing a double storefront with Bob Church's old saloon. Even white reporters acknowledged that Justice Sanderlin was an impressive man, a self-taught scholar of the classics who passed time between cases reading Greek and Latin, while "some of the white Justices, it is said, are seriously thinking about learning to read English."[6]

Peace courts were set up all over the city. Squire Charlie Gallina had one on Beale Street. Here citizens could swear out a warrant against an accused offender, and the court's deputies could then make arrests. Magistrates heard testimony and ruled to either dismiss cases or send them up to the larger courts. They functioned basically as a small claims clearinghouse.

When a Black Cap wanted to bring a charge of unlawful cohabitation (as miscegenation was styled) against an alleged offender, he swore out a warrant in Sanderlin's court. Sanderlin had a number of colored deputies attached to his court that he could dispatch to apprehend a suspect. And when the deputy hauled in the accused, who should await them but the Sanderlin court's prosecuting attorney—and Black Cap cofounder—Ed Shaw. Justice Sanderlin bound up numerous couples of white men and Negro whores to criminal court under indictment on miscegenation charges.

The whole racket outraged white citizens. A few showed up to Sanderlin's court to try to disrupt the proceedings. One described the scene July 11 on "the corner of Gayoso and De Soto streets,

> the very hotbed and breeding ground of negro vice in its worst and most hideous forms. Go there when you will and a horde of noisy and loitering negroes will be found in the vicinity. A thriftless, worthless, and insolent set they are, who lounge about the neighborhood, supported most of them by their wives and mistresses, and regarding work with a detestation that might become a prince of the blood royal. . . . The delight of humiliating a white man by a trial before a negro seemed to act upon them in a most rapturous way, and they could be heard congratulating each other upon the new dispensation of things. It was not a question of morality—the suppression of evil had no place in their thoughts—it was merely a race triumph.

This white visitor wondered, "Is Mr. Hadden powerless to put an end to this evil?"[7]

Next day the wheels of white justice turned—a hack pulled to the curb at De Soto and Gayoso. Three county sheriffs deputies hopped off and entered Sanderlin's court.

He glanced up from an ancient text to hear the deputies say he owed a ten-dollar debt that they were empowered to collect one way or another. Sanderlin didn't have the money or any property to forfeit and told them to not disturb his reading for such trivia. Sanderlin's deputy and the "horde of noisy and loitering Negroes" perked up. The deputies said they had to collect, and if Sanderlin could offer nothing of value, they would forcefully remove what they could get their hands on to satisfy the debt. The sheriff's men ripped down the railings. The courtroom klatch closed in, but Sanderlin ordered his deputies to stay back and allow the sheriffs to complete their business. The loafer chorus cursed the deputies as the witness stand and judge's bench marched out the door to a flatbed wagon parked outside.

Though the court was refitted and returned quickly to business, Sanderlin showed up to work two days later, July 15, and found a startling message. Someone had hung black crepe on the door and left a note.

Closed by Order of the White Caps

Sanderlin blew it off—it was a joke, he said. Most sensible folks echoed this view, "but there are some who firmly believe that there is in the city a secret league of white men who are acting in opposition, or rather as a check, to the Black Caps," the *Ledger* reported.[8]

The Black Caps refused to back down. White men fumed. "A spirit of hatred and revenge, aimed at the entire white race, and not a love of virtue, is at the back of these prosecutions," a man remarked. "They cannot successfully do what they have undertaken to do, and their efforts will sooner or later end in bloodshed."[9]

Black Caps still patrolled the district all night. They pulled over hired carriages and searched the passengers. In one they found a well-known city clerk with a pretty, painted octoroon on each arm. They pulled him out and arrested him. Ed Shaw and Reverend Nightingale split up to spy on the patrons at different resorts to fuel future warrants, while a burly Black Cap named Tom Anderson forced streetwalkers to run for cover. Catching one on the Gayoso bayou bridge on a stifling July night, Big Tom beat her unconscious.[10]

◆　◆　◆　◆

In police court, on the morning of July 21, 1889, during the height of the Black Caps' terror in the red-light district, a woman appeared before Judge Hadden on a streetwalking charge. She contested the charge, claiming she had a different vocation, as did many thus accused. "The washerwoman dodge plays out with this case," Judge Hadden thundered. "The next prostitute who tries to work it on me will feel my power."[11]

Up on his bench, the blue-eyed boss conducted business as usual but felt the gallows opening under his feet. A grand jury discovered a shortage of funds at the station house—$100,000 in bail bonds had been taken in, but $6,000 had vanished. Hadden's registrar of deeds, another fee taker, would soon be caught embezzling. After seven years of Hadden's rule, the papers were turning on the benevolent dictator. Rumblings had begun about a special Democratic Party convention being called to nominate a new ticket of Memphis taxing district officials.

On the seventh of August 1889, Hadden executed a grand finale. Per the *Ledger* report,

Everything was lovely and the goose hung high this morning in the court of David. The great man wore the same mixed suit he has been fining criminals in for many seasons. The coat is frayed at the sleeves and the pants kneed out, but they still cling to the great jurist's frame like they are stuck on him.

"Smoky Row" furnished the data for a trial this morning. "Smoky Row" is composed of five diminutive cottages at No. 202 Monroe Street. The houses are all right but the tenants are as crooked as a grape vine. Whites and blacks live huddled together and high revelry and low songs are indulged in throughout the night.

Festus Banks, an impish negro, and captain of a military company of "little coons," and Jack Rudliff, a lanky, flat-headed, and gingercake-colored mulatto, were tapped $10 each for boarding a street car on Beale street last night and trying to whip the driver.

Judge Hadden ordered the police to break up all such congregations as Banks now heads as captain.[12]

A subtle movement, by Hadden standards—by ordering the police to break up Negro militias, he sanctioned the destruction of the Black Caps without specifically naming them.

Ever more cleverly, closing Smoky Row had the effect not of eliminating vice but of moving it away from Monroe Street, away from the edge of respectable downtown. Hadden swept the brothels from the north side of town as well, and other than a couple venerable houses—old

No. 7 on Washington Street and the Ironclad at Front and Winchester
—he concentrated the venerable trade almost entirely into the Beale-
Gayoso sector.

◆　◆　◆　◆

Under threat from Hadden's ruling against black militias, the Black
Caps' fortunes sank deeper.

A man named Louis Radcliff, treasurer of Beale Street Baptist
Church and a leading Black Cap, had been siphoning funds off of his
employer, Buxbaum the clothier. Radcliff had developed at least one
other bad habit—he abused his woman. She blew the whistle on him
for stealing.

On the morning of August 9, 1889, Judge Hadden slammed Radcliff.
The offense might typically have resulted in Radcliff returning the purloined funds and spending a month breaking rocks. Instead, Hadden
set the Black Cap's bond at $8,000—a good decade's wage for most
colored workers. Even more terrifying, rather than keeping the prisoner
locally, Hadden bound the Black Cap over to the state.[13]

As everyone on Beale Street knew, getting bound over to the state
meant one thing:

> *They tell me Joe Turney's come and gone,*
> *Oh baby, they tell me Joe Turney's come and gone,*
> *Oh Lordy, he's got my man and gone.*
> *He come with 40 links of chain,*
> *Oh lordy, he come with 40 links of chain,*
> *Oh lordy, he's got my man and gone.*

Message received: the Black Caps vanished.

Chapter 8

THE TRUE SPARK
OF MANHOOD

A Negro newspaper called the *Appeal*, based in St. Paul, Minnesota, circulated nationally from offices in the twin cities, Chicago, Louisville, and St. Louis. Perhaps uniquely in the race field, it turned a profit. In her *Free Speech* columns, Ida sweet-talked the aging *Appeal* head J. Q. Adams, writing that he "once enjoyed the reputation of being the handsomest Colored man in America. . . . He is an indefatigable worker, of splendid physique."

It just wouldn't have felt the same coming from the Rev. Taylor Nightingale.

And lo, the *Appeal* not only ran that letter twice, it regularly posted Ida's subsequent work, lauded her efforts, and encouraged its readers to take *Free Speech*.[1]

But while she curried favor beyond Beale Street, Ida's mighty pen cost her dearly at home.

In late spring 1891, she authored a scathing critique of the city's black schools, still her full-time employer, berating its second-class facilities and incompetent teachers. Not only were amenities wanting, but many of her colleagues lacked the basic moral and intellectual qualifications to lead youth. A few had no more to recommend them than an illicit friendship with a white school board member. Ida knew her stuff but still preferred to keep the day job. She asked Reverend Nightingale to sign the editorial. He declined. The editorial ran anyway.

Hattie Britton was a black teacher whose white paramour served as an attorney for the school system. She boarded with her sister, music teacher Julia Hooks, and Julia's husband. Hattie returned home from a spree on Sunday morning, May 31, 1891, after Ida's critique had published. There Hattie's brother-in-law confronted her. He told her she was like a Gayoso Street whore to gallivant with a white man. Hattie ran to her room and shot herself in the head. Ida attended Hattie's funeral and coolly noted that the largest bouquet bore the name of the dead girl's white man.

The moral crusader still depended occasionally on contributions from her compromised benefactor. In the months before her critique of the schools, Ida asked Bob Church for an advance against her school salary.

Now with summer recess ahead and the town hot already, Ida got herself a press pass and hit the railroad. She spent the summer of 1891 canvassing for the *Free Speech* around the Mississippi Delta, Arkansas, and West Tennessee. "Wherever there was a gathering of the people," Wells recalled, "I was in the midst of them, to solicit subscribers for the Free Speech and to appoint a correspondent to send us weekly news," and so "the Free Speech began to be in demand all up and down the Delta spur of the Illinois Central Railroad."[2]

Ida returned to Beale Street to teach fall term and found herself persona non grata—the school board had voted her out of her teaching job. The black school exposé eroded her social life as well. As recently as winter 1889, a local colored paper called the *Watchman* had noted her presence at the Live Oak Club banquet, a gathering of Negro society. She was attired elegantly in blue surah and lace overdress.[3] Now the event of the season was approaching, and though Ida had once devoted much of her energy to running with the elite, no invitation to Mollie Church's wedding awaited her.

Out of the classroom and in social exile, Ida had little more to lose.

And just then news reached Memphis of an extraordinary event in the unfolding Southern race drama: a group of black men in Kentucky retaliated violently to one of their own being lynched. Ida wrote in the *Free Speech* of September 1, 1891,

> Those Georgetown, KY Negroes who set fire to the town last week because a Negro named Dudley had been lynched, show some of the true spark of manhood by their resentment. We begun to think the Negroes of Jackson and Tullahoma, Tenn., of Forrest City, Arkansas, Kentucky, and nearly the whole State of Mississippi, where lynching of Negroes has become the sport and pastime of unknown (?) white citizens, hadn't manhood enough in them to wriggle and crawl out of the way, much less protect and defend themselves. Of one thing we may be assured, so long as we permit ourselves to be trampled upon, so long we will have to endure it. Not until the Negro rises in his might and takes a hand in resenting such cold-blooded murders, if he has to burn up whole towns, will a halt be called in wholesale lynching.[4]

No black paper in the South had ever printed anything quite like it. It was perhaps the most inflammatory viewpoint yet published anywhere in the brief history of the American Negro press.

The piece had run without a byline, so the inevitable backlash hit Reverend Nightingale—a known rabble-rouser from his Black Caps days and still part owner of the *Free Speech*—rather than Ida. White editor A. B. Pickett, of the merged *Daily Appeal-Avalanche* wrote, "There are bounds beyond which it is unsafe for him to venture, and in the article published in his Saturday's paper, he has approached perilously near the danger line."[5]

White people weren't the only Memphians angered at Nightingale's impetuousness: the reverend's own congregation at Beale Street Baptist turned on him. Furious for jeopardizing their safety, they demanded he retract the editorial. But he stood by the *Free Speech* no matter the cost and refused to back away.

Ida's words "true spark of manhood" won hearts throughout the Delta. And if those words weren't enough to get the *Free Speech* noticed, she devised a gimmick to make the paper stand out even more. As the (St. Paul) *Appeal* editor, once the most handsome colored man in America, put it, "There seems to be a determination in the minds of the proprietors of the *Memphis Free Speech* that it shall be re(a)d so they are printing it on red paper. By the way the *Free Speech* is a good race paper and ought to be read all over the country."[6]

While the red-hot paper gained a wider following, it lost a partner. Reverend Nightingale left Memphis for the West and sold his share to Ida and a man named James Fleming. They had to move the paper from Beale Street Baptist Church and relocated it nearer the historic heart of the black community, at the corner of Beale and Hernando. Thanks to the Georgetown fire editorial, Ida now had fewer friends, one less ally, and all her money invested in the paper.

◆　◆　◆　◆

Ida and Mollie Church admired each other. Ida's friendship with Mollie's father notwithstanding, the two shared a sense of ambition and an idea of a woman's possibilities in the world that vastly exceeded the norm. (Though Robert Church endorsed Ida's activities, he wanted his daughter to be a Southern belle, one of his few wishes that would never come true.)

Remarkable Mollie, not yet thirty, had graduated from Oberlin College, spent years traveling Europe, studied at the Sorbonne, and taught at Wilberforce University before joining the faculty of a black school in Washington, D.C. For a colored girl born in the South during the Civil War, her life had been nothing short of extraordinary. Ida admired Mollie's combination—which was then thought contradictory—of uncompromised smarts and undiluted grace and femininity. Ida applied this to her activist journalism, wooing admirers as she sharpened her hatchet.

Despite the respect between Ida and Mollie, Ida became too controversial for Mollie to socialize with. The *Free Speech* nonetheless printed an account of Mollie's wedding October 28, 1891, to Washington, D.C., lawyer Robert Terrell.

Also in attendance that cool fall evening was a mutual friend of Ida and the Church family, Thomas Moss. Tommie carried mail on Beale Street and functioned as an informal tipster for the *Free Speech*—as soon as Moss picked up a story on his rounds, he delivered it to Ida. He was both a religious man and a race militant. He was a leader. He organized a colored militia, and not long before the Church-Terrell wedding, he assembled ten investors to form the People's Grocery. They located a store over a mile due south of the Beale district, in a frontier outpost beyond city limits known as the Curve. Moss and company were doing well. He gave a gift of six silver demitasse spoons to his childhood friend Mollie on her wedding.

Guests basked in the luxury of Mr. Church's home. Piper Heidsieck flowed, and tuxedos and gowns swayed to the Joe Hall and Jim Turner orchestra.

From that night on, Mollie Church would be better known as Mary Church Terrell.

◆　◆　◆　◆

Pappy Hadden no longer patrolled town on a mule-drawn buckboard, but his influence lived on, as prostitution prospered within the confines of Gayoso and its cross streets, St. Martin, Hadden, and Hernando. The 1891 city directory showed nothing but madams in residence on both sides of Gayoso, from Hernando to De Soto.

Even without Hadden's visible hand, Beale Street flourished. On November 10, 1891, Squire Charlie Gallina, Beale's de facto Italian ambassador, opened the most grandiose secular structure yet seen on the street. The Gallina Exchange stood four stories tall and sat four storefronts wide. Its elegant arched top peaked above the flat-roofed buildings beside it, with four cornices like flaming torches. Inside, it housed a burlesque theater and a restaurant specializing in roast lamb and macaroni. The squire held court up on the fourth floor.

It was still through Robert Church that the prosperity of colored Memphis projected to the world. A visiting entertainer had remarked to a *Boston Herald* reporter in 1889,

> In Memphis, Tenn., phenomenal progress has been made by the [colored] people. . . . In education, in music, in material prosperity, they are keeping pace with, if not outstripping, our people more favored in the North. . . . A Mr. Robert R. Church owns one of the finest hotels in Memphis. It takes up a whole block and faces three streets. Nor is this all. In the registry of deeds his name is on the books as the lawful owner of 60 brick and wooden houses. His note is good for at least $250,000.[7]

In 1892, after owning property on and around Gayoso Street for years, Church at last established a presence on Beale Street. He opened a new saloon right in the heart of whiskey row between Hernando and De Soto streets. He shared the building with Young and Morgan, the street's first colored dentists. A few doors away stood the shop of S. I. Jordan, colored shoemaker. Construction in progress across the street would, in a year's time, hold Wiley Abernathy's barbershop and musician Jim Neely's office. The black economy was still entirely entrepreneurial, small businesses and shops, but Beale Street amassed collective wealth.

The street's highest-profile venture was Ida Wells's and J. L. Fleming's *Free Speech*. Without classroom responsibilities, Ida spent much of her time on the road, engaging new readers. In the months since Reverend Nightingale's departure, subscriptions increased from 1,500 to 4,000, as the *Free Speech* grew into the liveliest connection between Beale and the black world around it.

Ida Wells was working in Natchez in this capacity March 9, 1892, when devastating news found her.

◆   ◆   ◆   ◆

The Beale streetcar line turned south at Hernando and arrived, after a mile and a half, at the Curve. There two competing businesses caused great turbulence, the colored People's Grocery co-op, led by former Beale postman and *Free Speech* tipster Tommie Moss, and the store of a white fellow named Bill Barrett.

Barrett repeatedly complained about the gambling going on at his competitor's business. On Saturday night, March 5, a dozen sheriff's deputies raided the People's Grocery. Moss and his key employees were trained militiamen, and the sheriff's men unwittingly stomped into a gunfight. Three deputies took severe gunshot wounds, including Charley Cole, who left the People's Grocery with one eye fewer than he'd brought. Eventually twelve Negro men were arrested in and about the store, including the manager, Calvin McDowell, and an employee named Will Stewart. Like Robert Church and Tommie Moss, McDowell belonged to the Tennessee Rifles black militia. McDowell was wearing fatigues that night, with his T.R. cap cocked.

The next morning's *Appeal-Avalanche* prematurely celebrated the city's lawful handling of racial violence.[8]

> If we had an inefficient police, if the courts had not always been swift to punish law-breakers, we have no doubt that Judge Lynch would have appeared speedily on the scene. No such affair had ever before occurred in the vicinity of Memphis. It was wholly unprecedented. It has been nearly 30 years since the lynching of anyone in Memphis, the safety of life and property here having come to be a matter of fame.[9]

Contrary to the white press outlook, paranoia gripped Beale Street. White men clumped on every corner, rifles and shotguns shouldered. Beale Street bards wove the tension into song—

They are roaming the streets with their guns,
Looking for us to shoot.
All we can do is pray to the Lord,
There's nothing else to do.
Oh me oh my, oh Lord have mercy on me.[10]

Sheriff's deputy Charley Cole, who'd lost an eye in the People's Grocery fracas, identified Tommie Moss as his assailant. Moss landed in custody on Sunday night, March 6, joining People's manager Calvin McDowell and clerk Will Stewart at the county jail on the north side of town.

At two in the morning of March 9, seventy-five masked white men silently surrounded the jailhouse. They slipped in, tied up the watchman, and found the cell keys. They rounded up Moss, McDowell, and Stewart and moved the three Negroes from the jailhouse up the C&O road to a field near Wolf River. There Moss told the masked men, "If you're going to kill us, turn our faces to the west."[11] And that was how they fell, three in a row, bullet-riddled, their heads to the west.

Though Moss was accused of inflicting the nastiest wound against the deputies, the masked white men executed Calvin McDowell most sadistically. No member of the masked posse would be identified or brought to justice for the lynching, but this circumstance suggests that the rivalry between the People's Grocery and Bill Barrett's had gotten personal.

McDowell, a proud, uniform-wearing member of the all-black Tennessee Rifles, had given an interview March 5, the night of the deputy raid and shooting at People's Grocery. "The trouble tonight had its origin last Wednesday night," he said, "when a difficulty occurred between some people living near my store. Mr. W. R. Barrett came that night. . . . Mr. Barrett struck me with a pistol. Being the stronger, I got the best of that scrimmage."[12]

Three days later the lynchers shot off McDowell's fingers and blew a hole through his right eye.

As news of the trio's disappearance hit the streets, the sheriff acted not to apprehend the kidnappers but to defend against Negro retaliation. Deputies crashed the Tennessee Rifles armory on Hernando and carried off every last gun and sword. They closed down Frank Schuman's shop on Main at Beale. Schuman had advertised his selection of guns, rifles, pistols, and pocket cutlery in Beale's black newspapers since the 1880s.[13]

Hundreds of white men armed themselves and, following the buzz of Negro insurrection, marched to the Curve. They found no proof of the rumor. The *Appeal-Avalanche* had applauded the lawful conduct of the white community in response to the People's Grocery raid, but as in the 1866 race riot, only the black population had behaved peaceably.

The dead men returned to the Beale district a final time. Three caskets lay open at the altar of Avery Chapel, displaying the grisly remains of white justice. Twenty-five hundred people packed the funeral. Four whites attended—a reporter, two policemen, and a fallen woman. She was curious, she said.[14]

Twenty-five hundred more clamored outside the chapel, packing the neighborhood all the way back to the *Free Speech* office. Inside, James Fleming echoed the response taking shape throughout the community. He counseled self-preservation and economic retaliation over race war:

> The city of Memphis has demonstrated that neither character nor standing avails the Negro if he dares to protect himself against the white man or become his rival. There is therefore only one thing left that we can do; save our money and leave a town which will neither protect our lives and property, nor give us a fair trial in the courts, but takes us out and murders us in cold blood when accused by white persons.[15]

Eight years before, a local judge ruled against a white-run big business, the railroad, in a black woman's favor. Now the truth was laid bare: the city had regressed.

By the time Ida got home from her barnstorming, Tommie Moss, Calvin McDowell, and Will Stewart were in the ground. She would recall:

I have no power to describe the feeling of horror that possessed
every member of the race in Memphis when the truth dawned upon
us that the protection of the law which we had so long enjoyed was
no longer ours. All this had been destroyed in a night, and the bar-
riers of the law had been thrown down, and the guardians of the
public peace scoffed away into the shadows. . . . The first feeling
was one of utter dismay, then intense indignation.[16]

Thousands of black Memphians followed Tommie Moss's dead-eye
gaze, west to land that was barren of civilization and the brutal preju-
dice that went with it—to Oklahoma. Their mass movement to dry soil
became known as the exodust.

Exodusters came from among the aspiring class. They were black
property owners, policemen, and entrepreneurs on the way up. Cash
Mosby, who'd supervised bonanza train excursions into Memphis, now
took up money to help others get out. "I have sent my family to Cincinnati and intend to follow them as soon as I can sell out," he said. "I was
born and raised in Memphis, but I cannot stay here any longer."[17]

Exodusters included the civil rights activists of their time. The Rev.
R. N. Countee, who had brought Ida Wells into journalism via his *Living Way* newspaper, owned one of the two black printing presses in
town and headed a large church. Now he sold everything and, with
his ministerial colleagues, led entire congregations of hardworking,
God-fearing people from Memphis to the West. Leaders like Taylor
Nightingale and policeman Townsend Jackson were gone. George Battier, Mary Burton Battier, and their children, symbols of wholesome
miscegenation, moved to New York.

For all the cynicism that Robert Church's business required, he
believed in Memphis. He operated in a nether region, exploiting ruf-
fians and visitors to help build the community. He had risked his life
and his wealth in aiding the city's recovery from riots and plagues, and
he derived great pride from watching modern Memphis rise. Tommie
Moss, who had been a guest at Mary Church's wedding not six months
earlier, had been carrying out Church's hopes for the bright side of

black life. Church also could not blame anyone for leaving. He donated $10,000—an astronomical sum—to Cash Mosby's Central Oklahoma Emigration Society.

The lynching and the exodust left Beale Street with a few well-to-do men and countless desperadoes. It left Ida B. Wells brokenhearted but fully militant. "I had bought a pistol the first thing after Tom Moss was lynched because I had expected some cowardly retaliation from the lynchers," she wrote. "I felt that one had better die fighting against injustice than to die like a dog or a rat in a trap. . . . I felt if I could take one lyncher with me, this would even up the score a bit."

Wells knew what a precarious position her people in Memphis occupied as of May 1892. She knew the *Free Speech* had no future there— "We had already announced that we would not stay in Memphis, but had not decided where to go."[18]

Wells had spent little time there lately, having been on the road selling subscriptions during the lynching, and she was away writing about the exodust afterward. She had investigated Mississippi lynchings of black men who were accused of raping white women and concluded that the rape charges covered up romances. Colored people who stayed in Memphis warned that her lynching stories caused them trouble.

Wells knew that more needed to be said about lynching, though— that the story couldn't die with Moss, McDowell, and Stewart. She gambled that the backlash would hit her this time rather than the people she would leave behind. In the office overlooking Beale, she composed her most shocking lines of the *Free Speech* yet. "Nobody in this section believes the old threadbare lie that Negro men assault white women," she wrote. "If Southern white men are not careful, they will over-reach themselves and a conclusion will be reached which will be very damaging to the moral reputation of their women."[19]

The bright blood-red issue, hot as fire, was published Saturday, May 21, 1892. Ida had just boarded a train to Philadelphia. Leaving may have saved her life.

The white Memphis press exploded. The *Commercial* and the *Eve-*

ning Scimitar called in no uncertain terms for the author of those lines to be burned like a witch on the busiest corner downtown.

One of two things happened next, both according to Ida's accounts. In early 1893 she would tell an audience at Tremont Temple in Boston of her Memphis horrors, saying that creditors had repossessed her printing press and locked up the *Free Speech* office. Her autobiography, published in 1970, almost forty years after her death, stated that a group of white citizens had stormed the *Free Speech* office on Hernando and Beale, destroyed the type and furniture, and left a warning to the paper's staff to leave town within twenty-four hours.[20]

Either action produced the same result. Though Ida B. Wells would not venture below the Mason-Dixon line again for thirty years, she was hardly through with the South. The *New York Age* of June 25, 1892, carried a front-page headline, THE TRUTH ABOUT LYNCHING: "The miscegenation laws of the South only operate against the legitimate union of the races; they leave the white man to seduce all the colored girls he can, but it is death to the colored man who yields to the force and advances of a similar attraction in white women."

The byline read: "Exiled."

The edition sold a thousand copies in Memphis alone. Other black papers copied the story, and Ida soon got on the public speaking circuit, beginning a lifelong campaign against lynching.

On October 31, 1892, a crowd filled the Metropolitan A.M.E. Church in New York to hear a much-anticipated lecture on Southern mob rule. They saw a slight, feminine form ascend the podium, a Southern lady of refined air. It was Bob Church's daughter, Mary Church Terrell, herself a distinguished educator and civil rights activist with gravitas enough to introduce the main attraction, Miss Ida B. Wells.

History would reunite them over the coming years, most notably in 1909, when they'd be the only females of color to sign the call to form the National Association for the Advancement of Colored People. While Wells's travels would take her across seas, and her message would keep her at the forefront of black civil rights activism, her connection to Beale Street would remain strong. The street had been indispensable—

its exceptional print culture and activist discourse had given her a voice
and nurtured it, while its rampant vice had supplied plenty of ammuni-
tion, and a little money, to keep her afloat.

◆   ◆   ◆   ◆

With Ida B. Wells, Beale Street made its first great contribution
to the world, but a chaotic age had reached its end. Beale Street had
lost its political clout, as Lymus Wallace left office with Pappy Hadden
in 1890 and Republican organizer Ed Shaw succumbed to pneumonia
in 1891. After the lynching and the exodust, Beale's activist journalists departed, leaving the street without a newspaper. The community's
confidence in the law—buoyed by Ida Wells's 1884 court victory—had
died with Tommie Moss, Calvin McDowell, and Will Stewart. Strivers
of the bright side marched their entrepreneurial spirit to Guthrie, Tulsa,
and unnamed corners of the Indian Territory. And yet Beale still had
assets, not least of which was a man who'd just opened a saloon on the
street and for some reason named it the New Era.

PART III

BIRTH OF THE BLUES,

1901–1918

*Any alert musician
could learn something,
even in that
sordid atmosphere.*

—WILLIAM GRANT STILL

Chapter 9

RED, GRAY, AND BLUE

Increasingly harsh racial segregation during the 1890s had the somewhat paradoxical effect of strengthening black communities, and nowhere would this fact come to life so colorfully as in Memphis. Between the turn of the century and the First World War, Beale Street would emerge as the mythical Main Street of Black America, hosting a renaissance in Negro business, a nationally powerful black political dynasty, and a new expressive culture that would revolutionize American popular music. Tremors that began on Beale would rumble to Pennsylvania Avenue in Washington, D.C., and Broadway in New York City.

The Beale neighborhood, while prospering in Negro uplift, also continued its underworld predominance. In fact, virtually all the great and memorable Memphis achievements were tied inextricably to vice and crime.

◆　◆　◆　◆

Throughout the 1890s, Memphis recovered from the political and social aftereffects of the yellow fever and the exodust,

regaining its city charter, abolishing the taxing district form of government, and enjoying renewed growth. Its population topped 100,000 as
of the 1900 census, making it, by the day's standard, a true metropolis.

In early 1901 new pavilions and auditoriums sprang up across the
city. As if anticipating a world's fair, speculators hastily constructed
hotels, and the city fathers fretted over how to raise $50,000 to cover
costs for a bonanza gala—a May reunion of Confederate veterans.
Amid all the activity, news that a former slave had donated $1,000 to
celebrate the army of the slave empire surprised Memphis and made
front-page news across the old Confederacy. Robert Church grinned, "I
never gave a cent in my life so cheerfully or gladly as I gave that check
to the veterans' entertainment fund."[1]

Church made the $1,000 donation at a critical moment in his career.
Nearing his sixty-second birthday, he recognized that time had turned
against him. He had begun to consider his legacy and wished people
would remember his frugality, generosity, and unobtrusiveness rather
than his whorehouses, saloons, and bullet holes. As for the thousand
bucks, it was the least he could do. He had entertained these men his
whole life: from the steamboats his father had run before the Civil War
to Gayoso Street at the dawn of a new century, old rebels had helped
make him rich and powerful.

A decade of narrow escapes led up to this moment.

Back in spring 1893, a county grand jury had indicted Church for owning properties used for disorderly and immoral purposes. But Church
came under fire with the best of company, for his name appeared on the
blotter alongside those of riverboat magnate James Lee, restaurateur
John Oakey, and major property owners Hu Brinkley, and Church's old
friend John Overton Jr. The indicted were pillars of Memphis society,
representing all major economic and political concerns as well as the
city's nobility. But while these gentry indictments were all rooted sub-
stantially in fact, they ultimately served to reinforce the power of these
few men in Memphis, for none of the indictments led to trial or even all
that much media attention, or created much lasting damage. Brinkley,

for instance, would donate $6,000 to the YWCA to purchase a charity boardinghouse for orphan girls the next year and win election as the city's police and fire commissioner.[2]

Church remained far enough removed from the money changing hands in his whorehouses to keep his deniability plausible. He still had steady Ed McKeever making the rounds. For nearly a decade, since he'd agreed to work off a gambling debt to one of Church's saloons, McKeever had dutifully collected Church's rents and supervised his gambling operations. The boss had four dice games rolling—one at the New Era on Beale Street, another at the old headquarters at Second and Gayoso, plus two more in the vicinity. "The way these games are run," McKeever explained, "is that if there are enough players without the house the man in charge of the game is not to play, as the rake-off is enormous, but if it is necessary that he should play, he goes in and takes his chances."[3] In other words, gambling with house money encouraged more potential profits than no gambling at all. The house kept a third of winnings, ostensibly for protecting players from the police.

McKeever floated, keeping the dice moving. He typically cashed out a hundred of Church's dollars at the beginning of a shift, to spice any lackluster games. His beat covered the six-block vice zone on Beale and Gayoso streets between Second and De Soto. In McKeever's nine years on the path, the Wild West wooden boardwalks had given way to brick on Beale and macadamized pavement on Gayoso. The scattered single-story brothels on Gayoso were growing into more spacious, luxurious abodes with second stories and balconies.

With inside knowledge of Church's brothel holdings and unsupervised access to his bank, McKeever was Church's most trusted employee. As the boss's real estate manager, he held a precarious spot as the middleman between legitimate business and prostitution. McKeever knew who would be scapegoated should a serious prostitution charge hit Church. He also seems to have grown frustrated with his role in the Church business, having worked his way up as high as he could.

On April 1, 1895, McKeever collected ninety-eight dollars from a Church sporting house. He stuffed the cash into his pocket, but instead of playing dice, he headed to the depot, caught a train, and left Memphis.

Church levied a criminal charge of embezzlement against McKeever and hired the Pinkerton National Detective Agency to find him. If Church had known his apprentice's true identity, he might have let him go. Nearly two months later the Pinkertons located him hopping bells at a St. Louis hotel. They sat on him there until the Memphis police came to make the arrest and escorted him back to the Bluff, arriving June 1.

The next day a news reporter called on the jail. McKeever, standing coatless in his cell, apologized for showing his shirtsleeves. He hadn't been expecting company or would have been ready, he said. The reporter noted his shrewd look and relaxed manner. He discoursed knowledgebly and pleasantly on a variety of topics, and weaved his tale of woe, beginning, "On Second and Gayoso streets."

McKeever explained his duties as overseer of Church's gaming franchise. He had lived among colored crapshooters, dandies, brawlers, and whores, passing himself as one of their kind. He said he'd landed in Memphis broke nearly ten years ago, adopted the name of a hanged Negro murderer, and chosen the life. He concluded,

> I have gone all the paces, much to my regret. I enjoyed life more in St. Louis, earning an honest living, enjoying the respect of everybody and respecting everybody, and I was only there six weeks, than I enjoyed the nine years of my life in Memphis. If I had worked in the hotel that I was employed in there for half the time I worked for Bob Church I would have been manager of the place.[4]

Ed McKeever, well known to the Beale Street Negro sporting class as a light-toned mulatto, was really Robert D. Roane, a blue-blooded white man with powerful family connections. Roane's grandfather Archibald had been governor of Tennessee, and a county of the state to this day bears their surname. His father, Archibald Roane Jr., though long deceased, had been an attorney in the nation's capital. Roane's uncle John T. Morgan served as U.S. senator from Alabama. Once the news of McKeever's arrest and the revelation of his identity broke, Roane's prominent relations converged on the Memphis jail.

A Capt. Roane of Oxford, Mississippi, arrived and said this Ed McKeever crook bore a shocking resemblance to Archibald Roane, late attorney of Washington, D.C. Capt. Roane of Oxford called Judge A. T. Roane of Granada, Mississippi, to the scene, and they listened as McKeever accurately delineated the roots and branches of the Roane family tree. The Roanes beseeched the court to let their boy go, but the court had no such power. That belonged to the plaintiff.

Attention swung to Bob Church. As if he had any choice, the Negro boss accepted reimbursement of the purloined funds and dropped his charge against McKeever.[5]

McKeever could have gone anywhere, done anything, had any opportunity opened to him in the halls of power or justice. That a white man had chosen Beale Street over white life attests to the allure, the magic, and the fun down on Beale. Though race switching was hardly unprecedented, the idea of a white man behaving as a colored one in the South and spending a decade in the Negro underworld remains extraordinary.

Savvy Church had maintained throughout the affair that he knew nothing of McKeever's alter-identity, that he didn't believe McKeever was white.[6] Privately, Church knew that he faced harsh retribution for debauching a young white man of such decent origin. Memphis's history up to this point indicated that gambling, prostitution, and liquor were okay, but a black man like Church encroaching upon the polite white world spelled trouble.

The McKeever episode occurred as a mixed-race man from Louisiana named Homer Plessy was in the midst of a protracted legal battle for his right to ride in a railroad car with white people. He would lose in his home state and lose in the U.S. Supreme Court; the latter body, in its 1896 decision, would essentially legalize racial segregation, coining the "separate but equal" phrase that would extend beyond trains to schools and public facilities, quickly worming its way into the national consciousness.

Church's own local scandal and the broader American trend compelled him to self-segregate. While McKeever-Roane was spilling his story to the papers in summer 1895, Church abandoned his longtime headquarters at Second and Gayoso, establishing himself on Beale at the heart of the busiest colored saloon district around. From that day forward, Robert Church and Beale Street were practically one and the same.

◆   ◆   ◆   ◆

Church greeted the deepening racial separation opportunistically. As the nineteenth century wore down, he rented out his colored saloons at either end of Gayoso Street to white men. In late 1898 the massive saloon-hotel-oyster bar-poolroom at Second and Gayoso, Bob Church's headquarters for nearly thirty years, welcomed a new tenant, Mike Haggarty. The saloon Church had run on De Soto and Gayoso the day of his vicious wounding in the 1866 riot went over to Haggarty's associate Bill McVey.

Putting white men and white saloons in place of colored joints had serious financial ramifications. Not only could white establishments channel a more prosperous clientele through their doors, but they could funnel a more prosperous clientele into the Gayoso brothels located between the two saloons. By the time Haggarty and McVey took over, Gayoso Street had grown from sparse one-story brothels to a row of two-to-three-story parlor houses.[7] "Its hundreds of lovely women," wrote Beale Street folk historian George W. Lee, "richly red-brown like the glow of the sunset, white like the snow of an inaccessible mountaintop, black and smooth like velvet with a soul, " were cycled into Memphis "to live in the twenty or more gaudy palaces of pleasure. . . . Their favors were offered to white men who were carefree and reckless in their spending." The clientele, according to Lee, ranged from "big white planters from the Mississippi delta, big merchants from Front Street, big names that were on the social register from New York to Frisco."[8]

◆   ◆   ◆   ◆

A visitor to Beale not long after the McKeever affair dubbed the street "the Jerusalem of Memphis and the negro's paradise."[9] A local reporter observed,

> Beale Street, from Main to De Soto, is the liveliest place in Memphis on Saturday. . . . The continual stream of humanity of both colors ebbs and flows all day, however, and reminds one not a little of the Midway of Chicago fame. . . . The line of brightly colored shops on both sides of the street are also pretty well filled, mostly by those of African persuasion . . . and the persuasive Hebrew merchants wear their most engaging smile. Recent improvements have been made in the buildings on this street, and some of the stores compare favorably with any in Memphis as regards to the class of goods for sale, and certainly there is anything one could or should want. Saloons, barber shops, shoe stores, furniture, candy, Chinese wash homes, dry goods, meat markets, drug stores, and bakeries are all sandwiched in together. . . . By walking very fast and wearing a metropolitan air one can manage to get through the crowds and avoid being pulled into a half dozen places by the earnest entreaties of the sidewalk artist.[10]

Some of the European-born merchants who'd set up shop on Beale in the 1870s assimilated into the white city, moving their businesses to Main Street in the 1890s, the Goldsmith department store and Schuman the gunsmith notable among them. The 1892 triple lynching of black entrepreneurs had chased scores of ambitious Negroes from the city, but it had the effect of concentrating those who remained in Memphis on Beale.

By 1894 white-run enterprises had given way to Negro enterprises. Established colored professionals like attorney Sandy Carter, justice of the peace Andrew Sanderlin, physician Thomas Cottrell, and shoemaker Nat Trigg moved their offices to Beale *after* the lynching, while Lymus Wallace, the stalwart colored elected official of the 1880s, returned to the street to run a Republican fund-raiser, as colored gaming saloons were derisively called. Colored ladies operated a fruit stand and a dress shop on the street.

The spirit of cooperation that had set Beale on strong footing in the 1870s helped reestablish its equilibrium after the exodust. At the corner of Beale and Hernando an Italian immigrant named Lorenzo Pacini assumed charge of the Pee Wee saloon, right across from Church's New Era tavern, while elsewhere in the same building the colored *Memphis Watchman* newspaper and the Chickasaw Cornet Band made their respective headquarters. The action stayed in three or so blocks, a layout that would remain intact for much of the next century—pawnshop row ran to Hernando, giving way to the saloon and theater block ending at De Soto, spilling into the black business and spiritual zone, centering on Beale Street Baptist Church.

◆　◆　◆　◆

As the Confederate throng approached Memphis in 1901, Robert Church was not the only notorious figure who engendered goodwill through charity. A fellow named James Kinnane pledged five hundred dollars to entertain the old boys in gray. Kinnane, at just over thirty years old, had risen from rough-and-tumble ranks to become the undisputed crime boss on the city's north side.

Though scarcely a mile stood between them, the city's north and south sides were worlds apart. While sumptuous south Memphis bred vice lord gentlemen, the north side gave rise to cold-blooded desperadoes and violent competition. Irishmen dominated north Memphis, with influential politicians hailing mostly from the Poplar Street merchant class. Their thugs came from a neighborhood known as the Pinch. North-side gaming action revolved through a few fancy casinos around City Hall, but most uptown gambling revenue was scattered in alleyways and dives. Uptown prostitution operated on a comparable scale. Aside from the Ironclad House at Front and Winchester and old No. 7 on Washington Street, the north-side operations paled in comparison to Bob Church's Gayoso Street palaces. The two worlds rarely met, unless upon a coincidentally scheduled court date.

Kinnane derived his power from politics. The Pinch encompassed the first ward, containing the largest batch of votes in Memphis. Soldiers from warring factions killed each other at *primaries*, fighting over a thousand votes. The Democratic primary of July 1894 found Ed Ryan, a gallant fireman and sadistic political boss, at his familiar post, the first ward polls, assisting voters in the correct expression of the franchise. Every election dispute ultimately came down to which of the opposing forces could induce a greater number of votes through currying, intimidation, and fraud.

A local letter carrier served that July day as the ward's election clerk, and he didn't care for Ryan entering the booth to help someone cast a ballot. The steel flashed. Ryan and the clerk fired their weapons at each other across a busy polling station, and as the stampede commenced, the clerk shot Ryan through the jaw.

Ryan spilled a trail of blood from the polls to a nearby firehouse, from where he hoped to retrieve his Winchester rifle. Instead, the police arrested him.

That letter carrier and courageous electioneer was James Kinnane.[11]

Kinnane learned that the Negro vote could be easily packaged. Voters needed to pay a poll tax and present their receipt for having done so at the polls, in order to cast a ballot. Kinnane paid hundreds of poll taxes for poor and politically uninterested citizens, collected the receipts, and offered his loyalty—and that of his constituency—to whatever candidate offered the most optimistic outlook on underworld affairs and Kinnane's prominence within the same. To show his devotion to a candidate, Kinnane's thugs worked the polls to discourage the opposition.

No political supporter delivered election-day results more effectively than those in greatest need of immunity from the police. After attaining ward political chieftain status, Kinnane dropped his letter pouch and opened a pair of north Memphis attractions, the saloon and boxing venue called the Phoenix Athletic Club, and James Kinnane's Dancing Hall, for colored. It'd be hard to determine where more blood spilled. Deposed Pinch boss Ed Ryan fought back, and the Kinnane and Ryan factions engaged in countless gun battles in those last years of the nineteenth century. During one such occasion, Ryan left a Kinnane lieutenant named George Honan with a shattered forearm and a bullet in the abdomen.

Just before the century's turn, the Kinnane-Ryan feud climaxed at the racetrack. In clear view of a full grandstand, Kinnane's trigger man Mike Shanley shot Ryan in the gut, leading to his agonizing death on April 9, 1899. Ryan was thirty-four, Kinnane a year or two younger.

Having dispensed with his rival, Kinnane acquired a prime corner of north Memphis—Front Street and Auction Avenue—and there opened a saloon, the Blue Goose. Kinnane paid $3,900 for the property, to one of Memphis's leading citizens, John Overton Jr.

Ed Ryan's death left Kinnane without competition on the north side of Memphis. Kinnane ran his pugilistic club, Negro dance hall, and the Blue Goose saloon with impunity. Now the power, opulence, and money in the Beale district tantalized him.

◆　◆　◆　◆

After word of the Confederate donation got around, a *Commercial Appeal* reporter found Robert Church on Beale Street, walking a vast tract of land he owned and supervising the construction of an immense concert hall. He carried himself with the same bulldog comportment that had gotten him this far. With his straight silver hair and his father's features, clad in a dark suit, white collar, and hard bowler hat, Church looked every inch the prosperous modern man. Nearby, laborers pulled down rickety old structures and landscapers planted hundreds of sapling trees. "It will be a resort for the colored people," Church explained.

He projected the image the city wanted the outside world to see. While other towns and cities throughout the South restricted black

education, black rights, and black opportunity, a black man could thrive
in Memphis. He could earn respect here.

Though Memphis newspapers typically rendered black speech in
minstrel show dialect, Church's diction appeared clean. Explaining his
motive for making the $1,000 donation to the Confederate gala, he said,

> My experience has shown that nowhere on earth will the colored
> man be treated better, or be given better opportunity to make some-
> thing of himself than in Memphis. . . . That is how I find the con-
> ditions here, those are the sentiments I feel, and that is why I, for
> myself and on behalf of my race, desire to be allowed to make this
> contribution to the cause in which all the people of Memphis are
> now interested.[12]

The media more than upheld its part of the dynamic.

As for the gift, it had invisible strings attached. If the city accepted
his money—*I desire to be allowed to make this contribution*, as he'd pas-
sively phrased the proposition—didn't Memphis also have to accept
how he earned it?

Church's Park and Auditorium—his "resort for the colored people"—
opened shortly after the Confederates left town. Carnival rides, gazebos, footbridges, and a playground graced the four acres of Church's
Park. Where Negroes once crowded into dark dives, they could now
stroll across manicured grounds breathing fresh air. Church's daughter
Annette recalled:

> Credit for the unusual taste in the arrangement of flowers in the
> park would be to my mother, who personally selected them and
> supervised the arrangement and planting of the beds. Perhaps
> the most conspicuous flowerbed in the park was round in shape,
> twenty-five feet in diameter, located near the bandstand. In the cen-
> ter of the bed was a large banana tree, surrounded by circular rows
> of red cannas and bordered with white periwinkle. Although there
> was no zoo connected with the park, tame peacocks strutted about

the grounds spreading their tails in fan shape and displaying their beautiful plumage, which attracted the attention and admiration of visitors.[13]

The centerpiece auditorium brought elegance and grandeur, without precedent, and another point of pride to Beale Street. It held 2,200 seats and a seventy-five-by-twenty-five foot stage. The drop curtain displayed the scene depicted on a painting over the mantel in Church's home, the burning of *Bulletin no . 2*, the Mississippi River disaster that Church had survived in his cabin boy days. As resident Robert Hooks recalled, the auditorium "had all the appointments, a stage, and beautiful trimmed curtains, and all the electrical lights, and spotlights, and everything. And he put in some boxes and a balcony. It was a wonderful place, I wish you could've seen it."[14]

Church's Park outshone any place in Memphis that white people prohibited Negroes from entering. It would soon attract national entertainers and world leaders to Beale Street. Not to be outdone, the city began developing a new park for white citizens. Memphis would name it after its grand old Overton family. But few knew how John Overton Jr. had helped make the Negro park possible, cosigning Church's loan to buy the land.

All the while Church's esteem grew. His reputation owed everything to his wealth, generosity, and power to shape public opinion. "The wealthiest of our colored citizens," a journalist remarked back in 1885, "has always given liberally to any enterprise for the benefit of the city."[15] His success and commitment to his hometown were intertwined, as described in an 1891 feature: "A firm believer in Memphis, war and plagues have never shaken his faith in her. . . . Whether it was to contribute to a fair, trades display, the reception of a president, republican or democratic, to a church, and orphan asylum, or to private charity, he has always responded promptly and liberally, regardless of whether the beneficiaries were of his own color or political faith."[16] By 1899, the local press had promoted his stature to "the wealthiest colored man in the state."[17]

His reputation expanded nationally through the *Colored American*, published out of Washington, D.C., and distributed around the country. It advertised Church's Park and Auditorium, and his daughter Mary Church Terrell wrote a column under a pseudonym for the paper. A *Colored American* feature in 1900 called him "one of the best known colored men in America." It touched also on his bond with Memphis. "No man of any race is more completely identified with the commercial interests of his community than is Mr. Church with those of Memphis. His name is connected with every great movement undertaken, looking to the growth and advancement of that city. In every printed statement touching its progress the name of Robert R. Church finds a prominent place."[18]

It cataloged his many courageous stands on behalf of his people and echoed the *Commercial Appeal* in its conclusion: "Today it would be difficult to state the extent of his wealth. There is little doubt that he is the wealthiest colored man in America."[19]

Chapter 10

DOCTOR SAID IT'D KILL ME, BUT HE DIDN'T SAY WHEN

They met at night in a tenement room down an alley off Beale, ten Negro men and women, maybe a dozen, all specially invited. Arriving little by little, they chatted until the entire group was present. They formed a circle around the room—"like Indians at a sun dance," said one.

They struck up a lullaby, humming. They pulled out little white cardboard containers and brassy, jeweled medicine boxes and passed them around the circle. They pinched out white powder and sniffed the grains off their fingertips.

Within minutes, as the boxes circulated, the lullaby intensified into a chant and built to a song. The phrase "take a whiff on me" captured the communal spirit, and as the sniffs passed the box, they passed the verse.

I've been drunk on absinthe, way down in New Orleans
I been drinkin' steamboat licker, since I was in my teens

I been drinkin' cordial, wine, and rum
But the quickest action and the most satisfaction is a little sniff
    of coke
It make me feel like ridin' on a cloud, floating through the air on
    wings
And I hear sweet voices a'singin' loud, and this is the song they
    sings:
    Honey take a sniff on me
    No more trouble will we see
    Baby, take a sniff on me, and we'll sail the jasper sea—
    Take a sniff on me![1]

"When I feel that coke working its way down to my legs, I want to dance," said one of the revelers.

> Then it goes to my mind and I want to sing. I see the clouds acomin' from the New Jerusalem, and I know the day is at hand. I ride the wheels of chariots and listen to the words of Moses in the wilderness crying out to save me. He says, Moses does, "You'se travelin' the wicked road." And then I feel so good! I see my dead friends in angel robes and doves a' singin'. The white folks gives way and you rides in hacks while they walk along burning bricks. You feel more powerful than white folks and figure you can lick four policemen.[2]

Cocaine arrived on Beale Street in the 1890s and quickly overtook bamboo—Beale Street slang for opium—as the preferred narcotic. Some attributed its appearance to New Orleans Negroes. Its inexpensiveness won over the economical partier who got wilder from a nickel box of coke than from a dollar bottle of whiskey. Devotees were called "sniffs" after the favored method of ingestion.[3]

Early on, Memphis's few coke fiends were depicted as harmless and colorful as town drunks, but by 1900 Cocaine Joe and Sallie the Sniff had overwhelmed local authorities: "In the eyes of the police, cocaine is more dangerous than morphine, more fatal than whisky, and more of a menace in public peace than the two combined."[4]

All-night drugstores and corner groceries legally retailed coke. One drugstore in the tenderloin paid a clerk seventy-five dollars a month to work an overnight shift to meet the high demand. Street drummers peddled the stuff, and police found little white boxes in holding cells, the sweatbox, and the witness stand. Law enforcers claimed that three out of four criminals arrested were high on coke. In court arguments, the old standby whiskey jag defense fell out of favor with criminals who now blamed cocaine for their actions.[5]

Coke party chants drifted down to the street corner, and as with Joe Turney and the 1892 triple lynching, Beale Street bards lyricized the coke craze. Lehman's drugstore supplied Beale Street's sniffs and got some free word-of-mouth advertising via the sidewalk banjo picker.

I went to Mr. Lehman 'bout half past nine
Said to Mr. Lehman I've only got a dime
To get my habits on, to get my habits on
I went to Mr. Lehman 'bout half past ten
Said to Mr. Lehman I'm back again
To get my habits on, to get my habits on
I went to Mr. Lehman 'bout half past leben
Said to Mr. Lehman I'll never get to heben
With my habits on, with my habits on.

Little white boxes stamped "Lehman's" littered alleyways, and coke song filled the air.

Sniff my cocaine, sniff it by the grain
Doctor said it'd kill me but he didn't say when
Hey, Hey Honey take a whiff on me.[6]

The coke craze coincided with high tide for the so-called coon song genre. As a Memphis critic explained, in early 1899, "The first coon songs sung on stage were really . . . negro songs. The music and words were composed by negroes, not in parlors or theaters, but as these natural minstrels worked. Some smart song writers began adopting the tunes sung by the negroes. . . . The success of the songs was instantaneous."

Coon song evolution exhibited a number of time-honored trends in American pop music, as the critic explained. "It was another case of the white man beating the negro. He made money from the sale of the songs, but the spontaneous coon songs of the negro are better than the written-to-supply-the-demand coon songs of the white man."

Coon songs took blame for promoting impolite language, publicizing sex, and eroding young minds. "They have brought the word 'wench' into much more frequent use," wrote the critic, his outrage giving way to sarcasm. "The man who wrote this song could think of nothing else to rhyme with what had gone before, so he slapped a couple lines of 'ram-a-jam, jam, jam' into the chorus. These are the actual words. There's intellectual food for a cultured audience."

Already, a noted Memphis physician warned that "a coke fiend would steal from his mother to get a good sniff," while a cultural gatekeeper hoped "coon shouting and its kindred evil the cakewalk have had their run."[7]

◆　◆　◆　◆

To rampant cocaine abuse on Beale, north-side gangster Jim Kinnane added a dash of violent boisterousness. Kinnane began operating the Tivoli at 81 De Soto Street, corner of Gayoso, opening it December 20, 1901. He hired a colored fellow named Alfred "Tick" Houston as manager. The Tivoli occupied a big two-story brick building that had housed the colored peace court of Andrew Sanderlin as well as one of Bob Church's old saloons.

Tick Houston was a renaissance man of sorts, managing under one roof a con game, a colored vaudeville theater, and a pimp hive. "On the first floor was a bar, and strung along the walls were a number of gaming wheels," as Beale Street's folk historian George W. Lee described it. "If the lucky number was caught on one of those wheels the winner was supposed to get an amount of money equal to what he carried in his pocket; but when he turned his roll over to be counted he was kicked out without receiving what he had won or what actually belonged to him."

Upstairs, pimps hung around waiting on their women to bring the money. "These 'sweet men' and 'easy riders' were always immaculately dressed in well tailored suits and expensive shoes," in Lee's rendering. "Each of them had from one to three women 'hustling' for him. If they failed to bring in the money, they were usually boxed in the ear and sent back into the night to search for trade."[8]

The Tivoli served opium upstairs while its orchestra played downstairs. For a time, early in Kinnane and Houston's occupancy, Lou Barnes—"a tall mulatto woman," according to Lee, "the most colorful figure in Beale Street's night life"—hosted "riotous parties nightly, and the girls of her house had a feminine lure that was like the tinkle of bangles, a call to Bohemia."[9]

Tick Houston's mimicked the scenery two blocks west at Second and Gayoso, where Bob Church had rented another saloon to a pair of Kinnane affiliates. George "Bud" Degg and Mike Haggarty were both just over thirty years old. Bud Degg was a horse-racing expert with connections in Chicago and Louisville. Haggarty had risen to prominence through political acumen, playing an important role in the 1898 mayoral election, packaging black votes by the bundle. The victor had tallied the decisive margin with a landslide in the fifth ward—encompassing Beale Street—thanks in part to Haggarty's work. The *Commercial Appeal* conceded, "[The Negro] came unexpected and captured the ballot box, electing whom he chose."[10] In the aftermath, Haggarty set up shop at Second and Gayoso.

Mike Haggarty would become one of the most criminally accomplished figures in the country, an energetic and enterprising man who fixed races, trials, and elections, a patron saint to con men nationwide.[11] He operated a saloon, a bawdy house, and the type of elaborate and lucrative long con dramatized in the movie *The Sting*.[12] His influence extended into the employment practices of the police force and, in time, up to the mayor's office. He became the city's fixer, having a hand directly in every activity that made the city famous, all emanating from on and around Beale Street.

On paper Haggarty owned nothing. Like many Irish-descended clerks and firemen in his quiet residential section, he lived in a modest home with his old mother. But he and Degg stepped out in the evenings, wrapped in silk shirts and white scarves. They rechristened Church's old billiard hall the Turf Saloon and Memphi Theatre and ran it as a midnight resort for white men, replete with a barroom adjacent to a dance hall and theater of improper vaudeville that featured a kick show starring ladies from nearby disorderly houses.

The Turf employed a floor walker named Frank Sweeney who explained that his duties were "to make the gentlemen take off their hats, and to protect the house." Sweeney raised the curtain to start the show and kept order during its raucous proceedings.

"The upper floor is let to lodgers," wrote a wry observer, "the majority of whom are females."

Haggarty's hall endeared itself to underworld denizens. On April 4, 1902, the police arrested Angelo "The String Kid" Arata in the Chinese Laundry opium den at 178 Beale. He stood accused of larceny and the theft of $125 from a streetcar passenger, and as the scenario implied, he was blowing these proceeds at Kee Sing's.

When Arata went to trial later that month, five witnesses appeared on his behalf, swearing he'd spent the entire night of the robbery at the Turf. The five were the Turf night bartender, the Turf bouncer, stage director of the Turf dance hall and variety sideshow, and two regulars, one a former Turf bartender. The jury voted against conviction, eleven to one.[13]

Other stars of the underworld, some shining, some just rising, orbited around the Turf. Paul Battier, a jewel thief active and well known from New Orleans to St. Louis, called it his headquarters. But a shadowy figure, soon to become the most feared man in Memphis, slept away the sunny hours there, too—George Honan.

Honan stood five foot eight or so. He had red hair and a thick red mustache on a boulder of a head stuck flush to his steamer trunk torso. He favored green suits, and like his colleagues', Honan's skin was night-life pallid. Honan, the enforcer, and Mike Shanley, the noted marksman who'd wiped out his rival Ed Ryan at the racetrack, brought an intense new violence to the Beale-Gayoso district.

In May 1902, Kinnane bought a two-story Italian grocery located on Beale in the heart of the saloon district between Hernando and De Soto streets. He called his place the Monarch—a reflection, perhaps, of his robust self-esteem. Mike Haggarty took charge. He would supervise Kinnane's Beale district holdings, and function as the key election fixer in the city's south wards just as Kinnane controlled the north-side.

The Turf and the Monarch gave the Haggarty-Kinnane crew prime locations within Memphis's two most powerful downtown wards, four and five. (Kinnane had the large first ward vote perennially sewn up since Ed Ryan's demise.) Ward four encompassed much of the white downtown business elite. The Turf became the ward four political hub, serving as a registration center and occasionally a polling place.

Ward five included the black saloons in the heart of Beale. The presence of the black vote in Memphis had as much to do with the city's unusual character and remarkable history as did its distinguished citizens. From the end of the Civil War on through the twentieth century, while virtually every other city in the South took legal and extralegal measures to keep Negroes from the polls, the black Memphis vote remained in play. Even when exploited, the black vote benefited citizens of color, as a generation of black creativity began, however indirectly, through the auspices of Negro divekeepers.

On top of the ballots cast for their candidates, the Kinnane-Haggarty gang deployed Harry Hartley and Harry Keene to intimidate voters and, failing that, to remove ballot boxes by might.[14]

The gang influenced the legitimate voting apparatus as well, with Jim Kinnane's brother Tom installed as an official election judge in the first ward, while Kinnane and Haggarty's muscleman George Honan solemnly served in the fourth.[15]

Memphis politicians, by tradition, protected their underworld friends, dating to an edict issued in early 1893. The city's leader at that time declared that only *local* criminal entrepreneurs could open gambling saloons, barrooms, or brothels. This nifty legislation prevented traveling gamblers from setting up shop in Memphis. Local underworld bosses could report to the police anyone operating an underworld venture without political sanctioning.[16] This law invested tremendous power in men like Church, Kinnane, and Haggarty, who rewarded political leaders with votes. Unlike outsiders, locals could be trusted to enrich the city, as described in a 1902 *Commercial Appeal* editorial:

> On the first of the month, the gamblers posted a [cash] forfeit, one for each place [they ran], at the police station. The name of the proprietor or some attaché of the house was placed on the docket, and he was charged with a misdemeanor . . . and in police court the following day the name was called out and the forfeit was declared, no one being present to answer the misdemeanor charge. The forfeit . . . was then turned over to the trustee, the custodian of the city's money. The same process was repeated on the 15th of each month.

The program showed real benefit—"The fire engine house on the bluff was erected from money secured from gambling houses, and the pavement in Court Square was paid for by the same process."[17]

◆　◆　◆　◆

Kinnane, Haggarty, and Church weren't the only major power brokers in the tenderloin saloon business.

Like the rise of Jim Kinnane, John Persica's tale hearkens back to that 1893 declaration of local vice independence.

Born in Italy around 1860, Persica debuted on the public record in Memphis as a result of his apprehension of a chicken thief. Stopping the suspect in the act, Persica shouldered his shotgun and vaporized the man's head. In a dangerous precedent, the killing went unprosecuted, and presumably, John Persica formed the idea that he could get away with murder.

To those who let his chickens be, Persica was a disarmingly warm character, well dressed in wool coats with brass buttons, his bear-greased black hair parted down the middle, and his handlebar mustache oiled and twirled catfish-whisker thin. Deep smile lines creased his face from the corners of his eyes, eyes that twinkled in merry mockery of his psychopathic nature. Or perhaps because of it.

Persica had arrived on Beale Street via the Italian pipeline—he tended bar at Charles Gallina's, and by 1891 he had joined the colorful cast at Vigelio Maffei's place, Pee Wee's. Persica took up residence there at 117 Beale, commingling with the Negro music ensemble known as the Chickasaw Cornet Band, plus the idol of the street, violinist Jim Turner.

Like Kinnane and Haggarty, Persica carved out an ethnic political niche. He made the Beale Street Market House his base. He saw to it that the Italian produce wholesalers, retailers, and peddlers connected to the market house registered to vote in ward five, regardless of where they lived, and he could deliver these votes to his candidate of choice. Persica thus received diplomatic immunity.[18]

By the turn of the century, Persica had built himself a three-story castle halfway between Beale and Gayoso on Hernando Street, where, according to one estimate, twenty penal statues were nightly violated. It provided work for Negro bands and blue vaudevillians. It gave vent to every known form of vice and some new twists. Persica ruled his castle himself, sleeping for maybe a few hours in the morning but otherwise always at the ready.

He needed no entourage or security force to maintain order and watch his back. If anyone wanted to fight in his castle, he dragged them out across the street to the cobblestone alley behind the market house and boxed them. One day Persica was chatting with a visitor in his saloon, leaning against a pool table, facing the bar and a mirror that ran behind it, as a disgruntled employee belly-crawled under the pool table, en route to stab Persica. Persica caught a glimpse of his assailant in the mirror and casually swung his foot back, bootheeling every tooth out of the attacker's head, without pausing his conversation.

Persica and Kinnane avoided conflict with each other. Persica stayed away from the black vote, concentrating on the Italian market house bloc, and Kinnane knew better than to waste time meddling with Italians. Persica protected the Beale Street joint where he'd gotten his start. Pee Wee's benefited from Persica's immunity, and Beale Street benefited from Pee Wee's.

Pee Wee's namesake Vigelio Maffei returned to the old country, leaving his lounge and lodging house to Lorenzo Pacini. As his predecessor had done, Pacini catered exclusively to a black clientele and was known up and down the railroads for his hospitality—he let hoboes sleep away the winter months around his woodstove. Saturday nights saw the bar packed. Thunderous crashes emanated from a back room where card games occurred around six or eight stands and victors announced a winning hand with a hammering fist on the table. When the noise reached the street and rattled police eardrums, drawn Colt revolvers made their appearance in Pee Wee's and chased everyone to the station house. Typically, by the time a court case rolled around, the officers could never identify the Negro sportsmen before a judge, and so it began again.[19] Whether they intended to or not, Haggarty, Kinnane, Persica, Church, and the divekeepers who flourished through their auspices enriched not only Beale Street political life but its culture, as politics and music became the building blocks of Beale Street's burgeoning national identity.

Less than a year after its opening, Church's Park Auditorium stood out prominently as a key stop on the emerging black entertainment circuit. Church brought internationally renowned Negro pianist Blind Tom to town, and on April 15–16, 1902, the most elaborate, perhaps the most successful, and the most widely traveled colored show graced the stage, the Black Patti Troubadors. Their dizzying, dazzling program featured "A Farcical Skit in One Act: A Filipino Mis-fit," plus a Slack Wire Equilibrist, and the Operatic Kaleidoscope, showcasing a chorus, expert soprano, contralto, tenor, baritone, and basso singers around the star, Sissiretta Jones, the Black Patti.[20]

Church aimed high in politics as well. He had served as a delegate to the 1900 Republican National Convention that nominated the ultimately victorious Theodore Roosevelt. The Roosevelt presidency proved momentous for colored America, as T.R. welcomed a black guest, Booker T. Washington, to dinner at the White House. On November 19, 1902, Roosevelt made an appearance on the Main Street of Negro America. A homecoming for Gen. Luke Wright, Memphis-born ambassador to the Philippines, occasioned the visit, and the celebration took place at Church's Park and Auditorium.

Buntings, flags, and patriotically colored flowers decorated the stage and balcony. Wright and Roosevelt sat on plush red parlor chairs brought from the Church home. The governors of Tennessee and Mississippi, the mayor of Memphis, and Memphis's first citizen, John Overton, graced the stage beside the honored guests. Beale Street music teacher John R. Love led the Young Men's Brass Band, and the crowd cheered "Dixie" as uproariously as it did "The Star-Spangled Banner."[21]

Following the speeches, a choir sang "God Be with You Until We Meet Again," but rather than close out on such a solemn note, Professor Love sent the president off with "There'll Be a Hot Time in the Old Town Tonight." Roosevelt stood, bowed, and clapped the beat. The audience jumped in unison, waved flags, and drowned out the band, yelling itself hoarse until the last note.[22]

Roosevelt's visit was another triumph for Robert Church. Guests at a 1902 party in Church's honor at the home of his son-in-law, Judge Terrell of Washington, D.C., had appeared to *Colored American* readers the previous month as "typifying in its broadest sense the education, the wealth, the moral culture, and solid worth of our progressive people." This story too emphasized Church's ties to Memphis. "Her people, irrespective of race, look to him for wise counsel, for substantial aid, and for inspiring example. His business enterprise there, his mammoth auditorium, his beautiful home, and his open purse for public benefit all stand as monuments."[23]

Church's name became associated with the high quality of Negro life in Memphis. "Floors are carpeted and pianos or some other musical instrument ornament the homes of three-fourths of our people," one reporter offered, with Church as his utmost example. "Five hundred thousand dollars would be a moderate estimate of his wealth."[24]

As the president's caravan turned out of Church's Park, heading down Beale, it passed an attractive two-story building decorated with a blond-brick-inlaid facade: the Monarch.

Inside, Jim Kinnane had designed a masterpiece of criminal carpentry. Mirrors lined the lobby walls, leading to a brass-railed mahogany bar stopping at a brick wall at the back of the joint. The Monarch had become widely known for its ornate decor and fancily attired clientele, contrasting Pee Wee's burn-scarred cigar counter and the heap of hoboes sleeping around a stove. Behind the brilliant foyer and barroom, Kinnane had installed a steel door that led through the brick wall to the tavern's gambling den. The gaming apparatuses were situated above trap doors designed to conceal them in the event of a raid.

Upstairs, the Monarch dance hall stayed open around the clock, its windows thrown open. Raggy piano spilled out onto Beale Street where the presidential parade passed below.

Chapter 11

PURIFYING THE
MORAL ATMOSPHERE

Memphis crime, politics, and culture crystallized in the summer of 1904. A sensational pair of murders started a chain of events that altered the city's political landscape and led to one of Memphis's signal contributions to American culture.

A posse of five hit Beale Street on July 11, 1904, a warm night. They could smell the rain blowing in.

These quasi-legal deputies were a step above bounty hunters, a notch below policemen or sheriffs. They worked for Justice Frank Davis, a county magistrate. They could make court-ordered arrests but had no legal power beyond that specific task.

A man named John Lawless led the posse on this night. Monday nights like this one whittled the Beale crowd down to young hopefuls, their newsboy caps worn sideways and backward. The heavyweight gamblers and star streetwalkers were nowhere to be seen. The posse carried warrants to raid Pee Wee's, the New Era, and a dump on De Soto Street, all suspected of hosting gambling operations. Up the Beale bricks with Lawless marched deputies Solly, Shoults, McDermott, and a Negro named Houston Mitchell.

Mitchell was the tallest, loudest, and most muscular and heavily armed of the bunch. On his right wrist he wore a leather thong tied to a lead ball. He had gotten his shiny black .41 Colt revolver out of pawn and holstered it to his hip.

The posse stomped through light traffic to Pee Wee's first. They burst through the front door ready to swing—and looked across the bare barroom at the lone figure in the place. An Italian barkeep cheerfully struggled to comprehend their business and sent them away.

They crossed Beale to the New Era, Bob Church's place, now under his brother-in-law's management. The ranch stood empty. News of the raid had traveled faster than the posse. Now Lawless and the lawmen turned up Hernando and stopped in front of Persica's to regroup.

They cursed and stared at one another, Houston Mitchell exhaling beer vapors and profanity. Deputy Solly announced he had personal business to tend to before it rained. He split off, heading left on Gayoso toward Haggarty's place, the Turf.

"Best not be layin' down on us," Lawless called.

The remaining four deputies turned right on Gayoso toward De Soto Street, heading through the muffled perfume, piano strains, and laughter seeping from Bob Church's red-light row—six new two-story brownstones cocked at an angle to the street, each with a brass-railed porch. The posse turned left on De Soto, arriving at a two-story brick duplex and their last appointment for the night.

They opened a glass door from the street and entered a cramped, unlit vestibule, where a couple of Negroes flattened against the wall to let the deputies pass. Inside, colored men and women, dressed for the field and the factory, were gambling around a series of long wooden tables with bench seats. An oil lamp flickered in the middle of each table, showing scatterings of metal money and dried corn kernels. Two white men stalked up and down the aisles, Harry Hartley and Harry Keene, supervising the action. The place was so dark, smoky, and noisy, none of the silhouettes looked up until Lawless jumped onto one of the tables and shouted that everyone was under arrest.

Deputies Mitchell, Shoults, and McDermott fanned out and separated the men to one side of the room, women to the other. The deputies began tying all the gamblers together for their trip to jail.

Just as they were ready to go, two more white men pushed into the game room: George Honan, with a smiling Mike Haggarty behind.

Minutes later at the police station, Capt. Oliver Perry caught a call reporting a gun battle in progress at 42 De Soto Street. Perry hopped into a carriage. A *Commercial Appeal* reporter dove in with him. Heavy rain fell as the buggy careened around tight corners, sliding along slick stones.

The captain and the reporter arrived at 42 De Soto and found a crowd outside. Whatever had happened was over. They entered the dive. The reporter lit a match: overturned tables, coats and hats, scattered corn kernels. The match died as the two men saw a body draped across one of the benches, its feet dangling toward the floor.

The reporter struck another, and he and the captain found the colored deputy Houston Mitchell bleeding to death from gunshot wounds.

More police arrived, and as they canvassed the neighborhood, they discovered another casualty—Deputy Thomas McDermott had caught two bullets in his side. He'd staggered next door to Lehman's drugstore, where he'd lain down on a cot in a back room and died.

The fracas became known as the De Soto Street Riot. No criminal event in the city's history up to that point had sparked so much outrage or such a massive response. Politicians and polite citizens alike cried that the city's crime had grown out of control. Criminal court judge John T. Moss, saying that Memphis positively vomited crime, charged the sheriff to "proceed upon your duties at once, and assist this court in purifying the moral atmosphere of this community."[1] Citizens rallied by the thousands to demand justice in the De Soto Street case.

No one could know that events surrounding the De Soto Street Riot would develop into a lengthy and elaborate power heist. Crime wasn't out of control in Memphis—crime was in control of Memphis.

◆ ◆ ◆ ◆

During the night of July 11, into the morning of the twelfth, the police apprehended Haggarty's Turf Saloon business partner George "Bud" Degg, who was soaking at Henry Loeb's Turkish bathhouse. Harry Hartley, supervisor of the De Soto Street game, awoke in a bed at Lizzie Sanders's sporting house on Hernando and opened his eyes to see a police officer standing over him. Hartley expressed no surprise and went along to jail without protest. Haggarty and Honan were found above a hardware store on the north side of town, next door to the residence of Jim Kinnane.[2]

The county grand jury returned fourteen indictments against Haggarty, Honan, Degg, Hartley, and Harry Keene for murder in the first degree and assault to murder. Two days after the riot, the suspects appeared in court. Nocturnal animals blinking in bright warm light of day, they faced their charges and pleaded not guilty. Degg laughed. The others appeared bored, with the exception of George Honan, whose eyes darted about the courtroom. Honan emerged as the primary suspect, and the court opted to try him first. Not even Honan disputed that he'd killed Houston Mitchell. He said he'd done it in self-defense. Trying a white man for a Negro's murder, however, was not an option. Honan stood accused of a homicide in the first-degree of the white deputy Thomas McDermott.[3]

The trial featured a flashy coterie of defendants and witnesses, all bringing notorious reputations to the proceedings. Honan was fresh off an acquittal for election-day antics, charges earned during the municipal contest that January. He and Mike Shanley had allegedly rioted in the ninth ward, instigating a squabble that led to an assault-to-murder charge against Honan, a pistol-carrying charge against Shanley, and a story about the two absconding with the ballot box and passing it to Keene and Hartley in a carriage.

Their performances from the stand went before a packed courtroom and a rapt reportorial brigade.

"George Honan is not a handsome man," one scribe noted, "but by no means is he ugly." Honan's face appeared "strong, and the features denote stubbornness of spirit and a temper that might on occasion leap the bounds of propriety." Honan's eyes were "small and alert and gray. A rather long nose and a receding chin complete the features." Honan dressed well. "In fact, he is somewhat vain. He wears a diamond ring and a diamond shirt stud."[4]

George "Bud" Degg showed up, "With tan shoes and a filmy shirt of silk," observed another journalist, "had he been coming to a social function instead of approaching the bar on trial for murder, he could hardly have looked more natty and wholesome."[5]

Then came the presumed ringleader: "No man has ever called Mike Haggarty a coward or known him to desert one whom he has classed as his friend. . . . He came up smiling, easy but not impertinent, and while imperturbably polite yet firm and adamant." His manner betrayed no scar of incarceration. "He is still the confident, well-fed, neatly-groomed man of affairs," a reporter fawned.

A famous and star-crossed pair of attorneys took up either side of the case, with U.S. senator Edward Carmack prosecuting Honan for the state and U.S. congressman Malcolm Patterson defending Honan. The two were engaged in a bitter political rivalry that would culminate when *Governor* Patterson pardoned an ally who shot Carmack dead on the street in 1908.

Senator Carmack made a great show of taking the arm of deputy McDermott's pretty young widow, attired in mourning garb with a broad black hat and full skirts, and escorting her to her seat. The packed courtroom in Southern summer conditions reeked of smoke and sweat, much like the dive where Mitchell and McDermott had taken their mortal wounds.

As the prosecutor reconstituted the events that had resulted in Deputy McDermott's death, he exposed connections between notorious crooks and trusted officials. Justice of the peace Frank Davis had signed the warrants sending Lawless, Shoults, Solly, Mitchell, and McDermott to raid Pee Wee's, the New Era, and the De Soto dive—the adventure that had dispatched Mitchell and McDermott to their graves.

Justice Davis had a strained relationship with Deputy McDermott but sent the young man anyway. Three weeks earlier McDermott had married Davis's daughter, over the old man's objection. Justice Davis meanwhile carried on a friendship with a rather compromised public figure: Jim Kinnane.

Completing the circle, Kinnane, known affiliate of Honan and Haggarty, had been hanging around Justice Davis's office much of the afternoon during which Davis signed the raid warrant. Triggerman Mike Shanley had been there too. Justice Davis would testify that he regularly smoked cigars and drank liquor with Jim Kinnane, but he insisted this always took place at the corner near his office and never anywhere else.[6]

When defendant George Honan took the stand, "those who looked upon him as he sat there waiting for the attorney to begin were compelled to acknowledge that, right or wrong, guilty or innocent, George Honan was still, in this supreme test, what he had always borne the reputation of being—game to the core."[7]

Thirty-three-year-old Honan testified that he took care of his widowed sister and her children. (He also made license applications for quasi-legal businesses such as saloons or gaming houses in her late husband's name, though didn't mention this on the stand.) He had been employed as booking agent for the floor show at Haggarty and Degg's Memphi Theatre. (This job entailed recruiting the Gayoso sporting women who desired the opportunity to show off for potential clients, but the title *booking agent* carried a faintly legitimate air to those otherwise unaware.) Honan bantered in vaudevillian style with the prosecutor.

"Isn't it a fact that you and Kinnane went after Ed Ryan, and that he shot you in the arm?" asked Senator Carmack.

"No sir, it is not," Honan replied. "He shot right here in my stomach."

"Isn't it a fact that you were convicted of highway robbery with Joe Blackburn, and that after conviction, you got a new trial?"

"No sir, it is not a fact. We were acquitted the first time."

Honan said he'd spent the evening of the riot at a nearby saloon. At about nine-thirty, a bartender had told him to come to the phone. Honan had heard Mike Haggarty on the line, asking him to meet up and walk to 42 De Soto Street to make bond for Hartley and Keene, their associates who'd been pinched for a gaming violation. Honan said that once he and Haggarty got inside 42 De Soto, Deputy Lawless and Haggarty leaped onto a gaming table and began grappling. Honan explained that the Negro deputy Mitchell attacked him at that moment.

Mitchell and Honan had wrestled for Mitchell's big Colt .41 revolver, and when Honan came away with it, Mitchell picked him up, threw him down over a bench, and began smashing Honan with the slung shot—the chunk of lead swinging from a leather strap around his wrist. "I turned the pistol on him and fired as fast as I could," Honan said. "He fell back off of me and staggered to a bench. I got up and walked out of the place."[8]

As Honan gestured, onlookers saw gunpowder burns on his right hand. The young widow McDermott bit her lip and stared at Honan through tears.

As for the fate of McDermott, neither Honan nor anyone else could definitively explain it. Everyone in the place had heard shooting, but the darkness and chaos made it impossible to know where it was coming from. Not even Deputy Lawless could swear to the fact that Honan killed McDermott.

The trial then brought forth a surprise appearance that sent a flutter through the rumpled heart of a newspaperman: "The next witness proved one of the warmest and most refreshing numbers on the programme. He was none other than James Kinnane."

Kinnane, now thirty-six, impressed the courtroom with his frank testimony. On the stand he faced a formidable opponent, to a reporter's apparent delight:

Then the junior senator from Tennessee took up the cross-examination, and the sparks flew. . . . Senator Carmack, glancing up from under his eyebrows, plumped the question full at the truculent witness:

"When did you get into the gambling business?"

It was a center shot, a 100-pounder of solid steel. It failed to pierce the armor of the case-hardened witness, but it stunned him momentarily and disconcerted him for a breathing space. Then he recovered his voice and nerve and answered with smiling defiance:

"I claim my privilege."

The judge interjected, "You must answer the question. You cannot claim your privilege farther back than six months, Mr. Kinnane."

"You're known as a wholesale gambler, aren't you?" asked Senator Carmack, to hearty courtroom laughter, including a chuckle on the stand.

Though the judge warned the attorney that Kinnane was a witness and not a defendant, Kinnane illuminated the issue. "Well, I know but very little about gambling," he said. "I can't play no game for money. I *have* made some money managing games." He listed the properties in which he held a stake, including his famous Blue Goose saloon in the Pinch, Tick Houston's at 81 De Soto Street, and 142 Beale Street, the Monarch.

"It's a Negro crap dive, isn't it?" asked the examiner.

"Well, yes, Negroes play there," Kinnane said.

Kinnane got to the part about his presence at Frank Davis's magistrate office the day of the fatal raid on 42 De Soto. He titillated the court with underworld gossip. He hadn't gone to Davis to talk about De Soto Street—he was there to snitch on Bob Church's New Era saloon.

"Bob Church had my place . . . closed last winter and I knew there was gambling going on in Church's place," he explained. "I wanted to catch him gambling when I was not."[9]

Kinnane thus established a certain level of credibility. Just a dishonest man making a fabulous living, Kinnane offered these tidbits so that he could obfuscate more crucial facts. His candor seemed to satisfy the prosecutor.

But if Kinnane hadn't offered the tip that sent the deputies to 42 De Soto Street, who had?

Deputy Lawless, leader of the raid, explained that a Negro named

John Smith had provided the tip. But John Smith never appeared at Honan's trial. No one could find him. Honan's defense deftly worked this against the prosecution, mocking its inability to produce such an important witness.

Attention returned now to Deputy Lawless, leader of the fateful raiding party.

Haggarty and Honan testified that after the riot, they had walked off *with* Lawless. Haggarty recalled ribbing Lawless. "I told him he ought to be ashamed of himself," he said, "going about with a nigger deputy that way, raiding places at night."[10]

Furthermore, Kinnane testified that Lawless had called on him the morning after the riot. That got Lawless back on the witness stand. "I went to see Kinnane about a personal matter," he explained. "I borrowed $20 from him. Kinnane said if he could do anything for us, financially or otherwise, he would be glad to do it."[11]

Meanwhile Honan's defense attorneys hoped to corroborate that Honan had killed Houston Mitchell in self-defense and fled.

A new witness materialized, a colored carpenter named R. H. Elkins. He frequented gambling establishments only to round up laborers for a job, he swore, and never to play, and that task had him at 42 De Soto during the raid.

Elkins testified that the Negro deputy Mitchell had acted boisterous and excited, while Honan attempted to settle things down. Elkins said that Mitchell had pulled a pistol and pointed it at Honan. Elkins said that as the two men scuffled, he heard gunfire, and the shots caused him and everyone else to flee.[12]

◆   ◆   ◆   ◆

The facts gestured toward conspiracy. Kinnane had been present in Frank Davis's office as the warrant was signed, sending Davis's unwanted son-in-law McDermott on the fatal raid. Prosecutors noted the fact that one of the deputies in the raid, Solly, had broken off from the group in the middle of the raiding expedition, heading in the direction of the Turf Saloon, where he could have alerted Mike Haggarty that the posse had headed to De Soto Street, not long before Haggarty and Honan arrived at the De Soto dive. But Solly never testified. Deputy Lawless had taken money from Kinnane the day after the raid. The connections between Haggarty, Kinnane, Honan, and the others were part of the public record, yet the prosecution made no attempt to link them in the De Soto Street story.

The whole scenario looks like a mutually satisfying deal. Justice Davis eliminated the man his daughter had just married over his objection, and Kinnane and company put the fear of death into anyone who might threaten the conglomerate's gambling houses. As a bonus, these events opened the mayor to criticism. "Mayor Williams is to blame for this affair," Justice Davis said, "because he has permitted the lack of enforcement of the municipal laws. The police have known of these places all along. Patrolmen have walked right past the doors of these hell holes and said nothing or done nothing."[13]

To close the prosecution, Senator Carmack reasserted that Honan had killed McDermott and artfully called for Honan's execution—"He should be treated to a monument of wood and a coral of hemp."[14] But Carmack couldn't overcome the colored carpenter R. H. Elkins's late testimony, describing the Negro deputy Houston Mitchell as the aggressor, and the jury couldn't see past the image Elkins rendered.

The jury returned a verdict of not guilty—acquitting Honan of McDermott's murder and dropping all related charges against Haggarty, Degg, Hartley, and Keene.

Elkins, the pivotal defense witness, explained how he'd come forward so late in the trial—an employee of Bob Church had encouraged him to testify, at least raising the possibility that Church had been the fixer.

Afterward the principal actors from the trial all seemed to tighten their bonds. Haggarty and Kinnane's influence at the police department received implicit testimony when John Lawless was hired onto the force and made detective. Kinnane placed George Honan in charge of his Beale Street establishment, the Monarch. Hartley, who'd testified that he controlled the 42 De Soto Street dump during the riot, installed his game at Bob Church's former Beale Street saloon, the New Era.

The De Soto Street Riot provoked a cry for reform among the citizenry, who critiqued mayor J. J. Williams's administration and its failure to enforce law. The next year would do nothing to quiet the clamor.

◆   ◆   ◆   ◆

Beale Street saloon owners—Church, Kinnane, Lorenzo Pacini, and Hammitt Ashford—gambled against one another, yet each comported himself in gentlemanly fashion in both triumph and defeat, never allowing the intensity of rivalry to bubble forth in public. Any display of profanity, ill temper, or violence could prove as injurious to their reputations as a display of cowardice.

The bosses imported sharks to play high-stakes card games, promoting them like boxing matches. Heavyweight champs Jack Johnson and John L. Sullivan shouldered in beside Beale Street pimps Tittiwee and Black Slick to watch epic twenty-four-hour tilts between locals Casino Henry and Mac Harris, the latter done up like English nobility, and itinerants Anthony Small, Slop Crowder, and the mysterious man from New Orleans, Nine Tongue.

Into this tradition stepped the patent leather shoes of Ed "Fatty" Grimes. Fatty hailed from St. Louis. He ran a saloon there but traveled wherever the game called. In summer 1905 he became the honored guest at Jim Kinnane's decadent Beale Street dive, the Monarch.

Fatty wore silk shirts and topcoats, a shiny diamond shirt stud, a diamond pinky ring, and a gold watch chain. Though Fatty's occupation was listed as bartender, his real job entailed beating every house other than the Monarch. Fatty was a mercenary in Kinnane's war against competing enterprises—such as Hammitt Ashford's.

Noted for its mahogany bar, crystal chandeliers, and marble-top tables, Ashford's place displayed numerous sculptures, paintings, and engravings celebrating female pulchritude. Ashford's stood four doors down from the Monarch. The battles involving Grimes and Ashford or

George Fitzhugh, Ashford's aide-de-camp, became personal. Not only did Grimes beat the house at Ashford's, he started talking to Fitzhugh's wife and became familiar with Black Carrie, an exotic dancer who frequented Ashford's.

As Saturday night turned to Sunday morning, September 17, 1905, Fatty Grimes received word that Black Carrie desired his company upstairs at Ashford's.

He made his way down the sidewalk, almost alone at the late hour, and passed through the front door into Ashford's decorous lobby. Gunfire blasted, at least ten rounds. People peeped out windows and opened their doors and saw Fatty high-speed-staggering down the sidewalk from Ashford's back toward the Monarch. They'd shot him at such close range and so many times that his coat caught fire, and flames rose from his back like wings as he fell facedown at the Monarch front door.

The Monarch emptied, and the street filled. A bartender cut Fatty's diamond stud from his shirt, relieved the corpse of its ring and watch chain, and disappeared.[15]

George Fitzhugh, the bartender at Ashford's, confessed that he'd shot Fatty Grimes but had done so in self-defense after an altercation concerning Fitzhugh's wife. The autopsy on Grimes unearthed four bullets of four different calibers. Each shot had entered the victim's back: so much for self-defense. The detectives went looking for Hammitt Ashford and Black Carrie.[16]

The case unfolded during a political war, as James Malone came to challenge incumbent J. J. Williams in the 1905 mayoral election. Both men were Democrats, as any serious white candidate for office in the South had to be. Both candidates grabbed on to the trendy political theme of reform, each claiming that he possessed the antidote to municipal government corruption, while doing anything to win.

During the early twentieth century, the progressive reform movement influenced political agendas from the local level to the White House. The progressive ideal inspired all sorts of political and social activity, from the creation of the National Parks to the increased momentum of the Prohibition movement—all with the goal of improving people's lives via an improved American society. At the local level, in cities all over the United States, reformers sought to combat the political power of saloon bosses, and Prohibition was wielded as one weapon in the fight.

A *Commercial Appeal* report linked mayoral candidate James Malone to Mike Haggarty. The paper's editor summarized the campaign's central paradox: "Could Mike Haggarty . . . convince any party that he is honestly working for the reform of Memphis?"[17]

The Grimes murder and search for accomplices empowered a district crackdown. Police raided the opium den above Tick Houston's, owned by Jim Kinnane. They found the place thick with sweet, nauseating fumes and Negroes laughing, dreaming, and sick. They cleared the bambooheads to the station house and arrested Tick Houston for felonious gambling, while another troop apprehended Pearl King, keeper of Robert Church's bawdyhouse around the corner on Gayoso.[18]

A judge ordered Pearl to leave town just as officers arrested Hammitt Ashford for the murder of Fatty Grimes.[19]

The whole scenario ripened for political exploitation as voters contemplated their choices. After a craps table shooting at Tick Houston's, the *Commercial Appeal* opined,

> The incident is a sad commentary on the present administration of the Police Department. . . . Tick Houston is a negro and of the same class as Hammitt Ashford and has been before the police for numerous crimes that have taken place in his joint. He keeps several dives and is one of the men the Civic League has made such a strong fight against. . . . Houston still remains at the old stand operating his notorious dives apparently under the protection of the police.

According to one reporter, despite the Grimes murder, the opium raid, the prostitution sting, and the shooting, "no effort has been made by the police to suppress these dives, and remove the stench of their lawlessness from the fair name of the city."[20]

◆ ◆ ◆ ◆

Eighteen Chicago crooks filed into Memphis prior to election day
of November 9, 1905. They were repeaters, each planning to vote in four
different wards. They carried a variety of registration papers and might
cast upward of twenty-five ballots. The papers associated the repeaters'
presence with Mike Haggarty, now prominent in national crime circles. "If there is any porch climber, second-story man, safe-blower or
confidence man in the country known to the profession, he can find an
abiding place in the Fourth Ward and [be] summoned when emergency
demands."[21]

Instead of being decided by the voters, the election fell into the hands
of Haggarty and Kinnane, who covered every possible contingency.
Between their repeaters, bundled Negro votes, muscle at the polls, and
influence in the legitimate voting apparatus, they guided their candidate, James Malone, to victory in the mayoral election. Kinnane and
Haggarty created the climate of reform, and they chose the reformer.

A thirty-two-year-old unknown named Edward Hull Crump had
worked for Malone's reform ticket from the fourth ward, Haggarty's
backyard. He won a seat in the city's lower legislative house, the public
works board. It was an almost unnoticeable beginning to one of the
more audacious political careers of the twentieth century.

Meanwhile, Hammitt Ashford's trial wore on in criminal court.

The evidence clearly pointed to conspiracy, but Ashford's prosecutors had a hard time finding witnesses. The alleged conspirators all
corroborated one another's stories, to the effect that the deceased Fatty
Grimes had pulled his pistol on them first. The late Mr. Grimes had
been the only other person with firsthand knowledge.

Finally one Mose Perkins stepped forward to contradict Ashford's
self-defense theory. He said he'd been at the Ashford saloon and had
seen Ashford and company ambush Fatty Grimes.

As at George Honan's trial, a witness with strong connections to
Robert Church had materialized to boost the defense of a murderer.
A man who worked at the Church's Park stables said Mose Perkins

boarded with him and had been home the night of the Grimes murder. Mose Perkins couldn't have seen what he testified about.

The next day the jury acquitted Ashford and friends.[22] Church, again—the fixer.

Church bought champagne, and every rounder and racetrack tout came to clink glasses and crack wise on Beale Street. Guitarist Charlie Bynum's band played. It was a good day.

Though Beale Street seemingly had no conscience, it had eyes. The piano thumper peering down at dead Fatty's flame wings from the Monarch window wove what he saw into what he sang. It was the street's story, the latest chapter, like a link in Joe Turney's chain, from prison enslavers to lynch mobs to cocaine. The Fatty story inspired a motif— diamond-studded man, two-timing temptress, bullets, and blood. It was Beale Street distilled—struggles of wealthy and powerful men pulling unseen strings.

Into this world dropped a well-regarded Negro professor of music named William Christopher Handy.

Chapter 12

THE GIG

W. C. Handy rode into Memphis on the colored car from Clarksdale, Mississippi, and got off at the Poplar Street station. Burdened with instrument cases, he walked to the station barbershop to meet a colored barber named Matt Thornton. Handy popped his perfectly round, shiny-bald head through the door to announce his arrival.

They boarded the electric streetcar on the river line. Handy, caramel colored and mustachioed, Thornton, tall, thin, and dark, stood in their section. A movable partition separated the races in the streetcar. The barricade could slide either way, depending on the number of riders that needed to fit in each section.

Out the window on their right, the Mississippi churned. Out the left, a city reached from the dirt: a few splendid structures like the Ottoman-style library and the imposing cotton houses on Front Street mingled with smoke-belching manufacturers. Scarcely a stitch of landscaping yet graced the streets.

Handy lugged a typewriter, conspicuous among his instrument cases.

Now in his early thirties, Handy had traveled all over the

continent, up to frozen Nova Scotia, down to old Havana. He'd marched in glorious parades and narrowly escaped lynch mobs. Every reader of the national colored newspaper the *Indianapolis Freeman* knew something of his exploits, playing lead cornet and fronting the popular Mahara's Minstrel orchestra, which he saw as the finest group of Negro secular musicians of the time. He fronted a thirty-piece parade outfit that advertised the minstrels' arrival in a town, specializing in marching band classics from the likes of John Phillip Sousa, and a forty-two-piece concert band for the night's performance, playing popular tunes like "A Hot Time in the Old Town Tonight" and minstrel classics such as "Carry Me Back to Old Virginny."

Handy had left the road and taken a job leading a band in Clarksdale, Mississippi, but he needed to supplement his income: thus the task of coming to Memphis to rehearse the colored Knights of Pythias band, Mr. Thornton's ensemble.

As the car turned up Beale, Handy's quick brown eyes took in the scenery—first the golden balls, thick as orchard fruit, on pawnshop row. As the city grew, the address numbers were changing. Pee Wee's went from 117 to 317 Beale without moving an inch, while quaint De Soto became urbane Fourth Street without becoming more upscale. Beale Street looked to Handy now much as it had fifteen years before, when he'd ridden the excursions up from Alabama, beckoned by the sounds and stories of fiddle-playing Jim Turner and the reputation Robert Church projected across the colored South.

Past Fourth, though, a shadow city was growing to match the rest of Memphis. Glorious Church's Park came into view, with its imposing auditorium, frilly gazebos, tropical flora and fowl. The Knights of Pythias met in a rented room just past it.

This environment suited the ambitious Handy. As he'd once explained to a reporter, he wished to do more than add to the characteristic harmonies of his race. He wanted to compose new, original music. The idea held a certain intellectual currency, put forth by the Czech composer Antonín Dvořák, who had predicted that the only great *American* music would come from Negroes.

Beale Street had more to offer Handy than upstart atmosphere. In his life and travels, he had become a musical forager, entranced by the blind streetcorner spiritual singers and footloose train station guitarists who populated his universe. Their styles ran counter to his training and ideology as a reading musician who played in formal ensembles. Their sounds nonetheless intrigued him. He possessed something like a photographic memory, only not for images but for sound—a phonographic memory, perhaps.

By nature or inclination, W. C. Handy had always hopped boundaries, moving between worlds. He had been a divided creature his whole life, pursuing music against his minister father's will, sinking to the common status of entertainer when his upbringing and education promised more. His devotion to written composition reflected his need to be professional despite his chosen field.

To Handy, folk airs were a fine novelty, and collecting them was something of a hobby next to the serious pursuit of music. Yet he could never fully escape the raw sounds all around him. And he had begun to see, in Mississippi, more value to black folk songs. Inspiration came not only from those raw sounds—"the weirdest music I ever heard," as he would describe it—but from the rain of silver dollars he saw falling at the feet of a rough little band performing a haunting rhythm for a dance at Cleveland, Mississippi. "Then I saw the beauty of primitive music," Handy would recall. "That night a composer was born, an *American* composer."[1]

The day he arrived to meet Matt Thornton in Memphis, though, Handy was all ambition and no delivery, a music teacher trying to figure out a new city. He moved there in late 1905 or early 1906.

◆　◆　◆　◆

Jim Turner lived on Fourth, less than a block from Pee Wee's and the Monarch. The fiddler Turner had drawn Handy to Beale Street many years ago, and now Turner would open the district to the ambitious maestro. Handy the forager, the *American* composer, could have found no better guide than Turner and no richer environs than these. A pianist named Ben French, who lived around the corner in one of Bob Church's boardinghouses on Gayoso, had gained underworld admiration as the best piano player on Beale Street.

At the moment, George Honan ran the Monarch for Jim Kinnane and surrounded himself with a cast of unstable characters. A barrel-bodied beast with long, muscular arms known as Cousin Hog ran the craps tables. His job as "back-out man" entailed scaring or punching out anyone who beat the house too hard.

The place never closed, and the music never stopped.

Another hub was spinning across Beale from the Monarch, where Lorenzo Pacini operated Pee Wee's. Nobody could pronounce *Pacini* correctly, so they called him Casino. This rang true in a professional sense, as Pacini derived much of his income from the Negro policy game that played around the clock in Pee Wee's. Policy players wagered on drawings of numbered balls, which a dealer pulled from a hand-spun hopper. Pacini spent most of his adult life under indictment but never stood trial. On the night of the De Soto Street Riot, deputies had gone to raid Pee Wee's but found nobody home. This sort of clairvoyance, and legal immunity, resulted from Pacini's friendship with John Persica. By now Persica was running a vaudeville theater-saloon-brothel for whites, but with black entertainment, halfway between Beale and Gayoso on Hernando Street.

Pacini helped whomever he could, and he enjoyed many warm friendships in return.

Pee Wee's had a cigar counter up front. An oil painting of a scene from *Othello* hung behind the bar. Regulars, apt to break into a favorite soliloquy or Edwin Booth monologue once the spirits loosened their tongues, appreciated the reference, as many intimately knew Beale Street's secret history and the Desdemonas of Gayoso.

Pacini permitted musicians to store their instruments in a cloakroom and to take calls at his extension, 2893, long before anybody dreamed up a Negro musician's union. "They had a wineroom back there," violinist Thomas Pinkston said, "where musicians used to go and drink wine with these cheap prostitutes, lay around and wait for someone to hire them."[2]

Policy game vernacular employed the term *gig* in a variety of fashions, noun and verb. A gambler referred to the sequence of numbers he wagered on as his gig. A winning sequence, they said, gigged. With a constant set of gamblers on hand, plus the prostitutes and musicians waiting to get hired, everybody hung around Pee Wee's looking for the next gig.

"Jim Turner introduced me to the place," Handy recalled.[3]

Now it served as headquarters for Turner's top competitor, guitarist Charlie Bynum, leader of Bynum's Superb Orchestra. Though Bynum gamely played the latest pop numbers, he also experimented. Beale folk historian George W. Lee wrote, "Bynum was the first leader on Beale Street to play the blues, but, not realizing their potential commercial value, he never thought of trying to set them to music."[4]

Dance halls like Persica's Garden Theater, Haggarty and Degg's Theatre Comique, the Dixie at Beale and Hernando, and Bill Harwood's Bremer Rathskeller all called for orchestral entertainment, while combos worked saloons such as Joe Raffanti's on Gayoso, Caradina's and Vaccaro's on Fourth Street, Ashford's and M. L. Clay's, the New Palace, Bob Church's old saloon, across from Pee Wee's, and such colorfully named joints as the Blue Light, the Drum, the Log Cabin, the Antler, and the Climax.

Between Hernando and Fourth, the street stayed as packed as the state fair nearly every night. Men could be seen sporting fancy hats laden with symbolic meaning. "That Stetson with the four-way crush," fiddler Thomas Pinkston said, "that meant 'I will not work.'"

Handy found Beale Street in renaissance, not just after dark and under ground but blooming with possibilities for optimistic race people. He saw the Beale Street of Ida B. Wells rekindle its promise.

Twenty years earlier Ida had crowded into the black section of the white-owned theater to catch the latest Gilbert and Sullivan production; but now a night at the theater dazzled the colored audience's sense of progress, along with their imaginations, as the Black Patti opera and virtuoso pianist Blind Tom brought high art to Church's Park Auditorium. Black performers played to black fans at a black-owned theater.

Along newly paved sidewalks, the soapy talc scents of a hundred barbershops curled around shoe polish tang, chicken frying at the Alabama Café, and sweets baking at Morat's.

The *Bluff City News*, a paper for colored, published on Beale and sold in every storefront. Undertaker Levi McCoy owned a mortuary around the corner on Fourth. He had at least one customer in the store at all hours. As a Beale resident recalled, "He had a dead man—deader than a doornail, honey—up there on the left with his back to the door. He was like a statue, dressed up like a model with a suit on. He didn't look bad. He just looked like an old man standing there. Levi McCoy had even taken his mustache and embalmed it."[5]

W. E. B. Du Bois, already a national figure thanks to the 1903 publication of his book *The Souls of Black Folk*, launched an unprecedented venture, a weekly Negro news magazine, from Beale Street.

While Booker T. Washington encouraged Negroes to sink their shovels into Southern soil and work for the white man's respect, Du Bois espoused higher education, classics, and the arts as the route to progress. He enlisted a former student named Harry Pace to carry out the message.

Pace worked zealously at whatever he did, energized by the belief that Negroes needed, and could support, elite institutions all their own. Along with Du Bois and Ed Simon, who owned a Beale Street printshop, Pace pooled $3,000 to launch *Moon Illustrated Weekly* out of 358 Beale in late 1905.

While Du Bois remained teaching at Atlanta University, Pace and Simon worked on the *Moon*. They designed an Egyptian-theme masthead, with obelisks and pyramids. The *Moon* illuminated the serious matters of disfranchisement and lynching, agitating for legal action against both. It took Teddy Roosevelt to task for remaining mum on the Negro question after such a warm, promising start to his progressive presidency. It applauded streetcar boycotts and professional accomplishments. The "Tidings of the Darker Million" shared news from the diaspora, like a Zulu uprising in South Africa. Unlike the city's white-owned tabloids, *Moon* spotlighted the *bright* side of the race, featuring stories about a Negro opera musician and a tribute to the late poet Paul Laurence Dunbar. Its advertisers included a real estate subdivision in northeast Memphis, Klondike, boasting property equal to anything opened for whites in the city and superior to any land marketed to colored.[6]

Handy also visited Church's Park. On warm nights, Mr. Church held dances. Handy heard Jim Turner's Orchestra and guitarist Charlie Bynum's band.[7] On cool evenings the dances moved indoors to the auditorium ballroom. Bathed in blue electric light, Bynum's Superb Orchestra whirled through waltzes, polkas, two-steps, and schottisches, playing "Little Johnny Jones," "My Oldsmobile," "Rufus Rastus Johnson Brown," and "45 Minutes From Broadway."[8] Church kept the police off his property and laid down the law himself, demanding the utmost in decorum from his patrons. He dictated closing time, and when he flourished his hand a certain way, the band knew to strike up "Home Sweet Home," and everyone went.

From the fiery illustration of *Bulletin no. 2* burning on the drop curtain at the auditorium to the new strip of buildings going up across Beale, testaments to Church's courage and prosperity appeared everywhere Handy looked.

Church had spent the first few years of the new century gobbling up Beale property, lots on the north side of the street across from his park. He owned most of the block by 1906 and deployed a parallel strategy one street north on Gayoso.[9]

In 1906 Church executed the boldest maneuver yet: on June 18 the Solvent Savings Bank and Trust Company opened its doors across from Church's Park, at 392 Beale. Church, now sixty-seven, installed himself as president. Memphis's first black bank boasted $25,000 subscribed stock and promised 3 percent interest on deposits.

A local newspaper editorial back in 1903 that cataloged Negro failures and foibles had cited the lack of colored financial institutions as proof of racial inferiority. Church had clipped the editorial and pondered the next phase of his career. As he aged, he realized he needed to do more for black Memphis, more for his legacy. Robert Church Jr. was off at school during these early years of the twentieth century, but once the heir returned, the boss would want to pass down more than a handful of saloons and the proceeds from their dice games.

The day after the bank opened, the white papers carried no word of what should have been a significant news story. Instead, the *Memphis News-Scimitar* served a regular diet of Negro stickups, shootings, and break-ins. A cartoon pushed comfortable stereotypes: the city Negro rounder tipping through saloon doors, and the simple rural Negro with his jug and rifle. A feature called "At the Bar of Justice," focusing on police court follies, mocked the testimony of one prisoner: "Ah is a good niggah an' never terrohizes."[10]

In a 1908 publication, *The Bright Side of Memphis*, colored educator G. P. Hamilton would note, with admirable rhetorical vigor, "as a rule, the bright side of the Colored Race is not given its due share of public-ity to the world. Its mistakes, misfortunes, weaknesses, and crimes are minutely published, while its abilities and worthy achievements are too often overlooked and unmentioned."

A two-story brick building painted white housed the bank, with lac-quered oak storefront and plate glass, gold-embossed with "Solvent Sav-ings." From inside, these windows overlooked the colorful flower beds, banana trees, and peacocks at Church's Park, but the building's back was turned to Church's brothels. Everything needed to undo Church, to drain off Beale Street's optimism and leadership in this new and hopeful time, was right there on Gayoso Street and not all that carefully concealed. The 1910 census taker marked the race of every girl and madam, all female boarders in the six two-story mansions on Church's strip from 220 to 234 Gayoso, with a big W.

Seemingly because of the white Memphis fixation on *Negro* short-comings, and the accompanying refusal to admit the white man's, Church avoided exposure. He had built a glorious park, established a grand theater, acquired swaths of valuable real estate, and gained con-trol of local politics like no other colored man in the country. Now the

Solvent Savings Bank stood as a monumental rejection of white racism. The foundation of that monument rested on the proceeds of Bob Church's brothels, on white men's moral failings.

◆   ◆   ◆   ◆

A Commercial Appeal editor frowned.

> For nearly eighteen months Memphis has been living under an era of "Reform." We all know what has happened here. Dives have been flourishing as they have never flourished before. Hundreds of lewd women, equipped with vials of chloral and knock-out drops, have been imported. Street-walkers have been thick as wasps in summer time. Pico joints have been numerous. The departments have been saturated with graft. Every Sunday morning, kids smoking cigarettes gather in the parks and shoot craps for hours in the pavillions and everybody comes along and sees it but the policeman.[11]

One politician in particular became the symbol of sham reform. E. H. Crump held a seat on the public works commission, the lesser of Memphis's two legislative bodies. He'd won it in 1905, thanks to Mike Haggarty.

"Mr. Crump doubtless has some inkling as to what took place in the Fourth ward"—Haggarty's base—"where he was working for his ticket," wrote the *Commercial Appeal*.

> Does he think the election in that ward was honest?
> Does he believe that the ballot box was switched there?
> Does he think the thugs with rifles were stationed there to ensure an honest election?[12]

Though the paper lambasted him, Crump won election to the upper house in 1907, taking a seat on the board of fire and police commissioners. Some saw Crump as a rubber stamp for his political benefactor,

Vice Mayor John T. Walsh. A grocer and wholesaler, Vice Mayor Walsh was involved with the liquor business, which tinged his political decision making. He needed commissioners to vote against Prohibition, an issue that had enjoyed great popularity in rural Tennessee and made its way into the city. Prohibition, along with the fight against political corruption, was one of the cornerstone concepts of the progressive reform philosophy.

Crump, an editor alleged, "is just this sort of young man the Walsh influence wants in the council, that it may 'eat him up.'"[13] This rankled Crump to his depths, as he possessed broad ambition and vision that had nothing at all to do with John T. Walsh. He seized reform as his mandate. On January 12, 1908, he put the lid on saloons and casinos, demanding that the police shut down gambling rooms, make sure taverns closed at their appointed hour and stayed closed on Sunday, and see that no one ran a saloon without license.

The police complied for a few days. By the night of January 16, however, Memphis reopened wide, as the police were "nodding at the corner," according the next morning's news. The report humiliated Crump, implying that Walsh had rendered Crump powerless: "Over a dozen all night saloons flourished and there were certain doings on Beal street [sic] that told more forcibly than words can that the Crump lid had gone the way of other historic lids and that Mr. Crump as a reformer is just as much of a success as a few of his predecessors in politics."[14]

Speaking of his predecessors, Crump shared more than a few of Pappy Hadden's outstanding attributes. Both were indefatigable, hands-on workers. Crump made rounds, inspecting the city just as Hadden once did, albeit without the mule—Crump motored around town in a Ford. They shared a gift for showmanship and mass psychology, both using the former in service of the latter. But their styles could not have been more different: Hadden's homespun witticisms and decorous language were frilly relics beside Crump's businesslike approach.

Still, Crump's first foray into the public spotlight looked like an homage to Hadden. The man who would be dictator—the critics had called

Hadden that, too—staged a theatrical raid on a saloon at Fourth and
Beale, the very spot Pappy Hadden had raided to appease concerned
citizens two decades before. If the police wouldn't follow orders to
enforce the lid on vice activity, Crump would have to do it himself.

On Friday night, January 17, Crump sent private detectives into the
tenderloin to note activities in the various resorts. He spent Saturday
rounding up twenty men, most hailing from his native Mississippi. They
met in Crump's office that night. There a justice of the peace deputized
the twenty as emergency officers for the purpose of suppressing illegal
gambling in the city.

Crump divided the men into three posses. He gave each team a
destination—one crew to Jim Kinnane's on Front Street, another to Bill
McVey's on Hadden Avenue—and to counteract leaks, he ordered the
teams to hit their targets simultaneously. Crump personally led a group
of six young Mississippi men to Hammitt Ashford's on Beale Street.

◆   ◆   ◆   ◆

Inside Ashford's, two pool tables in the back room, at a certain
hour, became craps tables.

A half-dozen early birds rolled the bones out of Hadden's Horn amid
marble-topped tables. Beneath paintings of naked ladies, they smoked
and jabbered as the dice crackled over the green felt.

It would be difficult to nightmare up a more dreaded scenario for
a group of Negro crapshooters than what burst through the saloon
entrance that Saturday night.

Strange white men, with guns pointed, one peckerwood for each
Negro. The dice froze, and trembling palms reached for the ceiling.
One of the deputies swiped the horn, the bones, and the cashbox. The
six deputies pulled the six gamblers out of Ashford's into the street. One
of the white men walked over to a tall, thin, redheaded fellow standing
under the streetlamp at Fourth and Beale—Mr. Crump—and passed
him Hadden's Horn.

Crump hurried to the police station. Just after ten o'clock, he threw open the station doors, hoisting Hadden's Horn like a trophy.

Jim Kinnane had been at home nursing a rheumatic flare-up. When word of the raid reached him, he gathered himself, grabbed his cane, and headed downtown.

He met Crump face-to-face at the station house. The young commissioner stared down the city's white criminal emperor and ordered police Capt. Oliver Perry to arrest Kinnane for illegal gaming. Instead of locking Kinnane in a cell, Crump removed him to an office in which the two conferred.

As Kinnane and Crump talked, another visitor arrived at the station, a heavily intoxicated George Honan. Barging into the office, he cursed and frothed at Crump, who maintained his equilibrium and promised he'd discuss the matter with Honan as soon as Honan sobered up. Kinnane bailed himself out, and he and Honan left together.

"We showed up the police department tonight," Crump crowed. "If Chief O' Haver and his men cannot suppress gambling in this town, I can."[15]

Crump's tenderloin sweep baffled his friends of easy conscience, for his campaign had raised funds from lawbreakers, and they naturally expected greater cooperation from him in return.[16] Instead, Kinnane and seventy-one Negroes stood trial for gaming charges that stemmed from the raids. Sixty of the gamblers drew $15 fines, the six rousted at Ashford's pleaded guilty, and Kinnane's case wiggled into legal ether.[17]

Crump's raids embarrassed the police out of their slumber, and they attacked saloons and gambling houses with fervor previously unseen. They visited Hammitt Ashford's, M. L. Clay's, Tick Houston's, the Monarch, the New Palace, and Pee Wee's—but found no illegal activity anywhere. The Beale bards had memorialized Fatty Grimes and lynching victims, chanted at cocaine parties, and warned that Joe Turney'd been here and gone. You'd better believe that Mr. Crump captured their imaginations.

◆   ◆   ◆   ◆

As Prohibition spread at the local and state levels, packs of nomad gamblers moved about the South. They followed the horse races in the spring and fall, or they left one town when the lid went down in search of a leak elsewhere. Lone itinerants fled sundown orders, warrants, and other legal or domestic responsibilities, and all learned from fellow travelers where their kind met welcome along the road. As musician Alex Simms explained, Beale Street was a gateway: "The sporting class of people brought music and dances from [around] the country."[18]

One such figure to land upon the Mississippi River shore was a New Orleans Creole, piano player, and pool shark called Winding Boy. He had split his hometown in 1908. "I decided to go to this Beale Street that I had heard a lot of talk about," he would say.

He proceeded cautiously, understanding that breaches of local custom spelled trouble. Once on the street, he found his way to the proper place and figured things out. "The Monarch saloon was ran by a white fellow by the name of Mike Haggarty," he recalled. "He was the tough guy of Memphis, Tennessee."

Winding Boy marveled at Haggarty's clout.

It was oftentimes that he would go and get some of his, his visitors or hanger-arounders, or, whatever you wanna call 'em, and gamblers that gambled in his place [when] the police picked [them] up. Why, he'd walk into the police station and say, "Turn him a-loose, and don't bother none of these people that hang around my place." And the police department didn't have any trouble at all in gettin' this prisoner out immediately.

He absorbed the Monarch for a few days—"nothin' went into that saloon but pimps, robbers, and gamblers." He wondered about the peculiar custom of rolling dice out of a horn and noted the dimensions of the gambling room Jim Kinnane had designed, "which was barricaded just the same, why I guess, even worse than the trenches, that is, in the wartime. Barricaded with steel and iron to keep policemens out."

He saw the craps table bouncer Bad Sam (whose predecessor Cousin Hog had been assassinated) shatter a man's jawbone straight out of the flesh. After a few days, Winding Boy picked his spot: "I first enquired, was there any piano players in the city? And they told me absolutely the best in the whole state of Tennessee was here."

This was Ben French. "Well, when Benny would show up, there would be a type of those low-class whores that would have a way of dancing when he'd play. They would run right directly up to the wall, with a kind of a little bit of a shuffle, and slap their hands together, and kick back their right legs and say, 'Oh, play it, Benny, play it.'"

Sauntering over to Bad Sam, Winding Boy asked, "Who is this fella?"

Bad Sam said, "That's Benny Frenchy."

"I never heard of him."

"Where in the hell you been? Never heard of Benny Frenchy?"

Winding Boy said, "What, is he supposed to be good?"

"Why, he's the best in the whole state of Tennessee."

Winding Boy said, "Why, that damn fool can't hit a piano with a brick."

Bad Sam said, "What? Can you play?"

"Well, I'm not supposed to be good. If that's playin'," Winding Boy said, toward Ben French, "I can beat all them kinds of suckers."

Bad Sam yelled, "Say Benny. Here's a little bum here, thinks he can play piano. Will you get up and let him try his hand, see what he can do? Because if he can't play, I'll kick him in the ass and run him out of here."

A chill came over the Winding Boy. French cut it and said, "Okay." He got up.

Winding Boy found his courage and told Bad Sam and Ben French, "Well, of course, you wouldn't kick me if I can beat him playin', because this, this guy can't play nothin' at all."

Bad Sam said, "This is a game kid, all right. Let him go down."

Winding Boy recalled, "I got out and played anyway, against Benny Frenchy."

With the city's toughest man, best pianist, and roughest whores looking, Winding Boy attacked the keys.

"I brought the house down," he recalled. "Don't believe me? Think I'm kiddin' you? I brought it down."[19]

Winding Boy became better known as Jelly Roll Morton. Though no one can say how much influence his music had in Memphis, his presence attests to undeniable but immeasurable influence of the wayfaring Negro sporting class upon emerging forms of American music.

Chapter 13

WE GONNA
BARRELHOUSE ANYHOW

A *few days before* the 1909 mayoral contest between E. H. Crump and J. J. Williams, the *Commercial Appeal* filled a half-page with a cartoon that showed a line of stoop-shouldered, thick-lipped black men marching single file, following a sign: "To The Polls."

Superimposed over this image, a sinewy black hand clutched a cat-of-nine-tails. The names Jim Kinnane and Hammitt Ashford were written along the whip's lashes. A tag shackled to the muscular wrist read "Nigger Dive Keepers For Williams."

The caption asked, "Shall Jim Kinnane's and Hammitt Ashford's low negro dive frequenters decide who shall be the next mayor of Memphis?"

Fine print credited friends of the E. H. Crump campaign.

"Mr. Williams' friends were exceedingly active in registering several hundred of the lowest class of negroes in the city," Crump asserted in a November 1 *Commercial Appeal* ad. He trotted out an affidavit from someone swearing that Williams held secret conferences with Hammitt Ashford, "the most notorious negro divekeeper in the state of Tennessee."

Crump wrote, "It is also a well-known fact that the negro dive-keepers in Memphis are solidly supporting J. J. Williams in this campaign . . . notably Jim Kinnane, who has grown rich out of this nefarious business under the Williams administration."

Williams, well aware of Crump's political background and bene-factors, retorted, "It is now too late for Mr. Crump to shake off the shackles and nefarious alliances which he himself has made with negro dive-keepers, so-called negro preachers, and with the notorious Hag-garty, Degg, and others."[1]

Beyond the typical mudslinging and a ho-hum turnout of 12,000 voters (around 10 percent of the population), the 1909 mayoral election brought about a pair of historic breakthroughs—the beginning of the Crump dynasty and the birth of the blues. These forces came together thanks to a most unexpected agent, an apple-faced Irish saloon boss named Jim Mulcahy.

As candidate Crump grabbed the public eye, W. C. Handy, ambi-tious instructor of the colored Knights of Pythias orchestra, stepped out of the crowd and onto the biggest stage on Beale Street, at Church's Park. Jim Turner, "who played many a dance for Mr. Church," got Handy the gig.[2] Turner now joined Handy's band, and Turner proved more than musically valuable. "Jim knew every pig path in Mississippi and Alabama," Handy recalled. "He had also played the river and was favorably known in Louisiana and Arkansas. All this territory we took under control and made it our stamping ground."[3]

Handy's popularity grew. A black Memphis business directory pub-lished in 1908 had called him "one of the leading bandmasters in Amer-ica." The author noted, "All Memphians take great pride in the fact that in Prof. Handy the city of Memphis has, as one of its citizens, one of the greatest musicians in the country, irrespective of race."[4] Handy's accompanying photograph shows him in Negro parade regalia, sporting a cab driver shako, epaulets dripping off his shoulders, his chest all ribbons and buttons, gold-brocade sleeves from elbow to cuff, cornet in his left hand, baton in the right. His scuffed boots, however, belie the many miles he'd marched.

Aside from dances at Church's Park, jobs around town lacked for glamour but never for color. Though Handy's profile increased, he couldn't refuse a gig, no matter how rustic the atmosphere. Via word of mouth at Pee Wee's, he made a fortuitous connection with Jim Mulcahy.

Mulcahy operated Blue Heaven, a joint on Polk Avenue, a mile or so south of Beale. More low-down than the fancy digs at Ashford's or the Monarch, Blue Heaven was best summarized by a term that could be used as a noun, verb, or adjective: *barrelhouse*—"where a certain type of people came to enjoy theirselves without any interference," explained Alex Simms, drummer in the Blue Heaven house band.

"Jim Mulcahy was a real sport," Simms said, and Blue Heaven reflected Mulcahy's interests. "They'd have rooster fights, prizefights, and barrelhousing contests." The latter had people rolling around on the floor, simulating copulation.

To comfortably host such activities, Blue Heaven needed to be protected from police raids. Legal immunity required political clout, and to accrue it, Jim Mulcahy exploited voting procedures that practically begged to be exploited. Legally, voters had to register and pay their two-dollar poll tax prior to election day. Upon completing these steps, they were issued poll tax receipts and registration slips, and these documents were the real currency of power. The receipts and slips had to be presented at the ballot box on election day, but the presenter had only to verbally verify that he was the person to whom the receipt had been issued. Ward bosses paid individuals to register, paid the poll tax, and kept the valuable receipt, to be bundled and delivered. Kinnane did it, Haggarty did it, and Ashford did it. On election day, underworld bosses sent handpicked delegates to cast votes for the candidate of choice. This *herding* or *bundling* was the true process behind the Crump campaign's accusation that keepers of low-class colored taverns were supporting J. J. Williams.

Mulcahy would bundle for Crump, but his support didn't end there. As Beale historian George W. Lee explained, "Mulcahy knew Handy and he admired Crump, and would say, 'All right Handy, let's play for Crump's rally.'"[5]

The Handy band featured a string-heavy lineup—three violins, a guitar, and a bass—to complement the clarinet, trombone, tenor sax, and trumpet. Once he'd been recruited, Handy recalled, he composed a campaign tune for Mr. Crump. He considered various patriotic rah-rah airs, but they wouldn't do. "Hot-cha music was the stuff we needed," he recalled. "Where was it to be found? Certainly not in any existing files."[6]

He shut his eyes, transporting himself back to a train platform in Tutwiler, Mississippi, where late one night years ago he'd heard a ragged guitarist. "I could hear what I wanted. . . . It was a weird melody in much the same mood as the one that had been strummed on the guitar at Tutwiler."

Handy quilted the Tutwiler melody to a musical motif heard widely among chain gangs and Beale Street saloon pianists, but alien to popular compositions, even those patterned on Negro ragtime. It was the twelve-bar, three-line form Handy had heard his violinist Jim Turner play on the old Beale Street song, "Joe Turney's Been Here and Gone."

The outfit performed the campaign song and got the folks dancing. While people liked the band, Crump's reform agenda lacked broad appeal to Memphians who liked their city wide open. Many feared Crump would close the vice trade, as Handy recalled: "I had heard various comments from the crowds around us, and even from my own men, which seemed to express their own feelings about reform. Most of these comments had been sung, impromptu, to my music."[7]

Handy wrote a lyric to his Crump campaign theme. Adapting underground music and street poetry into his own composition became Handy's standard recipe. The band practiced and mastered the number, and in late October or early November 1909, the song made its debut, complete with the new lyrics. "Thoroughly rehearsed and intoxicated by the new melody, my musicians arrived at Main and Madison riding in a band wagon," Handy recalled, in carefully chosen words, "and got set to play the blues to the general public for the first time in America."[8]

He remembered having a seven-piece group on the wagon, seated in chairs. The wagon stood at the city's busiest corner, in the shadow of office buildings housing the city's principal financial and business leaders. As the song swung to life, he saw bosses twirling their stenographers in the windows above. Colored dancers swayed on the sidewalk. Guitarist George Higgins shouted:

Mr. Crump won't 'low no easy riders here
Mr. Crump won't 'low no easy riders here
We don't care what Mr. Crump don't 'low
We gon' to bar'l-house anyhow—
Mr. Crump can go and catch hisself some air.

"The melody of *Mr. Crump* was mine throughout," Handy would explain. "On the other hand, the twelve-bar, three-line form of the first and last strains, with its three-chord basic harmonic structure was that already used by Negro roustabouts, honky-tonk piano players, wanderers and others of their underprivileged but undaunted class from Missouri to the Gulf. . . . My part in their history was to introduce this, the 'blues' form to the general public."[9]

The key phrase in Handy's claim is the repeated *general public*. He said he played the blues for the first time to the general public, that he introduced the already existing style to the *general public*—his code for "white people." Handy has become a controversial figure, his mythical title *father of the blues* much disputed. But his true claim to fame was never to have invented blues music outright but to have crossed the music over from Beale Street to Main Street, from colored honky-tonks to mainstream America.

Regardless of the many credible arguments against Handy—that he was more a thief than an artist—that was the way it happened. Other blues certainly had been performed prior to the Crump campaign dance at Main and Madison in the fall of 1909. Other blues compositions had made publication before Handy's would in 1912. But no performer—be it Jim Turner or even Jelly Roll Morton—had carried this Negro music to where it could be widely influential and historically recognized. No other blues composer's written work would be as important to triggering the wider trend in blues popularity or would prove as inspirational, oft-covered, and recognized (the stuff of *popular* music legacy) as the music W. C. Handy wrote in Memphis beginning in 1909.

At the moment, however, this episode looked to no one, least of all Handy, like an auspicious start. He felt so sheepish about the barrel-house "Mr. Crump" lyrics—with telling a powerful man to "catch his-self some air" tantamount to advising that he jump off the Mississippi River bridge—he wouldn't dare perform the tune for Crump himself. The tune proved politically ineffective as well. The Crump campaign had expected Handy to drum up the Beale Street vote, and that didn't work out, despite the catchy anthem.

◆　◆　◆　◆

In his public comments, Crump distanced himself from the colored vote, but on election day he monitored Negro voting personally, staking out the ward five polls near Beale Street. He caught a Negro named Robert Houston distributing official ballots outside the polls. Not only that, Crump would say, but these official ballots had already been marked J. J. Williams for mayor. After a brief and heated discussion, Crump punched Houston in the face.[10]

Poston Cox, then thirteen years old, recalled:

> I lived at 317 Hill Street and on a corner next to us was a grocery and a saloon and a livery stable in the back. That's the Eighth Ward and they were counting the votes there that night—this was the night of the election that Mr. Crump ran against Joe Williams. I was sitting up on a fence which was next to the livery stable . . . and was watching them count the votes and there was a detective named Lawless [a central figure in the De Soto Street Riot]. So Lawless saw me sitting up there on the fence—he'd been drinking—and he said, "Come here, kid, and tally this sheet, I can't see it." So I got down off the fence and came around down there and sat down and as they called off the votes I would mark them down. That is the election

that when they voted as I remember, the dead people that were in Winchester Cemetery.[11]

Crump lost Beale Street but eked out a seventy-nine-vote plurality city-wide, and at age thirty-six he became mayor of the thirty-seventh-largest city in the United States.

Almost immediately after the election, the much-maligned Beale saloon boss and J. J. Williams supporter Hammitt Ashford received a sundown order and fled to St. Louis. Even more disruptive to Beale Street, Robert Church slowed down significantly, resigning his presidency of the Solvent Savings Bank. Under doctor's orders, Church retired to quieter surroundings. Now seventy-one, he lived on milk, a digestive supplement called "prunoids," nitroglycerin, amyl nitrate, and hypodermic doses of codeine and morphine.[12]

Otherwise, the criminal elite remained intact—regardless of which reform candidate proved victorious, true reform never took. The combination of Ashford's exile and Church's illness put Crump's old crony Mike Haggarty in complete control of Beale Street.

Kinnane, Haggarty, and Honan were children of famine and forced migration. They had been kicking in their mothers' bellies during the 1866 race riot, and they had survived the 1878 and 1879 yellow fever epidemics. Their history told them life was neither long nor precious. Robert Church, however, came from plantation stock. His faith in a man's name and a man's connection to the land had descended with that. He believed in legacy. Though certainly vicious and amoral, he fought for his people. The Kinnane-Haggarty relationship with Beale Street, with black people, was strictly and narrowly exploitative. Now dying, and with his operative Ashford exiled, Church felt his control over this world slipping.

His heart pained him, his head throbbed, and he couldn't eat or defecate, but Church dressed every day and rode through the district in the back of a Pierce-Arrow, watching over it and making his presence known. He still had his ties to the land, property across Beale and Gayoso, the park bearing his name, the bank bearing his reputation.

He still had legacy and a card to play. He had been grooming an heir. If anyone on Beale thought Robert Church was done—that black power in Memphis had weakened—he had something to show them: another Robert Church. Junior's hour approached.

◆　◆　◆　◆

While men like Haggarty, Kinnane, and Church had made careers in the city's racial gray area, W. C. Handy lived closer to reality. Economically, the system circumscribed the colored workforce to low-paying, low-skill vocations, while (mostly) white merchants separated colored workingmen from their money with whiskey and cocaine. Just months after E. H. Crump raided Hammitt Ashford's Beale Street saloon for political theater, a white psychopath named Bill Latura walked into Ashford's and shot six Negroes, killing three. The killer received no punishment for the mass slaying, just as George Honan had beaten the charge of killing a white man by claiming self-defense against a black man (whom Honan also killed). Add to these wholesale outrages the million personal mockeries and degradations, the mass psychological accretion on both sides of the inferiority doctrine enforced in every facet of life, from housing, nutrition, health, and education to work and leisure, and then reinforced by the anger, ignorance, and violence that inevitably grew. In the words of Mary Church Terrell, "It is impossible for any white person in the United States, no matter how sympathetic and broad, to realize what life would mean to him if his incentive to effort were suddenly snatched away."[13]

W. C. Handy turned thirty-six in the first year of the Crump tenure. He shaved his head clean and tended a thick dark mustache that curled up at the corners of his mouth. With the clean pate and bedouin whiskers, he resembled W. E. B. Du Bois. Handy carried himself properly middle class, but white merchants on Beale mocked his exaggerated manner, calling him "parson."[14] His prominent job and best front failed to alleviate Handy from the normal burdens of Negro life. He lived in a small house in a squalid section of town. Handy and his wife Lizzie shared the home with their five children and Handy's brother Charles. The children played teeter-totter on their daddy's legs as he sat at the piano trying to work. The Handys would have had one more hungry mouth, but their one-year-old daughter Florence died in a whooping cough outbreak, during a punishing heat wave, on August 13, 1908. Handy had gone to work that evening, to play a dance in Mississippi, and when he returned, the baby was dead.

His Memphis years had brought possibility without vastly increasing his prosperity, though he and his family would move from a small shotgun shack to a slightly larger one. The new place had a little porch for air and a little fence to keep a few fowl in and strange dogs out. Neighborhood houses lined up in a row along unlit dirt streets. Even in the family's larger home, Handy struggled for enough time, space, and quiet to be creative. He spread his compositions out on the wooden floor and scribbled through his ideas. He struggled with chronic sleeplessness, performing and writing virtually around the clock.

Finally, Handy caught a break. His campaign tune may not have helped Mr. Crump get elected, but the song "Mr. Crump" vaulted Handy into higher office. Through its popularity, his band earned a regular gig playing the stylish Alaskan Roof Garden atop Memphis's tallest skyscraper, the Falls Building. The new job gave Handy access to a moneyed audience—to another world. White roof garden patrons, dressed in sharp tuxedos and evening gowns, enjoyed open views of the river, the sparkling city lights, and music mingling with the steamboat whistle at the landing below. Likewise, the Alaskan Roof Garden clientele under no circumstances hung out with rough Negroes at the Monarch, Pee Wee's, or Blue Heaven. "He used to come over to Blue Heaven when he got off from the Falls Building," recalled drummer Alex Simms, "he and his band." This would be the key creative dynamic for Handy's most fruitful, influential years as a composer, jumping from the Alaskan Roof Garden to Blue Heaven, hanging around Pee Wee's and passing by the Monarch, all in a day's work.

Chapter 14

LIKE A STONE CAST INTO THE SEA

In his last will and testament, Robert Church declared, "I give, bequeath, and devise to my wife Anna S. Church, all of my personal property of whatever kind and character and wherever situated, except my watch and chain and diamond stud, which I hereby give and bequeath to my son, Robert R. Church, Jr."

Church Senior also left his namesake in charge of the family home, Church's Park, the Solvent Savings Bank building, and the half-dozen whorehouses on Gayoso Street between Hernando and Fourth. With the jewelry, Church bestowed upon his son the mantle of black boss of Beale Street.

The bequest left Church's children from his first marriage, Thomas and Mary, feeling shorted. They had moved on to New York and Washington, D.C., respectively, and thus didn't figure in their father's succession plan. Hurt and flustered, Mary Church Terrell wrote to her father's attorney, "As you know, nothing but dilapidated houses sadly in need of repair were left us—on the other hand, fine houses in splendid condition, situated in the most desirable sections of Memphis were bequeathed the other heirs."[1]

She must not have known the character of these fine, splendid, well-situated houses. Otherwise it's hard to imagine Mrs. Terrell—she had been, by now, the first female member of the Washington, D.C., Board of Education, the only female of color to address the 1904 International Congress of Women at Berlin, and one of two black women to sign the call to form the NAACP and attend its first organizational meetings—lobbying to own her dad's brothels.

Church the Elder understood what embarrassment his "splendid houses" could cause a woman of his daughter's stature. Besides, he had carefully groomed his namesake to wear the watch and chain and diamond stud. These fine, splendid houses were the keys to power in Memphis, not to be left to absentee landlords in New York and Washington—they required a local presence.

Robert Church Jr. had enjoyed an extraordinary upbringing. Church Senior's riverboat youth and self-education served him well, and certainly river life in the days of slavery had afforded him and his friends P.B.S. Pinchback and Blanche Bruce the most adventure and liberty available to their kind. But Church had protected his children from the exploding boilers and coarse chambermaids and deckhands that had decorated his youth. Robert Junior and Annette spent far more time aboard transatlantic ocean liners than Mississippi steamboats.

The family attended the 1889 Exposition Universelle in Paris. They toured Europe from Antwerp to Zurich, Brussels, Cologne, Dieppe, and Frankfurt, up the Danube, down the Rhine, to the Mediterranean, to Milan, Rome, and Venice, carrying testimony of good character from Pappy Hadden and a blank check from John Overton. They returned the next summer and in London splurged on matching hosiery, sunshades, collars, linen shirts, and cashmere pant and vest sets for father and son and a sealskin coat for mama at Hope Brothers.

Overseas, they transcended race. Church, in 1890, rebuffed a German suitor for Mary's hand, a set of circumstances that virtually any other colored family in America would have found surreal. "Mary has been indulged all her life," Church wrote, explaining matter-of-factly his doubts that the German could sustain such a lifestyle. "Every wish of her bent has been gratified as far as the comforts and pleasures of life are concerned. She has never known a care of any kind."[2]

The Churches attended the 1893 World's Colombian Exposition at Chicago and most summers avoided the Memphis heat in Atlantic City.

The children enjoyed educational advantages, too. They had private tutors at home and attended private academies beyond the South, and all graduated from Oberlin College in Ohio. Robert Church Jr., after completing Oberlin, went to business school in New York and returned to Memphis in 1906 at twenty-one. His father awaited his return, having accomplished a remarkable image overhaul. Church Senior had retired from the saloon business and entered the bank business. He had saved Beale Street Baptist Church from foreclosure, buying up the note at its due date and extending the historic black church financing on gracious terms.

Differences in upbringing cultivated differences in manner. Church Senior had grown up hot-tempered, sharp-tongued, and pugilistic, contrasting with Junior's stately, elegant charisma. At the core of each man's character, father and son shared a dogged determination: Church Junior would be a fighter like his daddy. But rather than brawling on Beale Street or in a saloon, he would take his fight to the country's highest stations of power.

Everyone called Junior "Bob," just like his father. He stood six feet tall and weighed two hundred pounds. He had perfectly straight hair and light skin. He looked like a white man. An accident had cost him the middle finger on his right hand, and he reflexively balled his hand around the missing finger, making him appear ready to throw a blow at any time. He smoked cigarettes constantly, clenching the butts between his thumb and forefinger.

Junior had assumed proprietorship of Church's Park by 1908, around the time W. C. Handy's band first took the stage. He booked weekly local dances and negotiated contracts with traveling units. Around this time, Senior officially named his real estate firm R. R. Church and Son, turning over to Junior many of the day-to-day responsibilities of managing the family brothels, Beale Street commercial properties, and residential rentals around the city. He also hired Junior to cashier at Solvent Savings Bank. In 1908 Senior pushed his son's candidacy for a federal appointment as Memphis port inspector. Though unsuccessful, the effort stoked Junior's passion for politics.

In early summer 1912, Church Junior forged his own identity, apart from his father's ventures. He put up a fight at the Republican state convention in Nashville and won a seat as Memphis's delegate to the 1912 Republican National Convention. He returned home from the national convention in Chicago in time to bid his father goodbye.

Robert Reed Church Sr. succumbed to heart disease on the blistering twenty-ninth day of August 1912. He had survived slavery, the race riot, and lynching hysteria. He'd avoided incarceration despite numerous arrests and an indictment, in addition to operating illegal businesses for decades in open defiance of the most sacred Southern taboo. To die at home, in a mansion, of natural causes in old age amounted to a tremendous victory.

Church's death gave birth to his sobriquet, "The South's First Black Millionaire." The *Chicago Defender*, reporting that Church left behind over $1 million, dubbed him "The South's Richest Negro" and called guesses that he'd left between two hundred and three hundred houses "conservative."[3] A later estimate put the value of the estate at $1.5 million.[4] Whether or not the estimates are accurate, Church's status as the South's first black millionaire represented the truth in the public mind.

The morning after his father's death, Junior read the locally penned tributes. The *Commercial Appeal* noted, "He was true to his race, yet never counseled them into the foolishness and folly of politics."[5] The *News-Scimitar* followed the same line: "Only once did he show an inclination to become politically interested and that occurred when he was sent as a delegate to the Republican national convention that nominated William McKinley for president. He returned from the convention and resolved never again to participate in any political election or campaign. He kept his word."[6] The obituaries seemed designed to prevent two potentially dangerous trends—white people thinking that a black man had been powerful and black people thinking they should try to follow suit.

The funeral brought condolences and visits from Church's friends over the years. Cash Mosby, the train excursionist who'd left Memphis after the 1892 lynchings, returned; and Hammitt Ashford sneaked back in from St. Louis to send off the boss. Ida B. Wells sent uplifting wishes. Despite his grief, Junior rose the next morning and returned to the office he'd shared with his father in the Auditorium.

A note of condolence awaited him there.

> He was indeed a strong man, and we shall all be the poorer because of his taking away.
>
> It was a great satisfaction to me to hear from so many sources when I was in Memphis that you are a man of the type that will reflect credit upon your father and continue to enrich our race through your efforts.
>
> Yours Very Truly,
> Booker T. Washington[7]

With his father's passing, Robert Church Jr. became the one and only Bob Church.

◆　◆　◆　◆

In the nearly three years since Mayor Crump's election, W. C. Handy's "Mr. Crump" had become a regional, word-of-mouth hit, so much so that the composer stood at the cigar stand in Pee Wee's, jotting out the score by hand to give to visiting bandleaders, or to send out the door with bands he booked to play dances around Mississippi, Arkansas, and West Tennessee. As the tune's popularity proved resilient, another source of income gradually dawned on Handy.

A few months after Bob Church Jr. took his first steps toward public prominence, W. C. Handy tried pushing his music toward a wider audience.

In taking "Mr. Crump" from the stage to the printing press, he hoped for success beyond the boundaries of Mr. Crump's name recognition. He also wished to avoid offending a character who loomed large across Beale Street. He shopped his song to the publishers, but without success, and finally he paid to print a thousand copies of the score. On September 28, 1912, "Mr. Crump" appeared in sheet music form, though under a new title—"Memphis Blues"—and without its catchy lyric, advising the title character to catch hisself some air.

On the strength of this song, and the blues craze it helped spark, Handy staked his claim as an originator, an innovator in the style. But another song that Handy knew well had more likely been the first real blues. He would explain that his "Memphis Blues" composition

is fashioned after an old tune that we used to call "Joe Turney," here [in Memphis]. That was not called a blues, but it was a folk tune. More than a folk tune, it was Tennessee history. Because Joe Turney was the brother of Pete Turney, governor of the state of Tennessee. Joe Turney took prisoners to the penitentiary, and went down to labor camps and carry prisoners to work. He used to hang around Memphis and pass niggers in crap games and get them arrested. And had a hand chain with forty links on it, to take 'em down the river.

This is the story that Jim Turner told me. I played with Jim here in Memphis years ago. When [women] came home and missed their husbands, said "wonder where's my husband?" "Well, they tell me Joe Turney's been here and gone." So they made up a tune. And Jim Turner played it:

> They tell me Joe Turney's come and gone,
> Oh baby, they tell me Joe Turney's come and gone,
> Oh Lordy, he's got my man and gone.
> He come with 40 links of chain,
> Oh lordy, he come with 40 links of chain,
> Oh lordy, he's got my man and gone.[8]

Violinist Jim Turner, Handy's early mentor and later colleague, is the missing link in American music, an unknown, unrecorded artist who bridged the improvised, unlettered Beale Street sound of the nineteenth century to mainstream, twentieth-century pop.

Turner had become a traveling professional musician by the 1880s. He ranged throughout the states neighboring Tennessee, where his song about Joe Turney would be remembered as "Joe Turner." Joe Turney, the song's inspiration, had been Tennessee penitentiary agent as far back as 1885 if not earlier, and he continued in that capacity through the rest of the 1880s.[9] Turney was well known and widely feared on Turner's home turf, Beale Street, for pressing Negroes into the chain gang.

Though little is known of Jim Turner's career as a traveling musician, Handy saw him perform in Florence, Alabama, no later than 1890, so Turner had clearly gotten beyond Memphis. Turner joined forces with Handy's Memphis band in 1907 or 1908, by which time, in Handy's recollection, "Jim knew every pig path in Mississippi and Alabama . . . had also played the river and was favorably known in Louisiana and Arkansas." He had spread his music along these routes, where black musicians born in the late nineteenth and early twentieth centuries learned it.[10]

Handy adapted the twelve-bar blues song structure of "Memphis Blues" from Turner's "Joe Turney." As Handy would recall, the atypical twelve-bar structure frightened publishers away from the song—sixteen-bar tunes were the rage; it wouldn't be the last time the mainstream music industry initially rejected a concept that would nonetheless conquer it. The twelve-bar blues became the bedrock of American pop. Through jazz, boogie-woogie, rhythm and blues, rock 'n' roll, and soul, it held sturdy for more than sixty years.

Jim Turner didn't survive to see his music ascend. He died of pneumonia on May 20, 1910, in a tiny rear apartment on Turley Street, behind Church's Park.[11] He was forty-one. He left a wife and daughter and one of the great, unknown legacies in American music. Today he rests in the same neglected, overgrown cemetery as W. C. Handy's infant daughter and the three Negro merchants lynched in 1892.

◆   ◆   ◆   ◆

Mayor Crump's early days in office overlapped with the arrival of a
new law in the land of Tennessee, expressed in one staunch word: *Prohibition*. The legal prohibition of alcohol had evolved out of the temperance movement, embodied in such national grassroots organizations as
the American Temperance Society and the Woman's Christian Temperance Union, both founded in the nineteenth century to encourage individual abstinence from liquor. The issue achieved significant political
traction in 1881, when Kansas outlawed alcohol in its state constitution.

Tennessee banned booze and beer in 1909, initially via the "four-mile
law," which criminalized the sale or consumption of intoxicating bev-
erages within four miles of a school, and later via a bill that outlawed
alcoholic beverage manufacturing. These measures emanated not from
Tennessee's urban centers but from its rural constituencies, and they
either created or amplified a sense of rivalry between the largely pasto-
ral state and its few cities. As anti-alcohol factions gained strength in
town, anti-Prohibition forces developed rhetoric to sway the masses.
The city of Memphis availed itself quite naturally to those who opposed
Prohibition. Rather than enforce the four-mile law, Memphis might
sooner have banned schools.

Of course the great flaw of Prohibition—the disconnect between the
ideal of alcohol prohibition in the minds of its proponents and the reality
of prohibition in practice—is that it directly led to flagrant, widespread
illegal activity. Bootleggers supported Prohibition with the enthusiasm of a temperance evangelist. Circumstances in Memphis in 1910, a
decade before national Prohibition took effect across the country, foreshadowed the rise of organized crime in conjunction with illegal liquor.

Instead of following this onerous law to the letter, the mandated
reformer Crump ignored it, and Memphis became Prohibition's
worst-case scenario. After a year of Prohibition, a reporter from St.
Louis named Silas Bent investigated Memphis, wishing to observe the
social ravages of this law. And where might a visiting reporter witness
the corruption that clings to restricted booze? "In the district where vice

flourishes openly, along Gayoso street, from Third to Wellington, and along Rayburn boulevard, from Beale to Linden avenues," Silas Bent explained, adding, "I saw policemen enter saloons with women, and saw women stand with men at bars and drink. It is the boast of some of the saloon proprietors in this district that they never close their doors."[12]

Brightly illuminated signs and strings of electric lights beckoned Silas Bent to John Persica's Garden Theater. Inside, he noted the prize-fight advertisements and the stage at the back of the dance hall, "where moving pictures are shown, with indecent vaudeville turns at intervals." He watched a stout blond woman walk into the dance hall, holding the tasseled chord of a policeman's stick. "The stick was over her shoulder and the policeman held the other end." They found a table, through laughter and warm-hearted jests, and were served drinks, at no cost.

Following the indecent vaudeville, the floor was cleared of chairs and sprinkled with sand, and women wearing skirts that failed to conceal their knees led patrons out to dance. Couples seeking privacy scurried up stairs to one of the private boxes that overlooked the dance hall.

Silas Bent left Persica's and walked across the district, noting various activities. At the Climax, he heard a Negro pounding the piano, and everywhere the slot machines pinged, while saloon doors stood invitingly open, even on Sunday.

Bent caught up the next day with the mayor. Mr. Crump framed his refusal to abide by Prohibition as a sovereignty issue. The state had conjured the "four-mile law" to please a few noisy rural constituencies, the mayor said. The people of Memphis had never voted on it and wouldn't stand for it. If the state wanted the four-mile law enforced in Memphis, the state would have to come and do that itself. Still, no one could have guessed his level of commitment to vice.

◆　◆　◆　◆

The new "Memphis Blues" sheet music was right at home in the parlor of Alice Folliard. Two blocks south of Beale, she ran an elegant brothel, entertaining a male clientele of means. She enjoyed maximum security from the law, thanks to her friends, and felt little concern for her livelihood. But one warm summer night, one of Folliard's boarders sneaked out of a second-floor window and escaped.

Rachel Kerr, originally from Peoria, Illinois, had come to Folliard's under the pretense of respectable employment. Folliard pressed her into duty and kept her captive with threats of exposure to her parents or arrest. Folliard, who had half a dozen other girls doing the same thing, kept all the money made in her house. She intercepted inmates' attempts at communication with the outside world. After Kerr escaped, federal agents arrested Folliard on July 3, 1913.

The agents rounded up every inmate of Folliard's house and presented them to a circuit court judge. In an explosive Fourth of July hearing, one of the girls said Folliard regularly shared their proceeds with Memphis police officers. The girls all said that these payments protected them from arrest. In light of the revelation, Police Chief Hayes promised a thorough graft probe. He refused to suspend the accused officers, however, valuing the word of his lawmen over that of the sporting women.

The internal graft investigation lasted a day. The police commissioner announced the severance of one of the patrolmen implicated. "We have had some trouble to keep [Officer] Light sober and alert to his duty," he said. The firing emanated from their own findings, he emphasized, and not from the testimony of Folliard house inmates. "There was nothing conclusive in the statements of the girls and I would not discharge an officer on mere hearsay evidence."[13]

That was just about that. One head rolled. The police saved face. Mayor Crump recommended that the force hire a female detective to surreptitiously survey the street mashers and flirts hanging around.[14]

Meanwhile, the feds had released Folliard and the women who'd testified against her, but U.S. marshals continued investigating the madam. In her possession they found a letter addressed to Julia Gentry, a young woman living at the Folliard house. It had come from Gentry's mother, who had not heard from Julia for months. The mother had written the postmaster begging for information on her daughter's whereabouts.

In following days, red-light gossip had it that Folliard paid a rail-road engineer $1,000 to silence everyone who testified against her. The railroad man threatened to break the girls' pretty young jaws, but they talked to the marshals anyway. Federal agents arrested Folliard once again, this time for intimidating witnesses.

Despite the stifling heat, she donned full bawd regalia, arriving at the marshals' office in a lace dress and jaunty hat, her gaudy jewel rings and pins glittering. Traces of both beauty and kindness clung to her features, but her pretty lips spewed venom. She hissed that she'd spend her last penny proving that the government was persecuting her. She threatened to expose all the higher-ups allied with her.[15]

By now the situation had managed to elude the local fix and threatened to go higher, a distressing circumstance for Mr. Crump. He sat in his office at City Hall and dashed off a note to his best friend with federal pull, his district's U.S. congressman, Kenneth McKellar. Crump urged McKellar to head to the Department of Justice and "personally explain to whoever has this matter in charge that my only interest is from the standpoint that unwarranted publicity of this character not only hurts our city, but it also hurts in securing results in the suppression of the evil that the Department [of Justice] is trying to eradicate."[16]

But Crump's interests in the case extended well past bad publicity for the city. A full investigation of Folliard's business could lead to the saloon that Crump and his chief strategist Frank Rice owned.[17] The feds wouldn't have far to go—the back door of Crump and Rice's saloon led straight to Folliard's house. The clamor quieted and the Folliard case went nowhere, but Mr. Crump developed a healthy fear of federal authority.

◆ ◆ ◆ ◆

Though the Folliard case had vanished from the news by summer's end, the underworld stayed jumpy throughout the fall of 1913.

November came to Beale Street with the traditional harvest-time herding. Police arrested loafers with Mayor Crump's blessing—"the demand of cotton pickers is satisfied to some extent," he cracked.[18] The police enthusiasm for this task exceeded necessity, and Crump had to order his police commissioner to tone down the men. "No less than three negroes have been killed by officers within the past few weeks," Crump wrote in a memo. "I want to suggest that you make a talk to them, the mounted men as well as the patrolmen, and just give them to understand that we will not stand for the killing of negroes, or anyone else, unless there is a very, very good reason for it."[19]

For the first time in years, since Prohibition anyway, John Persica's Garden Theater was closed, its shutters pulled tight—black crepe fluttered on its doors. On November 10, just before five in the morning, Persica, two "actresses" in residence at his theater, and a police sergeant were on a joyride, with Persica's chauffeur at the wheel of a six-cylinder Thomas Flyer. Persica's car collided with an ice wagon on Madison Avenue, flipped upside down, and twirled fifty feet. As the wreck came to a rest, "John Persica, epitome of all that gayety and power represent in the underworld lay silent and crushed beneath the pride of his garage."

Persica's death brought forth a shower of journalistic bouquets. His district joint had reportedly achieved a state of dissolution equaled only in the frontier saloons of Gold Rush lore. The former New Orleanian hosted the rowdiest Mardi Gras balls. Scribes marveled at his legal immunity. The circumstances of his death—riding with a police sergeant and a pair of sporting women—spoke volumes of his life.

Underrated at the time, Persica had played a crucial, if indirect, role in the growth of Memphis music. "The statute against music in a place where liquor is sold was passed for the especial purpose of stopping such places as his, and it stopped all but his," an obituary stated. The statute silenced the fine string orchestra at the deluxe Peabody Hotel, but Persica's place "ran with his music, dances, and drinks."[20] In spite of the law against live music, a Negro touring act, Osceola and Berliana Blanks, had picked up "Memphis Blues" at Persica's. From there the Blanks sisters put "Memphis Blues" into their show and spread its popularity as they traveled around the country. Other bandleaders picked up the tune and added it to their repertoires.[21] Fans heard the tune in shows and bought the sheet music to play at home on the parlor piano.

The proceeds, however, went not to W. C. Handy but to Theron C. Bennett—who had slicked Handy out of the "Memphis Blues" copyright.[22]

After every music house had rejected the strange, twelve-bar "Memphis Blues," Handy had decided to self-publish the sheet music and sell it himself. While trying to find retailers, he encountered Bennett, a song publisher who traveled around the country promoting his sheet music and plugging his songs—that is, playing his songs on the piano in various stores, demonstrating them for the music-buying public, and trying to get them performed in stage shows, all to encourage sales. Bennett offered to have "Memphis Blues" placed at Bry's department store in Memphis and plug it there for white shoppers. Handy shook on it, paid for a thousand copies, and waited for good news.

An ad for the song appeared in the paper in late September 1912. Bennett, however, reported that people found the tune too complicated— it wouldn't sell. Handy was crushed. Bennett offered Handy fifty dollars for the copyright to "Memphis Blues," giving Handy a small profit on the venture after he'd spent $33.50 on printing.

Decades later Handy accidentally discovered that Bennett had ordered not one thousand but two thousand copies at the initial printing that Handy had paid for. The song in fact had sold briskly at Bry's, but whenever Handy had gone to see about sales, Bennett had shown him a stack of a thousand copies of "Memphis Blues," so as far as Handy knew, the thing was dead. Bennett soon split Memphis for New York, where he ordered ten thousand "Memphis Blues" sheets under his own copyright.

Losing his rights to "Memphis Blues" might have been the best thing that had ever happened to Handy and the song.

In order to promote sales of sheet music for his new composition, Bennett launched a national tour that showcased "Memphis Blues," sung by a white minstrel. He sold fifty thousand copies in his first year.[23] In 1914 the song debuted on a new medium—the Victor Military Band recorded it, and the Columbia Recording Company's house band followed suit.

Five years after Handy had played "Mr. Crump" to a crowd at the corner of Main and Madison, and two years since he published the tune as "Memphis Blues," the song was completing a remarkable evolution. The idea for it had begun deep in the black experience, from the clinking forty links on Joe Turney's chain. It had gone on to become a folk phenomenon through fiddler Jim Turner's pig path repertoire, then crossed into polite society as Mr. Crump's campaign theme. Now a white man had conned a Negro out of its ownership. "Memphis Blues" was a microcosm of American music.

Though it stung Handy to see someone else make the money from his hit, Bennett's song-plugger tricks brought "Memphis Blues" to a broader audience than Handy could have done. While the song's success didn't financially enrich him, it did wonders for his name. Bennett added a new lyric that touted the city and its musical charms—"They had a fellow there named Handy with a band you should hear."

The sheet music prominently displayed Handy's composer credit on its cover, and that, along with the lyrical name-drop being heard in theaters colored and white, boosted the bandleader's reputation.

Handy exhausted himself on a grinding schedule, playing riverboat cruises by evening, the Alaskan Roof Garden's white dances at night, and Jim Mulcahy's Blue Heaven dive for Negroes until nearly dawn. The routine strained his marriage. After one of his twenty-four-hour shifts, he'd return home to find Lizzie waiting for him with her rolling pin at the ready. Nevertheless, new musical ideas wouldn't leave Handy alone, and he needed time and quiet to write. Sounds haunted his mind, as his history played and replayed—the blind woman singing spirituals on the corner, the preacher intoning at his boyhood church in Alabama, the dance caller he heard as a youth in Kentucky. Beale Street color inspired him, but it made work impossible. He couldn't get anything done at Pee Wee's, and his tiny cottage full of children was no more amenable to the creative process.

Handy needed help. No Negroes had song-publishing experience, so he turned to someone who at least had publishing experience. If Harry Pace had been good enough for W. E. B. Du Bois, certainly he was worth a shot for W. C. Handy. Pace and Handy formally entered into business, taking an office over the Solvent Savings Bank on Beale, and Handy went to work.

He blocked out the strains of piano, the flickering colorful lights, and the chitterlings cooking. He channeled his past, picturing himself broke and raggedy in the St. Louis cold. He remembered a drunken woman's lament, sung as she staggered along: *My man's got a heart like a rock cast in the sea.* Cold, hard, true poetry.

The opening lyric of "St. Louis Blues" resonated with Beale Street's memory of Hammitt Ashford, who'd gotten a sundown order and left— for St. Louis.

I hate to see that evening sun go down.

◆　◆　◆　◆

On a hot August Saturday night, Handy's rounds from the office down to Pee Wee's would have taken him underneath a huge roll of canvas ringed with electric lights, stretched from outside the Monarch over Beale Street. Two-foot-high letters read: "Write it this way: RIECHMAN."

Riechman was Mayor Crump's candidate for county sheriff. The opposition had struck his name from the ballot, and so the Crump machinery began an ambitious campaign to elect Riechman as a write-in candidate.

Inside the Monarch, Mike Haggarty coordinated a cynical Negro voting school. He sent out a horse and buggy carrying a man with a blackboard and a supply of chalk. Blaring red torches attracted attention to the buggy, and the crowds gathered around to take instruction in the proper spelling of Riechman. Other instructors worked the crowd like carnival barkers or store pullers, grabbing passersby to offer the quick German lesson.[24]

Behind Haggarty and the Monarch, the city's political puppeteers were fine-tuning a machine.

Mayor Crump stood out as the most visible symbol of the machine, but his shadowy backer Frank Rice held significant power and strategic influence. "Frank Rice owned a lot of joints around in Memphis, and the black votes, we didn't have many votes, but Rice controlled many of the black votes, and Rice did more to build the machine than Crump did, as I see it," said Blair Hunt, a powerful minister and educator who served as a Crump booster in the black community. "Mr. Rice paid poll taxes and had control of using the poll tax receipts. That's the way the machine was built, and then the government was very efficient and the majority of white people liked it."[25]

Tall, redheaded Crump cut a dashing figure. Short, plump, older Rice looked as though he belonged behind the scenes, and there he worked, in the unassuming clerical office of county register. Rice had managed Crump's successful campaigns up the ladder from the lower public works board to the police and fire commissioners' board and finally to the mayor's office.

As campaign manager emeritus, Rice collected and maintained a sizable war chest. He supervised the organization's tenderloin property, owned in a number of trusts under various names, and in his official role as register, he controlled the property records to keep incriminating evidence out of sight.

Poll tax collection featured prominently in the register's job description, and it played splendidly with Rice's talents. Poll taxes equaled votes, plain and simple. Voters paid their poll tax, and the register collected the tax and issued the voter a receipt, without which no one could cast a vote.

Since machine officials themselves were in no position to explicitly acquire poll tax receipts and registrations en masse, this duty fell to saloon operators and divekeepers. The machine had saloonkeeper operatives in every ward. It fell in cahoots with Mike Haggarty and Tom

Dockery, Beale Street saloonists at the Monarch and Panama respectively; a colored divekeeper named Amos "Mack" McCullough out in Shinertown; and Beale Street mass murderer Bill Latura, who ran a saloon on the north side and gathered hundreds of registrations. They turned the registrations over to the police. (Jim Kinnane reportedly held on to his bundled registrations and poll tax receipts, personally distributing them on election day.) The machine reputedly stored away seven thousand registration slips during the effort to write in Riechman. All paid bulk poll taxes, with Haggarty adding $1,000 to the war chest as well. Rice, the official poll tax collector, was their liaison.

With the machine's guidance, police intimidated politically unfriendly saloons, smashing bottles, draining liquor, destroying furnishings.

The collective of machine-picked officials and their police cronies became known as "the boys."

In fairness, this corruption in no way hindered the performance of government. Memphis's material welfare improved, through Crump's standard progressive platform of highly functional public works and a business-friendly climate. The city's prosperity could be seen etched across its skyline in a number of ten-to-twenty-story buildings that sprouted during the administration. Its population growth continued rapidly if not explosively, from 100,000 at the turn of the century to nearly 150,000 by 1915. Streets, parks, utilities, and services all improved under Mr. Crump's despotism. And Boss Crump and the boys sure could clean up an election, as they wrote in Sheriff Riechman in fall 1914 by a comfortable 10,000-vote margin—a remarkable milestone for the machine, considering that a total of 12,000 votes had been cast for both candidates in the mayoral election Crump had won just five years earlier.

The write-in Riechman campaign showed the boys' guile but caused substantial collateral damage. The machine had conducted most of its prior chicanery more subtly, but the nature of the write-in Riechman campaign angered the public and infuriated good reform-minded people, who began calling Crump "Napoleon the Red."

Chapter 15

I'd Rather Be There
Than Any Place
I Know

George Honan stalked the red-light district, still the most dreaded character among stiff competition. He had earned his reputation in gun battles and political rows. He had survived a murder trial and countless other criminal inquests, for illegal liquor sales, numerous shootings, and a morals charge stemming from his brief cohabitation with two young girls. His exploits inspired mass meetings and safety committees and fed into reform fury.

He'd dominated the streets for over a decade, since before the De Soto Street Riot, where he'd killed at least one lawman, to his period as "booking agent" at Haggarty and Degg's Turf Saloon, a barely glorified brothel. Now he hung his hat at the Monarch, where he pit-bossed for Jim Kinnane and Haggarty.

Time had done nothing to diminish his ferocity. Age thickened his build, and now he looked like a gnarled cedar trunk, with a thick knot for a head, a stout barrel of a body, and a crippled limb—his gunshot-shattered left arm—jutting from his side.

On a cold morning, at just about three a.m., he made his way from the Majestic, a rowdy pool hall and rooming house on Hadden Avenue, across Beale and up a block to Mabel Harris's place, a brothel known as the Maidwell House, on Hernando Street. He arrived in a foul mood. He'd phoned a Maidwell resident named Grace Frazier and asked her to meet him at the Majestic. When she told him no, he went after her.

Honan started kicking in the door to her room. She opened up—and Honan shot her point-blank in the stomach. She wasn't alone. Her guest, a twenty-nine-year-old bookkeeper named Robert Embleton, ducked behind a wardrobe. With Honan firing, Embleton pulled a small automatic pistol and emptied the chamber into Honan.

"It was my life or his," Embleton would explain. "I had to kill him, and God knows I hate it."

The police quickly arrived to investigate. They found Grace Frazier bleeding out and asked her to make a dying statement. "No," she laughed, "I'll get well."

For the great bully of the town, the news wrote a chilling epitaph: "Honan, when under the influence of liquor, was one of the most desperate men that ever lived in Memphis."[1] Surprising no one, Honan's obituary identified him as an operative with the forces currently controlling city politics.

Through his role in the De Soto Street Riot, Honan had started the reform wave that first carried Crump into office. His reputation had kept Crump's opposition in check ever since. The loss of this muscleman and protector was an ill omen for the Crump machine.

◆ ◆ ◆ ◆

W. C. Handy and Robert Church Jr. developed a relationship like that of Ida B. Wells and Church Senior, though it was stronger and more personal. Church helped to sustain Handy, hiring him to play at Church's Park, and he shared business advice that would help make Handy wealthy. He rented an office to Handy, and the two were neighbors during working hours for the groundbreaking years of their respective careers.

While Handy built his music company at 392 Beale, Bob Church worked across the street at 391, developing a strategy that he hoped would elevate black power in American politics. Their remarkable synergy gained momentum as Church and Handy both tapped Beale Street's natural resources. Beale Street might never have become known as Home of the Blues or as the Main Street of Black America without Handy and Church, and yet Handy and Church would not have accomplished what they did without the people of Beale Street.

Handy's struggles continued. He mortgaged his home for funds and corralled fractious band members to take low-paying gigs. The lasting money could be made from music on paper, he knew, not from the stage. He continued to write songs and publish music to supplement his gigs.

He returned to the "Mr. Crump" formula, drawing on underworldly argot to spice his lyrics. He listened to Sonny Butts and Benny French play piano at the Monarch.[2] He remembered the lean, loose-jointed Negro he'd heard on a train platform at Tutwiler, Mississippi, perhaps a decade before, singing his intentions to go where the Southern cross' the Dog. Having no idea what this meant, Handy had asked the hobo, who smirked but patiently explained that the Southern and Yazoo Delta railroads met at Moorhead, Mississippi. Travelers had changed Yazoo Delta to Yellow Dog, abbreviating it as Dog.

A song called "I Wonder Where My Easy Rider's Gone" was a huge hit on Beale Street, played alike on the avenue's upscale stages at the Metropolitan and Savoy theaters and by the down-home string band jamming in Pee Wee's wine room. In late 1914 Pace & Handy published "Yellow Dog Rag" as a musical answer—that easy rider'd gone where the Southern cross' the Dog—based on the Monarch piano style and Mississippi hobo geography.

In April 1915 Pace & Handy made its presence known in a high-profile fashion, at least to the world of colored entertainment. It placed an ad in the *Indianapolis Freeman*, a nationally circulated black newspaper with correspondents reporting from theaters all over black America.[3] The pair coined a distinctive slogan for their firm:

PACE & HANDY MUSIC CO.
"Home of the Blues"

◆   ◆   ◆   ◆

Napoleon the Red's excesses caught up to him.

Tennessee's internal conflict over Prohibition had continued since Mr. Crump's election in 1909. Prohibition enforcement had been at issue in the 1912 gubernatorial election. The Republican candidate, Ben Hooper, made it a campaign pledge, to "clean out every saloon and low-down dive in Memphis." Crump supported the Democrat, who lost. The next year Governor Hooper pushed the so-called Nuisance Act through the state legislature, which suppressed saloons, brothels, and gambling dens by state injunction. The act failed to take hold in Memphis. Crump drew the ire of the Anti-Saloon League as well as Governor Hooper's successor, Tom Rye, who in early 1915 signed the epochal Ouster Law. Now any person holding office in the state, at any level of government, "who shall neglect to perform any duty enjoined upon such officer by any of the laws of the State of Tennessee," particularly Prohibition and related statues against gambling and prostitution, "shall be ousted from office." From that moment, any judicial official at the city, county, or state level could file a petition of complaint against a neglectful officeholder. In fall 1915 the state attorney general demanded Crump's ouster. A local judge initiated the proceedings, filing suit against Crump for failing to enforce Tennessee laws against alcohol, prostitution, and gambling, and a local chancery court ruled that Crump had to leave office.[4]

The ouster suit stated, among other things, that Frank Rice, Crump, and other associates owned property that was leased to tenants who used it for immoral purposes. It further stated that these properties were held in trust under various names, including that of P. H. Kelly, a Crump politician. Records of properties purchased by P. H. Kelly or the P. H. Kelly Trust during the early years of Crump machine rule, 1910–15, are extraordinarily spotty. Many have disappeared altogether, although property records had been systematically recorded in the county for a half-century and remain largely intact. The man in charge of accurately recording property deeds during that time period was the county register, Frank Rice.

Among the properties owned by the trust, the ouster suit listed 342 Second Street, the brothel of Alice Folliard, "Queen of the White Slavers," who'd bragged about "higher-ups" backing her venture back when the heat found her a couple years before.

The ouster suit opened the inner workings of Crump's machine to public inspection. At the heart of it was the voter-registration-slip racket. Stories circulated about a $200,000 slush fund, collected by Rice from "dive keepers, law violators, and office holders."[5] Rice allegedly paid a thug out of the city treasury to shadow an uncooperative local judge in order to scare the judge or to gain leverage by learning the judge's private habits.

As the ouster suit ricocheted up to the state Supreme Court, the city erupted into bacchanalian festivity, the Crump gang's last hurrah. The night of February 12, 1916, the party practically took over the city, filling the streets and invading the halls of government. Revelers brandished half-pints, and music flowed as freely as the liquor. As the party wound down, a Negro string band serenaded the city jail. A bemused reporter looked on. "They played 'Mr. Crump,'" noted the journalist. "The few remaining 'boys' applauded. The hat was passed and the boys disappeared. 'Where Has My Easy Rider Gone?' was the last number."[6]

The state Supreme Court found Crump guilty, and Crump forfeited office on February 22. Though scandalous, the ouster ultimately failed to undermine Napoleon the Red. It did carry an important consequence, however, as it unplugged the machine from its source of power: the saloon bosses who'd helped to elect Crump in 1909 and write in Riechman in 1914. Since the ouster was based on Crump's refusal to enforce Prohibition, subsequent leaders could not openly enable saloon-

keepers. Crump's ouster thus stripped political power from Jim Kinnane, Mike Haggarty, and Jim Mulcahy. Crump would look to others
for future political favors.

◆ ◆ ◆ ◆

Throughout fall 1915, as news of the Crump ouster dominated
headlines, Bob Church Jr. quietly assembled a new black political organization. He gathered business leaders—undertakers, grocers, lawyers,
and Solvent Savings Bank executives. They met after hours in the bank
(underneath W. C. Handy's writing room) and devised a strategy to
educate and organize Negro voters. They hoped to take the Negro
vote away from the divekeeper and create a large, politically significant
force. Church and his group adopted a thoroughly Republican platform
and named themselves the Lincoln League.

On February 14, 1916, two days after Mr. Crump's citywide blowout,
the Lincoln League went public with a mass rally at Church's Auditorium. The speakers outlined a simple platform: promote the principles
and candidates of the Republican Party and protect the interests of colored voters in the state of Tennessee. The organization wanted Lincoln
Leagues in every Tennessee town, from Memphis to Bristol. Anyone
who could support the party, legally register, and pay his own poll taxes
could join. Women attended the rally in great numbers.[7]

Lincoln League leaders set an optimistic goal of casting ten thousand votes to tip the polls their way in November.

Precinct by precinct, the league mobilized a mass colored voter registration. Brilliantly tapping into female enthusiasm, they employed
women to conduct voting classes and practice ballots in every Negro
church or fellowship hall in every black neighborhood of the city. Deal-
ing realistically with obstacles, they instructed illiterate voters to place
"single shot" ballots, voting for a single candidate to avoid invalidating
the ballot by voting for too many candidates in a given race. Voting
school instructors made weekly reports to a central registration committee at Church's Auditorium to specify the number of new voters trained.

Lincoln League momentum built, and excitement grew throughout the summer. Weekly rallies at the auditorium attracted fervent attendance. To distract from such subversive activity, Church lavishly displayed his patriotism and generosity.

On August 9 a detachment of colored soldiers stopped at Memphis, en route from Washington, D.C., to the Mexican border. Church organized a welcoming committee, including Sam Carnes, a white citizen of great esteem, theatrically playing the race chip in a way that would have made his father proud. They feted the colored soldiers at Church's Park, treating the doughboys to an afternoon of amusements and serving sandwiches, fresh coffee, bananas, oranges, and ice water. Church filled the soldiers' pockets with cigarettes on their way out of town and led a motorcade to Grand Central Station for the send-off. There Church had arranged a surprise for the soldiers.

Waiting at the station, sweating through their stiff wool uniforms on this hot afternoon, was the W. C. Handy Band. As Bob Church led the parade into sight, they launched into a set of Handy hits—"Memphis Blues," "Hesitation Blues," "Joe Turner," and "Yellow Dog Blues."[8]

The leader brought a string-heavy ensemble to the station, featuring some of the most important figures in Handy's career, as well as a pair of American music heroes. Matthew Thornton had been responsible for bringing Handy to Memphis over a decade earlier. He played cornet in the band, and his son Powers played violin. Charlie Bynum played guitar. He had been a prominent bandleader on Beale Street at the time of Handy's arrival, and old-timers would say that Bynum's, not Handy's, had been the first orchestra to play the blues. Finally, a cello player not twenty years old had lately joined the band from Little Rock, Arkansas.

William Grant Still would go on to become the most renowned African American classical music composer. He would conduct the Los Angeles Philharmonic Orchestra, win a Guggenheim Fellowship, and see the New York City Opera perform his *Troubled Island*. Still tinged his symphonic and operatic works with Negro musical idioms, embodying, perhaps even more than Handy, Antonín Dvořák's 1893 statement, "I am now satisfied . . . that the future music of this country must be founded upon what are called the negro melodies. This must be the foundation of any serious or original school of composition to be developed in the United States."

◆   ◆   ◆   ◆

The Lincoln League threw white Memphis into an absolute panic. A Negro political organization of such verve and dash had no precedent in white minds.

Shortly before the fall election, as Lincoln League activity reached its peak, the *Commercial Appeal* infiltrated the league, using several white Republicans and half a dozen Negro operatives to report the inner workings. The investigation confirmed the direst white Republican fears. Black voters equaled white Republican power in the city and drubbed white Republicans in the rurals five to one.[9] The GOP's local white faction was doomed. Even worse for would-be opponents, the Lincoln League boasted financial independence, with funding coming straight from wealthy Negro pockets. Using the league's momentum to attract national party attention, Church made significant inroads into the highest GOP councils. He received a telegram at his office, summoning him to New York for an October 6 meeting at which he joined the national advisory board of the Republican Party.[10]

The Lincoln League showed its force, sending a powerful message prior to election day. Nearly two thousand colored voters packed Church's Auditorium, filling every aisle and the balcony, plus standing room at the back. League members held high their registration certificates and poll tax receipts. Scores of others sent in their names but said they couldn't afford the tax. As their names were read, a pastor laid a ten-dollar bill on a table at the head of the hall, and everyone else knew what to do. They filed forward and covered the table in cash and coin.

Nearly a half-century before the modern civil rights movement, a black man, through his own financial resources and acumen, organized the most extensive registration of Southern Negro voters thus far in U.S. history.

The Lincoln League energized the entire region. It activated old voters who'd grown indifferent and inspired youth from the bright lights of Memphis to the hinterlands where slavelike conditions dominated.

"To black people, next to God and church, was the Republican party," said Herbert Brewster, born in 1897 and raised in cotton farming West Tennessee. "It was the party of Lincoln. They were by the Republican Party like Moses was by the burning bush." To rural, black youth like Brewster, Bob Church symbolized the incarnation of such powerful imagery. "It was one of the most inspirational names I'd ever heard," he said.[11]

Though he'd grown up less than fifty miles from Memphis on the map, Brewster's life seemed worlds and decades away from the big city. But as the Lincoln League's influence spread, Brewster and his classmates got the opportunity to attend its mammoth rally on the eve of the 1916 election.

"I had never seen an auditorium," Brewster recalled. "I didn't know what it was." The crowd outnumbered the population of the town he had come from, and though he and his classmates were hours early for the program, they could scarcely push inside for a seat. "We wedged in and as we looked up, saw it was a beautiful place," he said. The patriotic decor, buntings and flags, dazzled him.

The band roared into action. A lump filled his throat, and his eyes welled with tears. "After they played 'Battle Hymn of the Republic,'" Brewster said, "there strode out to the edge of the platform a young man of great carriage and personality."

Bob Church appeared, resplendent, his hair parted and slicked down, the incessant cigarette trailing blue smoke in the spotlight. Though Church preferred negotiation to oratory, he captured, in this moment, the ambition of his race while expanding what many within it thought possible.

"The Lincoln League," he said, "is founded for the good of the masses and not the classes of men. You don't have to be a black man nor a white man, a banker or a hodcarrier, a preacher or a blacksmith, but any qualified voter, be he black or white, rich or poor."

Church's understated performance amid the grandeur of the surroundings and the gravity of the moment changed Brewster's life.
"When I heard that speech and saw that young Negro man I went back
and resolved that night to be somebody some day," Brewster said. "That
determination was inspired by Bob Church and that crowd of people in
that black auditorium.

"I never knew before that I had a chance. I never knew before that it
was possible for a man to come from nowhere and end up somewhere."

Brewster went on to lead the congregation at East Trigg Avenue Baptist Church of Memphis for almost fifty years. He wrote gospel songs,
and his "Move on Up a Little Higher," recorded by Mahalia Jackson,
was the first million-seller in the genre. Brewster's easy chair, where he
liked to write, sits today in the Smithsonian Institution.

◆ ◆ ◆ ◆

Meanwhile, W. C. Handy harnessed Beale Street music, not only
drawing inspiration from the barrelhouse muse but opening his ear to
young talent on Beale, inviting vagabond child gangs in to sing their
play rhymes, and surreptitiously auditioning pit band musicians in
nearby theaters.

Handy discovered a twenty-year-old cornetist named Johnny Dunn
playing in the Metropolitan, a theater next door to the Monarch. Dunn
was the son of a prominent Beale Streeter, headwaiter at the Peabody
Hotel, Simon Dunn. The elder Dunn also ran a fellowship hall on the
street that opened the life to Johnny. The son's improvisatory flights
infuriated Handy, who remained at heart a marching bandleader. He'd
shout, "God damn it, play it like it's written!"

Johnny joined the Handy band in 1916. He eventually fronted Mamie
Smith's Jazz Hounds, just as Mamie's "Crazy Blues" sparked the first
frenzy for blues records.

Handy recruited an even younger Beale Streeter to the band,
fifteen-year-old clarinetist Buster Bailey. These gifted young men
would travel to prestige gigs with the main orchestra, pick up early

strains of jazz in New Orleans, and rouse Chicago with the "Memphis Blues." Bailey would quit Handy in Chicago and move in the highest jazz circles, playing clarinet in the bands of Joe "King" Oliver, Louis Armstrong, and Fletcher Henderson. He would record behind Bessie Smith and Ma Rainey, the two brightest blues stars of the 1920s and 1930s. Though Bailey never returned to Memphis long term, he never forgot the sordid, disreputable roots of his music, commemorating the district and punning his mentor in the composition "Hatton Avenue and Gayoso Street," recorded on his 1958 solo album *All About Memphis*.

Handy also recognized William Grant Still's capabilities as an arranger and put the young man to work in Pace & Handy's Beale Street headquarters. "This certainly would not seem to be an occupation nor a place where anything of real musical value could be gained," the erudite Still recalled. "Nor would nearby Gayoso Street, which was then a somewhat disreputable section. But, in searching for musical experiences that might later help me, I found there an undeniable color and a musical atmosphere that stemmed directly from the folk."[12]

As always, Handy haunted the Monarch. As he passed by one summer night in 1916, the piano rhythm struck him as something extraordinary. It captured the weary, wary feeling of these tumultuous, uncertain times punctuated with sudden thrills, like life on the street.

He went upstairs to listen more closely. He found a dark, wiry man at the piano: Son Wright. Son, in his early thirties, had played at Jim Kinnane's Blue Goose in North Memphis, and like the renowned Benny French, he rotated from joint to joint in the Kinnane belt, logging twelve-hour shifts at the piano. Though Handy would soon forget Son Wright's name, if he ever knew it, he recalled, "It would take quite an artist to hold such a job, and this artist, his name unknown to me, was the inspiration of *Beale Street Blues*."[13]

Heavy hours *slowed* the pace. Son Wright switched out his piano stool for a cushioned chair. He developed little tricks to sneak some rest. He kept his left hand on the keys, gently splashing an insistent beat with his thumb and forefinger. He swung his right hand to the high notes, pounding an equally insistent, quicker-paced groove. He rode the notes. And that was what Handy heard as he strolled below the Monarch window, headed from the office to Pee Wee's.

Handy asked Wright about this peculiar attack. Wright simply said he was resting one hand and the other, alternating between the deep bass groove and the manic high-note chirping until the boss came through, when he would resume playing with both hands. Wright kept a cigarette burning and would grab a puff with the free hand and toss a wink to the audience.

The budding composer William Grant Still studied Handy's methods up close. "Any alert musician could learn something, even in that sordid atmosphere," Still said. "W. C. Handy listened and learned—and what he learned profited him financially and in other ways in succeeding years."[14]

Beale Street had served Handy well, but that world as he'd known it began to slip away. One night the Monarch went dark. With no warning, and no going-away party, after nearly twenty years, Haggarty just left. In the seven years since "Mr. Crump" had vaulted Handy to the top, the illustrious cast of Beale Street characters, seemingly invincible at the time of Handy's arrival, had suffered brutal casualties: Hammitt Ashford exiled, Jim Turner dead, Bob Church Sr. dead, John Persica dead, George Honan dead, Mr. Crump ousted.

As Handy walked downstairs from his office late one night, he saw a light on at Martin's barbershop across the street. He poked his head in and cheerfully asked if it wasn't quitting time yet. The barber shot back, with typical relish, that nothing closes on Beale Street until someone gets killed. Handy used it.

Handy built the "Beale Street" lyrics around Beale Street talk, Beale Street imagery, and Beale Street attitude. He evoked the scenes, scents, and spirit of a hectic, turbulent avenue. Hog nose cafés and pickpockets. Leading men of black America and fallen women. Honesty and thievery. Secrets—"If Beale Street could talk . . . ," Handy's lyric muses. He spun it all out, culminating with the words,

I'd rather be there than any place I know.

Pace & Handy published the score of "Beale Street" on March 23, 1917, the composer's tribute to a vanishing world. It would punch his ticket out.

◆   ◆   ◆   ◆

Two months later, on a sunny early afternoon, a crowd of Negro men in their shade hats and shirt sleeves stood chatting on the corner of Beale and Hadden Avenue. An auto carrying three white men slowed to the corner. One of the men shouted, "Take this with our compliments," and threw a package at the Negroes. The auto sped off.

The crowd looked down and saw the severed foot and head of Ell Persons.

W. C. Handy was walking up Beale toward his office. He saw the crowd. He got close and saw the head.

Persons, a woodcutter from out in the county, had confessed to murdering a young white girl. The authorities had arrested Persons. Knowing that mob sentiment would run high, the mayor and two judges appealed to the state for protection and hid Persons across state lines, to no avail. Armed mobs grossly outnumbered law enforcement. They captured Persons, brought him back to the scene of his crime, and burned him at the stake.

Thousands of people attended the lynching. Vendors sold sodas and sandwiches, and after Persons's body burned, the people rushed his corpse like buzzards. They tore at his clothing, severed his fingers, poked out his eyes, cut off his ears and nose.

"Stunned, deeply resentful, I walked slowly to the office," Handy recalled. "All the savor had gone out of life. For the moment only a sense of ashes in the mouth remained."[15]

Handy was forty-four years old. Though he always enjoyed good health, attributable to hard work, long marches, and the respiratory workout of playing trumpet, he had just about ruined his eyesight and had to squint his once-quick brown eyes. He had battled dire poverty and privation, fought against the current, depended only on his own terms and talents, and largely succeeded. He was an independent black man. Though he felt in control of his life, he knew that forces beyond his influence could destroy him at a whim. He remembered every insult, injury, threat, beating, and bloodletting he'd witnessed.

Fear, frustration, and confusion mounted in the days following the lynching. Beale Street had become everything to the people, a source of pride, a source of jobs, their lifeblood. But if they could be burned, maimed, and dumped here, why remain?

A crowd flocked to Church's Auditorium, more people than had come to see President Roosevelt or Booker T. Washington. They filled the building, and thousands more jammed the park, crowding the gazebos and climbing lampposts. Their collective anguish burst into a tearful, deafening roar as Bob Church walked onstage.

"I would be untrue to you and to myself," he said, "if I should remain silent against the shame and crime of lawlessness, and I could not if I would hold my peace against either the lynching or burning of a human being." His calm demeanor soothed the furious masses. "We must not lose hope, but keep our eyes open and press forward." He promised to stare back into the face of intimidation and continue everything he had set out to do, *"without a shadow of turning."*[16]

He notified everyone that the time to fight for their human rights had arrived with Ell Persons's head on Beale Street.

Church proposed a local chapter of the organization his half-sister Mary Church Terrell and the former Beale Street journalist Ida B. Wells had helped bring to life: the National Association for the Advancement of Colored People.

◆ ◆ ◆ ◆

During the weeks following the lynching, the longstanding aristocrats of the Beale Street underworld joined the ousted Mayor Crump in exile.

The state pressured the mayor, the police chief, and the force to crush the openly conducted bootlegging trade. Fortunately, local officials understood its methods and actors from having watched it for so long, and though the bootleggers took to increasingly deceptive distribution modes, the police captured wagonloads of Shorty, as the demimonde called whiskey, and grounded the midnight blockade-running Mississippi River boat known as the *Gypsy*.

Though Jim Kinnane had kept a low profile in recent years, he made it known that he was shifting his operations beyond the city limits.[17] Haggarty, a man who'd gotten away with murder, every election violation, and a veritable blizzard of liquor and fighting infringements, was reduced to selling half-pints of Shorty from a stash on the roof next door to the Monarch.[18]

Law enforcement squeezed the tenderloin district into a more confined area. Federal agents unleashed a narcotics sweep unlike anything loafers had hitherto seen, curtailing the free trade of cocaine and bamboo. Beginning in summer 1916, law enforcement stopped the music, banning pianos and Victrolas. They outlawed drinking and dancing. Police cleaned out Hernando and Hadden, concentrating underworld activity on Gayoso.

In the first six months of 1917, police even began arresting men who entered the fine houses—and now Gayoso Street got panicky. Finally, on July 14, 1917, the police chief ordered all bawdy houses to close for good. Telegraph boys wheeled from red awning to red awning, collecting messages from inmates seeking wired funds and insight about where to go. Many headed to Chicago or St. Louis, as word spread that New Orleans was adopting similar restrictive measures.[19]

Despite the tremors throughout disorderly society, polite white dancers still did the fox-trot and grizzly bear atop the Alaskan Roof Garden nightly. Professor Handy grinned at them and blew his golden cornet— and very seriously contemplated following the bawds out of town.

If the severed head hadn't quite scared him off, maybe the feds, the local police, and their destruction of his creative world would force the issue. Memphis without pianos was no good for him. He struggled with the details, but knew: "Some day I would be gone."[20]

PART IV

THE LID,

1918–1940

. . . that three or four
Memphis city blocks
in comparison with which
Harlem is a movie set.

—WILLIAM FAULKNER

Chapter 16

ALL THE PRETTY GIRLS
LIVED GOOD

Six months after the end of his mayoral reign, Mr. Crump returned to public life as Shelby County trustee, a low-profile administrative position.

Crump and his top aide Frank Rice, still a county official, realized they should exercise power without subjecting themselves to the heightened level of scrutiny the mayor's office attracted. They would now sponsor or support candidates, working behind the scenes.

In 1918 they chose a candidate to run for Memphis mayor—an odd man—a failed poet and successful undertaker, the current county sheriff, Frank Monteverde. As sheriff, Monteverde had insisted on personally conducting executions, though the job held no such requirement.

Crump needed to rebuild a power base to get his man elected.

The Lincoln League made Bob Church a political force at just the time Mr. Crump began retooling his local machine. The Lincoln League boasted five thousand members and claimed to have registered ten thousand black voters in the city, one-third of the entire electorate.[1] Crump needed votes to get his candidates into office, and Church aimed to help his people.

The two leaders recognized an opportunity to help themselves by helping each other. Their alliance would define the next twenty years on Beale Street, culminating in a biracial partnership decades ahead of its time, then collapsing into a tragedy with far-reaching implications.

◆   ◆   ◆   ◆

Church and Monteverde discussed what sort of advancements the city might offer Negroes for their votes. Church realized that change had to occur in Memphis gradually, and he proved quite the reasonable smoky-room negotiator. He understood the psychology on the white side and knew his people.

He thought the possibilities through. Virtually every facet of colored life could use improvement—black people clamored for better schools, housing, and public recreation—but anything deemed too ambitious or expensive could alienate white voters. The issue of law enforcement had both practical and symbolic value. The police force terrorized black Memphis. The last colored officer had left the force twenty-five years earlier. A new crop of colored officers would create tremendous good-will for Church and for the administration from the black population. Church indicated as much to Monteverde. White Memphis could be easily mollified—the colored officers would patrol only a colored beat. New black cops would alleviate some black tension without provoking white tension, the very definition of sound policy.

Church persuaded Monteverde to promise to hire six Negro police-men in exchange for Church's support—six colored cops for a few thousand Negro votes. Monteverde shook on it and won.

Bob Church and Mr. Crump made for peculiar allies, the kind that only politics could unite.

In Church's political strategy, race outranked party affiliation. He recognized that no Republican candidate could win a local election—the GOP simply did not have enough voters, as was the case throughout the South. Marginal political power in Memphis was better for Church's black constituency than none at all, and thus the black Republicans would function as an election tiebreaker, with Church packaging black votes en masse to white candidates in exchange for black Memphis upgrades. Partnering with a white Democrat emerged as a far more appealing option than partnering with the so-called lily-white faction of Church's own party, who sought to eliminate colored participation in the GOP.

Mayor Monteverde delivered halfway on his end, hiring three colored detectives who lasted barely a year on the job. Still, the agreement between black Republican and white Democrat represented a breakthrough.

By *not* destroying Church either on traditional racist grounds or in direct political competition, Crump empowered black voters by the thousands and helped to create a black political symbol unlike any the nation had seen. The Crump-Church alliance suggested a new promise for bipartisan, biracial cooperation: if it could work in the South, it could work anywhere.

But just as the alliance pushed Beale Street in an optimistic direction, Crump also represented a potent threat to the black community. Behind his rural charms, his dandy appearance, and his gentlemanly grace, Crump was a thoroughly political creature. Machine operative Guy Bates said that his boss possessed a single, indispensable core value.

I think that the one thing Pendergast, Daley, Roosevelt, Crump, the one characteristic that they all had in common was the ability, when necessary, to be absolutely and completely ruthless when it came to the organization. I don't care how close a person was to them, how loyal they'd been, how much they had accomplished—as soon as he felt like they were no longer politically advantageous, out they went.[2]

◆   ◆   ◆   ◆

Any system, however complex and mysterious it may appear, comes down to people—their psychology, backgrounds, motives, philosophies, personalities, and goals. Crump and Rice's Democrat political organization would in time dominate every elected office in the city, county, and surrounding rural districts, plus the state legislature, the governor's mansion, and Tennessee's seats in the U.S. House and Senate. The states delegates to the Democratic National Convention, and numerous federally appointed jobs, were beholden to Crump for a period of time far longer than Huey Long controlled Louisiana, Tom Pendergast ran Kansas City, or Boss Tweed chaired Tammany Hall in New York City. By measures of time in power, extent of influence, and immunity from punishment, the Crump organization must be considered among the most successful political machines of the early twentieth century. It began quietly with the Monteverde campaign and expanded gradually over the next ten to fifteen years. Yet for all its power, influence, and secretive inner workings, the machine belonged to two men.

The people of Memphis expected to see a certain type of man in charge, and Ed Crump delivered the proper image. He gave them bread and circuses (or watermelon and barbecue), projecting the persona of a flashy Southern gentleman and modern capitalist. Crump appealed to folks' sense of tradition, since he hailed from the country, but also to their sense of progress in his civic success. He echoed rural life in his cutting political discourse, saying of one rival, "He'd milk his neighbor's cow through a crack in the fence."[3] Tall and lanky, now approaching fifty, his shock of red hair had given way to an unruly cloud of white. As ever, he attired himself fashionably, favoring wide hats, thick, dark-rimmed specs, a gold-headed cane for gesturing, colorful suits with all the trimmings—ties, handkerchiefs, and socks to match— two-tone shoes, and always a fresh boutonniere. He epitomized ancient plantation authority.

Crump stood for photo-ops, riding the roller coaster at the fair or leading his throng of friends aboard a Pullman car for the ride to the gambling resort town of Hot Springs, Arkansas, bringing his favorite jug band along to entertain. "On the train, they'd shoot craps," recalled Poston Cox, a machine politician from the 1920s. "I never will forget one time he walked in and saw them shooting dice. So he said, 'Let me shoot one time for fifty dollars.' And he laid it down, shot it out, and made a seven and picked it up. And said, 'That's all.' He said, 'The trouble is they don't know when to quit.'"[4]

Crump had no public speaking ability but no other discernible weaknesses. To compensate, he worked his crowds in person. He developed a mnemonic system with which he learned seemingly everyone's name in the city. He spoke in a high voice, his bushy eyebrows bouncing with every word. Health conscious, he daily walked the ten-mile round trip to his downtown office, abstained from strong drink and tobacco, and ate vegetarian. His formula for vitality included "a little orange juice and a little buttermilk," he said. "That, and work, work, work."[5]

Crump would enjoy business success on par with his political gains, rising in the decade after the ouster to the presidency of a successful insurance and real estate brokerage, while building a sphere of political influence that would reach the White House. He would be called Mr. Crump to his face and Boss Crump in the papers, while organization insiders spoke of "the man on the corner," referring to Crump's palatial business offices at Main Street and Adams Avenue.

Frank Rice played old-school politician to Crump's modern businessman. Born in Memphis in 1868, Rice's sad, watery eyes had seen the yellow fever nearly destroy his hometown. He'd survived a bout of it himself. Not long afterward Rice legendarily ended his high school education at age fourteen. When a teacher gave him the choice of forty lashes or forty lines of Latin, Rice jumped out the second-story window and kept running. He nevertheless obtained entry to the University of Virginia, which he endured for all of a semester before returning home.

In Memphis, Rice's path crossed that of every significant political figure. He began as a runner for Pappy Hadden's Manhattan Bank in the 1880s, and he worked with fat cat mayor J. J. Williams in the early twentieth century. Rice met Crump—where else?—on Beale Street, corner of Main, at the 44 Guards Hall above the ornate Grand Opera House, where they were both escorting friends to a gala.[6]

Rice had managed Crump's earliest election campaigns in 1905 and 1907, raising funds from gamblers and saloonocrats. He likely developed the "Nigger Dive Keepers for Williams" advertisements that had helped Crump take the mayor's office in 1909.[7]

Rice's sense of fashion and his personal habits contrasted with Crump's. "There was as much difference in the two men as daylight and dark," recalled Poston Cox, who worked for both.

> Frank was quite a drinker. He was afraid of Mr. Crump. He was his manager, but he was afraid of him. He didn't want him to know about the drinking or anything else. At campaign headquarters Frank always had whiskey and stuff, but if he saw Mr. Crump coming down the street that whiskey got taken out right quick. No sir, he wasn't going to let him see anything like that. Mr. Crump was on him all the time about it.[8]

Rice wore rumpled suits, haphazardly knotted ties, and slouch hats. He countered Crump's buttermilk and orange juice diet with cigarettes and Coca-Cola. Crump invited his most important men to a Battle Creek, Michigan, resort annually, to rest, relax, and regain their health. The resort forbade smoking, so Rice spent most of his stay on a bench outside, puffing away.

Rice's rheumatism and gout often flared up, so he catnapped throughout the long workday, accepting visitors while reclining on a beat-up sofa in his office, an unmarked windowless room down a dark back corridor of the courthouse. Only a plain table and seat, two leather chairs for visitors, and the old couch furnished the room, no filing cabinet or typewriter. "My father never wrote anything down," Rice's daughter recalled.

Tennessee's U.S. senator Kenneth McKellar, a Crump-friendly Democrat who held his seat from 1917 to 1953, said of Rice, "He had an uncanny power of understanding men. He could talk to a man 10 minutes and usually could tell in that time just what that man would do in almost any matter in any given state of circumstances. I have sometimes thought that he was almost a mind reader."[9]

Rice possessed a dark wit. After surviving a plane crash, he remarked,

"I always said I'd only be in one plane accident, but it looks like you can have two."[10]

He provided trustworthy leads to reporters but demanded they avoid citing him by name, and so he remained virtually unknown to most Memphians, as his tips were attributed to "a person with knowledge of the Shelby County organization."

Rice and Crump were staunch segregationists as a matter of social normalcy and public policy, but black Memphis had a place at the table with Rice. Whereas Crump affected a patronizing love for his colored people in classic plantation boss manner, savvy Rice served colored taxpayers sincerely.

Rice's responsibilities within the Shelby County organization were manifold. He functioned as black liaison, underworld contact, and chief strategist for all campaigns. He rose to his full height on election day. "Mr. Rice controlled all the precinct and ward activity for the organization," former ward captain Guy Bates said. Throughout the 1920s and 1930s, Rice held a variety of official titles but always performed his functions well beyond his job description.

Old friends called him Roxie. Newspapermen called him Colonel. Organization boys called him Generalissimo.

◆   ◆   ◆   ◆

In the spring of 1919 a Negro soldier returned from the Great War with a citation for bravery but no job. He wished to remain in the army but had been discharged during the postwar military downsizing. His only hope was to find a politically connected benefactor to get him reappointed. Though he had been on Beale Street just briefly, it didn't take him long to figure out who that would be. And so Lt. George W. Lee called on Bob Church.

The spacious waiting room outside Church's private office contained more books than Lee had ever seen. Church's two men sat there, Mr. Wilson and Mr. Wade, Wade's desk guarding the front door, Wilson's guarding the door to Church's suite. Wilson was a tall, imposing figure, a former policeman who collected Church's rents. Crisply folded newspapers were stacked neatly on a nearby table, and two more well-dressed young Negro men sat there, each poring over a section, not noticing Lee. Wade asked Lee what he wanted.

Lee explained his need for help to get rehired by the army. He said he'd sit and wait as long as necessary to see Mr. Church, taking an open chair and setting his rigid dress hat on his lap. He was a small, neat man, five foot six and 115 pounds, and looked younger than his twenty-five years.

Lee fidgeted. The young men at the newspaper table clipped articles and filed them into various envelopes. Finally Church emerged. He greeted Lee generously, and invited him into his office. Everywhere Lee looked he saw a prominent citizen's photograph personally inscribed to Church—Teddy Roosevelt, Booker T. Washington. Church looked as glamorous as any Negro that Lee had ever seen.

Church regarded Lee, the discharged soldier yet in uniform, bemusedly at first. He remained on his feet, pacing as Lee spoke, but he found himself drawn into Lee's story. He sat down, looked at him, and listened.

Lee, as a member of the famous 92nd Infantry, popularly known as the Buffalo Soldiers, ranked among the relatively few colored veterans with combat experience in World War I. He reviewed his wartime exploits for Church, highlighting his rare status as a black officer, and regaling him with accounts of Negro heroism in the Argonne Forest. He told him how he'd dislodged a German sniper, for which he received a citation for bravery. Church cracked a grin, enjoying the young lieutenant's brashness.

But this attribute, Lee explained, had nearly gotten him killed back at home. He'd traveled to Vicksburg, Mississippi on leave. Sporting his uniform as ever, he strolled through the town, swinging his swagger stick, his lieutenant bars gleaming on his lapel. These theatrics attracted the wrong kind of attention.

Lee went to the picture show, climbing into the buzzard's roost with the other colored moviegoers. Then he noticed the other Negroes filing out, until he and the janitor were the only colored folk remaining in the theater.

"Why is everybody leaving?" he asked the janitor.

The janitor pointed down the stairs. "The white folks are waiting down there, to get you and throw you into the river."

Church raised his eyebrows and blinked at Lee.

Church's clipping service, out in the lobby, had filled his files with stories of colored soldiers who'd come home to the South, having risked their necks overseas only to be burned alive or hanged, some in uniform, by white Americans.

"You could help me," Church said. "Forget about that military situation. You need to get on the firing line of racial activities and racial progress."

Lee smiled. "I'm sold," he said.[11]

Instead of getting Lee reappointed to the army, Church found him a job selling insurance with the largest black-owned firm on Beale Street. The talkative Lee rose fast, swiftly becoming a manager, then a vice president of Mississippi Life.

Just as fast, he became Church's right-hand man—a confidant, political colleague, and friend. While Church preferred working behind the scenes, Lee was a born raconteur: to him, a Saturday crowd on Beale "would move down the street like molasses poured out of a jar," while the women varied from "black Shebas, soft as teakwood and whose blackness was as velvety as the night, and girls fair as the evening sunset overladen with a veil of silver mist." Church enjoyed Lee's exuberant warmth, storytelling, and decadent language, while Lee found Church's aura of wealth and accomplishment inspiring. They shared a strict, fundamental faith in the Republican Party, grounded in capitalist doctrine.

One of Lee's top responsibilities in Church's political organization was to serve as liaison to the Crump machine, and so he could be seen navigating the dark back corridors of the courthouse near the unmarked office of Frank Rice.[12]

On Beale Street, from this point on, Lt. Lee would be known by his wartime rank, now given with new meaning.

◆ ◆ ◆ ◆

To strengthen the machine, Crump and Rice first addressed its vulnerabilities. The State of Tennessee had dealt them a powerful blow with its ouster law in 1915, and so they adapted. Rice gained appointment to the General Assembly, Tennessee's state legislature, in 1919. From there he organized the Shelby County delegation. His legislative team would come to dominate state politics, pushing an urban, progressive agenda against the narrow, fundamentalist rural constituencies, the sorts of people who'd clamored for Prohibition and later for Crump's ouster. As the state's metropolis, Memphis controlled the lion's share of statehouse power, and the Rice delegation named the chairs of all key committees. The state would scarcely bother them again.

The delegation functioned not only as legal insulation for the machine but as its factory. Rice selected the best and brightest attorneys from Memphis to serve as state senators and representatives, and groomed these young officials for life in the machine. He and Crump moved their acolytes from job to job—mayor, police commissioner, U.S. congressman. Watkins Overton and Walter Chandler both began their political careers in Rice's delegation before serving as Mr. Crump's mayors in the 1920s, 1930s, and 1940s. Chandler would also serve as U.S. congressman from Memphis's district, as did Clifford Davis, a Crump machine choice as Memphis police commissioner and vice mayor.

Rice also diversified the machine's vote-gathering mechanisms into a vastly more sophisticated operation than Haggarty and Kinnane's saloon-based vote bundling. Every ward in the city had a captain who reported to Rice, precinct captains who reported to the ward captain, and block captains who reported to the precinct captain, so that every voter in the city was registered and accounted for, all the way up the organizational ladder. The machine appealed to every voter on an individual basis and kept records of how every voter cast ballots. It leaned on city employees, registering everyone from basement custodians to clerks on the top floor of the courthouse. Teachers were encouraged to publicly support Crump candidates. All knew that a lack of political enthusiasm would cost them their job.

Most important, Crump and Rice redirected money and power from the city and county coffers into the machine war chest. At this early stage in the machine's metamorphosis, they both held inconspicuous but important jobs with regard to county finances—Crump was county trustee, and Rice was county register—and it was likely here that they devised their formidable fund-raising strategy.

The normal county taxation process dictated that businesses were levied either on the value of their inventory (as in the case of retail establishments) or on their capacity (as in the case of restaurants and hotels). Rice's tax office determined the dollar value of a business and issued an amount that that business could be taxed. Here's where he turned the trick. Though he knew, for example, that a certain liquor store carried a $10,000 inventory, he saw to it that the store was taxed on only half that amount, thereby creating a sense of indebtedness in the businessman to the machine. This paved the way for an organization representative to come collect a political contribution. The machine designated specific campaign fund liaisons for every industry. "I don't care what business you were in, you were called," machine operative Guy Bates explained. "And you gave. Either that or when you needed a favor you couldn't find one."[13]

The machine wielded its power over government contracts and all licenses and privileges. "If you were, say, in the building construction business, building houses out here, who you got to depend on?" Bates said.

You got to depend on that city inspector that comes along and says, "Your electrical work looks all right. Your plumbing looks all right. Your footage looks good, so go ahead." But if you didn't go along, then say an inspector came out there and said, "I don't think these footings are quite deep enough." Or you'd get the whole damn frame up and then the electrical inspector would come and say. "I don't think this meets the standards." Why, you'd never get through with anything.

The machine would punish stingy retailers, or those who voted wrong, with police presence. "After the election's over," Bates explained, "it just happens that the police stop right in front of your store and sit there waiting for a call. Well, nobody is going to walk in your store— there's not a black in Memphis that would walk in a liquor store with a police car sitting in front of it."

County trustee Crump collected property taxes and business license fees. The city and county ended up with less than it should have taken in taxes while the political organization took in a rapidly growing fortune via gifts from grateful, fearful business owners. In addition to granting businesses tax breaks for campaign contributors, Rice and Crump worked such wizardry for individuals as well, granting huge discounts, even total property tax forgiveness to generous or helpful citizens.

The organization found another segment of enthusiastic donors among the city's underworld.

"My daddy," Bates explained,

who had been a law enforcement officer and a Prohibition agent, knew every law violator and bootlegger in Shelby County. He was what they called the bagman. That's the people he called on. And they had people that called on the houses of prostitution, just like they had people that called on pharmacists and people that called on doctors, and people that called on architects. They were part of the business. Maybe they gave a little bit more liberally than the others, but they contributed.

The machine lifted the lid and appointed bosses of the vice trade, regulating crime as a dictatorship would a heavy industry. Violent flare-ups occurred, but for the most part, the sanctioned bootleggers and gamblers worked in conjunction and eliminated competition through their own security forces, with a little help from law enforcement. Police also regulated the brothels in their precincts, periodically checking inhabitants' clean cards—medical verification of their freedom from venereal disease—and collecting their poll taxes at the appropriate times.

And so vice returned to Memphis with renewed vigor, and as Beale Street musician Thomas Pinkston would say, "All the pretty girls lived good."[14]

◆   ◆   ◆   ◆

Since the police closed down Gayoso Street in 1917—emptying tenants from Bob Church's lucrative red-light rentals—the district had looked abandoned. On a Saturday night in mid-July 1918, however, a reporter noted, "Down on Gayoso Avenue, in the old segregated district, women of the underworld stood in front of their houses to welcome visitors."[15]

That summer a white boy could be seen pedaling his bicycle toward Gayoso Street, a large wicker picnic basket rigged to the handlebars, heavily packed with fragrant, steaming packages. Frank Liberto, fifteen-year-old son of a Beale blacksmith, got himself a job delivering restaurant food to the girls—"None of them cook anything," he explained—and watched the district repopulate from his bicycle seat:

> A man named Robert Church had opened up a whole bunch of these houses . . . on Gayoso, starting at Hernando, and they'd go all the way down to Fourth. You could hardly tell them apart because they all had the brass rail in front of the houses and every one of them was built just alike, a little bit like the old houses you see around Baltimore, right on the sidewalk, right next to each other, no yard, nothing, just a porch with a brass rail.

The women as well left a vivid impression on young Liberto:

> Well, was some of the prettiest women that I guess you could find anywhere. They were gorgeous. The ones that used to sit out on

the front porches during the summer time, they was just hard to describe, they were just beautiful women. All of them were white.

Now, they had a red light district on Hadden Avenue, they was nothing but colored and what they called creoles. Creoles was just about as white as you can be, but they were colored. And one that I knew was real, real famous was Mamie Smith, and she was right there at the starting of Hadden Avenue in a big house. Now she catered to all kinds of people, white, everybody.

Liberto made his deliveries in the parlor. "And that's where the people gathered," he said, "and they'd have a drink and they'd get acquainted with each other and this piano would be going and I'd bust in there with the food."[16]

◆　◆　◆　◆

A thousand miles away a gorgeous eighteen-year-old woman stepped into the spotlight at the Winter Garden Theater in New York City, wobbled her bare shoulders, and sang—

I've seen the lights of gay Broadway
Old Market Street down by the Frisco Bay
I've strolled the Prado, gambled on the Bourse
But take my advice, friends, and see Beale Street first.

When people asked, "What is that dance?" she replied, through a Polish accent thick as sausage, "I'm shaking my chemise." Her mother and father had named *her* Marianna Michalska, but she was called Gilda Gray now, and she and the Shimmy and W. C. Handy's "Beale Street Blues" were all debuting on Broadway in *Shubert Gaieties of 1919*. And here is another parallel between Handy and Church: their use of white women as conduits to the white man's money.

An exploration of his options after Ell Persons's head had rolled on Beale in 1917 brought Handy to a rented desk in the Gaiety Theatre

Building in New York. This humble situation nonetheless lent the Pace & Handy music company the pretentious address of 1547 Broadway.

The desk grew into a five-room suite thanks to a little Beale Street magic. Handy persuaded a cabaret singer in Chicago to sing his "A Good Man Is Hard to Find" on stage. Her name was Alberta Hunter. She'd been in the Windy City since 1911 but was born in Memphis and raised on Beale. The gleaming brass and bright red uniforms of the Handy band had opened a new world to her. "We'd hear that ta-da, ta-da of the band, and Lord, we'd be out the door so fast," Hunter said.[17] She returned the favor to Handy in 1918. He estimated that, after Alberta Hunter broke it, "A Good Man Is Hard to Find" sold half a million copies.[18]

As much as Handy owed his artistic inspiration to anonymous, low-down musicians of color, his business success and cultural importance were due to the white audience. A white jazz band's recording of "Beale Street Blues" got him to New York. His own recordings never amounted to much, nor did his stage presence. Instead a pair of flappers crossed his music over to the mainstream.

The year after Gilda Gray shimmied through "Beale Street Blues" on Broadway, a white bombshell named Marion Harris—called the Jazz Baby or the Jazz Vampire, depending on who you asked—recorded Handy's "St. Louis Blues," another song he'd written on Beale. The song was six years old, just about to slip into the American cultural abyss. But Harris's version hit, and from there it'd be hard to name an important artist who *didn't* cover the tune: Bessie Smith, Louis Armstrong (who also played cornet on Bessie's classic version), Fats Waller, Rudy Vallee, Django Reinhardt, Benny Goodman, Bob Wills, Ella Fitzgerald, and Judy Garland, among many others, recorded "St. Louis Blues" or performed it in their stage acts. Thanks to a bit of savvy business advice from Bob Church, Handy had copyrighted "St. Louis Blues" in his own name rather than that of the Pace & Handy company, so he alone profited. The royalties sustained him for much of his life.[19]

Emotional depth distinguished Handy's blues from the one-tone maudlin ballads and syrup pop songs of the early twentieth century, and the same quality resonated with later generations.

The First World War had separated young men in white America from their homes, forcing families to live with a void and the fear that they could never be whole again. The war showed young men of all backgrounds death and told them they were disposable. The war subjected white America to what Beale Streeters had felt for generations. It was as if Joe Turney had come for everyone.

Handy's blues became a cultural password for a new age. It spoke to the lost generation, artists who grappled with the experiences of war, witnessing grand-scale human atrocity, and coming home psychologically scarred and physically changed. F. Scott Fitzgerald referenced "Beale Street Blues" by name in *The Great Gatsby*. William Faulkner subtly evoked "St. Louis Blues" in the title of a short story, "That Evening Sun." Gershwin inscribed sheet music for "Rhapsody in Blue" to Handy, saying thanks I couldn't have done it without you.

◆   ◆   ◆   ◆

"The traveling man looks upon Memphis as 'a free and easy going city' where persons interested in prostitution may find it without difficulty," an observer of the city's commercialized vice would remark. A local businessman opined:

> There's an area we call our red-light district. It's located at the lower end of town. Some of our young men go there to drink and fool around with the girls. Married men who step out go to less conspicuous places. . . . You can get women in most any hotel in town. You'll either find 'em living there or the nigger bellboys will call them for you. I'm sorry to say, but our best hotel, one of the finest places in the entire South, is nothing but a whorehouse.

When New Orleans's Storyville closed in 1917, Memphis became the last Southern city to host wide-open houses of ill fame—"frame and brick structures which are easily identifiable as brothels," according to the observer.

Each resort has the house number painted in red on the transom over the entrance. At night all shades are drawn, but the interior lights seep out into the pitch-black streets. The music from the automatic phonograph may also be heard along the street and many places resort to the old method of window roping. A man may not pass through any of the district's streets without being attracted by inmates sitting in the windows, calling and tapping and in some instances imploring trade to enter.

Within this realm, Gayoso Street was perhaps the last place anywhere that you could enjoy the genteel old-Southern-parlor-house experience, a specialty of the six identical brownstones on the north side of Gayoso between Hernando and Fourth.

Here commercial transaction masqueraded as jovial hospitality. When a party stood below the red-numbered transom and rang, a Negro maid inside called out, "Company, girls!" The chippies, some wearing lingerie, others in pajamas, scrambled to the reception room, and as the maid opened the door, the callers and the landlady took their places.

The madam, almost invariably a heavyset, diamond-dripping woman of middle years, welcomed the guests warmly, inviting them to a seat and introducing the girls. Custom dictated that the men immediately purchased beers, wine, or whiskey, by the drink or by the bottle, at outrageous prices. In the course of drinking, girls and guests got familiar with one another, sitting and chatting or dancing, the men supplying the automatic phonograph with nickels.

As subtly as either could, the visitors and guests determined one another's interest either in old-fashioned or "French" sex. "Parlez vous français? Oui, oui?" a more worldly client might inquire. Once the pending transaction achieved some clarity, the couple excused themselves upstairs, typically at the chippy's invitation, to become better acquainted among quieter surroundings.[20] "Some of them had mirrors all around the rooms, the bedrooms," Frank Liberto recalled.

The contrasts—the finery and decadence of the furnishings and conversation compared to the crassness of the deal—made an impression on one Gayoso visitor who purportedly never mounted the stairs.

A young William Faulkner came for the company. He heard the hidden history of the street, tales of Madam Mae Goodwin, a brothel keeper and a fence for black market diamonds. An associate known as the Russian Fox had come to visit her home unannounced, via Mae's roof and bathroom window. Still, the Fox failed to perfectly conceal his entrance, and so several of the lady's boarders saw a man wearing a blue bandana to cover his face but otherwise bearing numerous memorable features, including a scar running from ear to eye and a thumb half cut off. He murdered Mae anyway, leaving a bloody four-and-a-half-finger handprint. The Fox hunt began.[21]

Faulkner, young, bushy-haired and soft-spoken, lived a hundred or so miles away in Oxford, Mississippi. He had a pointy nose and dark eyes, and he sported kneed-out trousers and threadbare coats. He gave off no indication of prosperity, looking like a tag-along to his flashy chums. The girls didn't work him too hard. When they did proposition young Faulkner, he played on his decidedly unsporty appearance, quipping, "No thank you, ma'am, I'm on my vacation."[22]

Chapter 17

In a Class
by Himself

It was before five a.m., on June 10, 1920, at the Republican National Convention in the Chicago Coliseum. A bleary-eyed session of the credentials committee would decide Bob Church's immediate political future, ruling whether he would take his seat as a delegate to the presidential nominating convention from Tennessee's tenth district, or lose this prestigious position and perhaps his power.

Now in his mid-thirties, Church had gained increasing importance within black affairs across the country. While forming his local alliance with Mr. Crump, he had established a chapter of the National Association for the Advancement of Colored People in Memphis. The branch received its charter in January 1918, with his wife, mother, and sister as charter members. In 1919, with the Memphis branch boasting more than a thousand members, the NAACP invited Church to become the first Southerner to join its national board of directors.[1]

The Lincoln League expanded, with large branches in New Orleans and Chicago. Taking a national perspective, Church filled a void in top-level black leadership. Headline grabbers like W. E. B. Du Bois, Ida B. Wells, and Marcus Garvey focused on segregation and lynching, espousing a variety of solutions from integration to separatism, even a return to Africa. Church focused solely on the ballot as the Negro's ticket to equality, and the practical organization of black voters.

Church could have chosen the playboy life, but instead he undertook dangerous pursuits on behalf of his people, funding Lincoln League expansion and NAACP activities out of his own pocket long before federal grants and subsidies for civil rights work or minority improvement existed. His driving ambition was to see black America become politically alive, he liked to say, conscious of the ballot's potency. His challenge was that virtually no one outside the race wanted colored people to become politically active.[2] Even the sole Negro political sanctuary, the Republican Party, was growing ambivalent toward black participation. Nevertheless the GOP had provided the only vehicle for black political mobility, and so it was the only source of hope for Church's Negro uplift strategy.

Nonetheless, he'd lately enjoyed greater cooperation with Mr. Crump's local Democratic organization than his own party, as the Republicans were engaged in a brutal internal conflict. Across the country, groups like Church's Lincoln League battled a rising faction known as the lily-whites that hoped to racially purify the GOP. A Memphis attorney named John Farley had published a treatise of lily-white doctrine called *Statistics and Politics* in which he argued that Negro participation in Republican election efforts served only to inflame white Democrat voters, thus turning out the opposition in greater numbers and harming the Republican cause. The lily-whites preferred to dump black Republicans, despite their party loyalty and potential numbers.

Church and his Lincoln Leaguers had fought their way through the ranks of the local and state party conventions, despite lily-white opposition at both stops, to gain recognition as the Memphis district's delegates to the Republican National Convention. As of that predawn June 10 committee hearing, they had one final hurdle to clear before joining the nomination process.

The lily-whites had sent their own delegation to the national convention claiming to be the official Memphis Republicans, forcing the committee on credentials to rule which group could help nominate the next Republican candidate for president.

Yet another change in the nation's political atmosphere was making Church's involvement in prostitution even more contradictory to his activism and untenable to a political career. Memphis and Tennessee had so far proven hospitable to the woman suffrage movement. The state had legally extended women the right to vote in April 1919, with statehouse support from Memphis delegates. Church had encouraged women to participate in the Lincoln League since its founding in 1916, employing female teachers in his voting schools.

The money made on Gayoso Street, the cornerstone of the family fortune and the Church political dynasty, was now intertwined with far-reaching good deeds in the political and civil rights arenas. On that early Chicago morning in June 1920, his contradictory business practices and human rights goals intersected in dramatic fashion.

Church arrived to the hearing with Lt. Lee and twenty or so other supporters. He'd chartered them a Pullman car to avoid Jim Crow seating during the Southern portion of the journey. The Coliseum was decorated for festivity, with red, white, and blue bunting, American and state flags hanging from the rafters, and paintings of Abraham Lincoln. Tension filled the Coliseum, though, as candidates and their proxies scrambled to solicit votes amidst a hotly competitive convention. No clear front-runner had yet emerged from among a crowded presidential slate, featuring Gen. Leonard Wood, Illinois governor Frank Lowden, and dark horse Warren G. Harding, a U.S. senator from Ohio. Standoffs between various warring delegations took place both inside hearing rooms and hallways as lily-whites ejected numerous colored groups. Negroes quipped that the Lincoln portraits should be turned to the wall.

In the credentials committee hearing, Church and his opponent would each have five minutes to state their case. Instead of lily-white theorist John Farley and the Memphis white Republicans, though, a group of five white women approached the committee to dispute Church's legitimacy as a convention delegate. Mrs. Eddie McCall Priest stepped forward and addressed the fifty-man tribunal. She attacked Church not on politics, though he openly supported Democrats in Memphis elections, but on moral grounds.

Disreputable, she called him, echoing the adjective oft applied to his Gayoso Street rentals. He operated the biggest Negro dive in the city and profited from gambling revenues, she claimed. If the party sat him, ladies would leave the Republican Party rather than associate with Bob Church.

It was a poignant political execution. With black Republican participation under assault, and women potentially gaining the vote in time for the presidential election, women might easily surpass blacks as the Republican minority of choice.

Having gotten the most out of her five minutes, Mrs. Priest ceded the floor.

Lt. Lee, Herbert Brewster, and the other Lincoln Leaguers stood in shocked silence, wondering what Church would say. The opposition's use of a white woman cornered Church. A black man simply could not argue directly with a white woman. Mrs. Priest did in fact represent a voting bloc numerically superior to Church's, and her claims against his moral character contained a few grains of truth.

"It was pretty rough in those days," Brewster recalled. "But [Bob Church] was the kind of fellow who could stand the roughness and keep his cool."[3]

Privately, Church would mock his lily-white Memphis opponents for hiding behind Mrs. Priest's skirts. Publicly, he took the floor and made his statement to the record as a gentleman and a party man through and through. White suit, soldierly posture, boater in hand, Church said that he would not be the one to hold up an entire convention. "I know that I am entitled to a seat in the Convention from the Tenth Congressional District," he said, "and I am going to carry my fight back to Memphis, Tennessee, and settle it there."

He walked out to great applause.[4] The credentials committee, comprised of GOP leaders from every state, appreciated Church's unwillingness to promote his local dispute over national party business.

The debacle in Chicago would soon force Church to make a deeper sacrifice.

In the weeks following the Republican National Convention, woman suffrage went from political issue to law of the land. As the presidential race intensified over the summer, the Nineteenth Amendment neared ratification. The Tennessee legislature convened an emergency session in August 1920, and with a Memphis congressman named Joe Hanover leading the charge, the House voted in favor, thus adding a new amendment to the Constitution, bringing women the franchise.

Church, singed by Mrs. Priest's attack at the convention and now very concerned about how women might affect the Negro's Republican status, took a bold but necessary risk. He closed down his family-owned brothels on Gayoso Street and converted the six mansions into Negro apartments. "The parlors that were hung with French-blue silken drapes," wrote Lt. Lee, "have passed into decay, and the bare feet of street urchins scamper across the dirty hardwood floors where once merrymakers danced to the weird chants of the jungles."[5]

The shift from lavishly prosperous tenants to poorly compensated ones must have harmed Church's income. Gayoso Street had bankrolled the bright side of Negro life on Beale from Church's Park and Auditorium to the Solvent Savings Bank. Now free of moral liability but with his personal fortune in decline, Church gambled that national political power could carry his empire.

◆　◆　◆　◆

Following the convention, Church might understandably have quit politics. Instead, he went to work. With much of his own party against him, he would orchestrate a multistate black voting campaign, the scope of which had few if any precedents in black American political history.

Church put Lt. Lee in charge of the Memphis campaign. Lee, just twenty-four, brought vital energy and impressive oratorical skills to the task. He adapted insurance business tactics to political mobilization, sending Lincoln League volunteers door to door like salesmen to register Negro voters and campaign for candidates. Church's Auditorium showed moving pictures and served lemonade every night free of charge to draw crowds to hear speakers extol the virtue of the vote. Lee likewise took the lead at the podium, assuming the role of chief motivational speaker at the many Negro rallies around Beale Street.

As Republican nominee Warren Harding battled Democrat James Cox, it became clear that the GOP effort still needed Negro support, despite lily-white rhetoric. On September 22, 1920, a cryptic telegram arrived in Church's office. It came from one of the party's chief national strategists, Republican National Committee chairman Will Hays. "I wish you would go down to Maryland right away for me," the note read. "There you get in touch with Senator Weller. See what the situation is in a particular matter which Senator Weller will mention to you and I wish you would go into this very thoroughly."

Church went to Maryland and helped Hays get out the black vote there. He also organized Negro-voting campaigns in Kentucky, Indiana, and Illinois. He ventured wherever else the party needed him, energizing black constituencies without asking for a penny from party headquarters.

Harding won the presidency on November 2, 1920, and the election results showed a stunning breakthrough: after five decades as a Democratic stronghold, Tennessee's electoral votes had swung into the Republican column. Not only was Tennessee the sole former Confederate state to go for the party of Lincoln in 1920—this was the first time *any* Southern state had gone Republican for president since 1876. Church also helped elect the state's first Republican governor in the twentieth century, with an estimated 170,000 black Republican votes statewide.[6]

Compared with Negro voting elsewhere in the South, the political climate in Tennessee was extraordinary. In Georgia, colored Republican leader Ben Davis had told a Senate committee investigating election irregularities in his state earlier that year, "Many a Negro voting the Republican ticket has disappeared and no tidings have ever been heard of him." In Orlando, Florida, a white mob murdered a Negro and torched a black section of town to intimidate colored people from the polls on election day. But in Memphis black voters peacefully cast their ballots and made a significant difference in the election's outcome.[7]

In a handful of weeks, Church had transformed himself from a discredited Republican delegate into the most powerful black politician in the country. The black media and high-ranking white Republicans alike took notice. The Associated Negro Press reported:

> Mr. Church is unquestionably in a position of power. But he has let it be known that he is not going to use his advantage for selfish ends. . . . He is letting the administration understand that the American colored people are expecting certain results, and if these results are not forthcoming . . . neither he nor those with whom he works can go back to the people in 1922 and lay before them a mere array of excuses.[8]

RNC chairman Hays wrote to President Harding to laud Church:

> He is in a class by himself, in the colored race of this country, as to matters political. . . . Without in any way discounting the splendid work done by a great many colored men, the fact is that the one outstanding man out of all the colored people in the quality of unselfish and efficient work done is Robert R. Church. He goes about largely at his own expense on political errands, never taking a salary, and he is a very exceptional individual.[9]

Hays, who would soon go on to achieve great infamy as the "czar of motion pictures" in Hollywood, let it be known that Church would handle all federal appointments in Tennessee and among Negroes nationwide, covering jobs from federal judges and district attorneys to postmasters and postal delivery workers, thereby granting Church the real but unofficial title of spoils dispenser. Patronage would make up a major part of Church's political life, as he reinforced the Memphis black middle class with stable letter-carrier jobs and protected himself by supporting a number of public officials who became indebted to him.

Sensitive to the caricatures of corrupt Negro politicians, most recently and pointedly dramatized in the 1915 motion picture *Birth of a Nation*, Church made his cleanliness and honesty well known. He steadfastly refused sweetheart spoils appointments for himself, like a federally funded vacation to the Virgin Islands, ostensibly to research economic conditions there, and as Hays noted, Church declined reimbursement for his party activities.

Another fact became clear in the election aftermath. Democratic boss Crump did *not* have his state locked up. Church, with his federal prestige, could challenge Crump on his home turf. With the city, county, and state legislature under Crump control, federal power represented the only real threat to the machine—Crump needed Church's friendship as insulation from the feds. With Church out of the prostitution business, Crump also needed to find a new favor to offer his friend.

To signal his continued helpfulness, Crump solved one of Church's black community issues to everyone's satisfaction. The city bought Church's Park in 1921, making it a public recreation facility for Negroes and filling Church's pocket with $85,000.

While Church enjoyed respect from the highest office in the land and cordial relations with the local boss, he received a low and vicious threat. As news of his influence spread, a length of rope, fashioned into a noose arrived at his Memphis office.

Church was in Washington when the noose landed. Lt. Lee cabled him about it, to which Church replied, "The rope episode has not disturbed me in the least. . . . It is not the first time I have received such presents, and just as soon as my work here is completed, which I hope will be shortly, I am going to return to the mighty Beale St. because I have never rung a backing bell and never will."[10]

*Robert Reed Church
in the late 1860s*

"HAVE TAKEN DOWN THE HORNS."
The Finest Billiards, Pool and Saloon owned and controlled by
ANY ONE COLORED MAN IN THE UNITED STATES.

CHURCH'S NEW BILLIARD HALL,
Corner Second and Gayoso Sts.   MEMPHIS, TENN.
R. R. CHURCH, Proprietor.

Church's saloon at Second and Gayoso

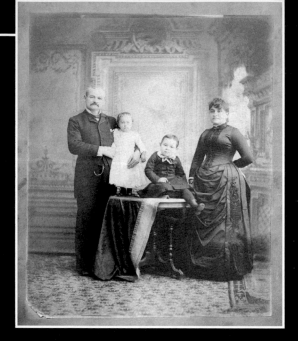

IDA B. WELLS.

An illustration of Ida B. Wells published in 1891.

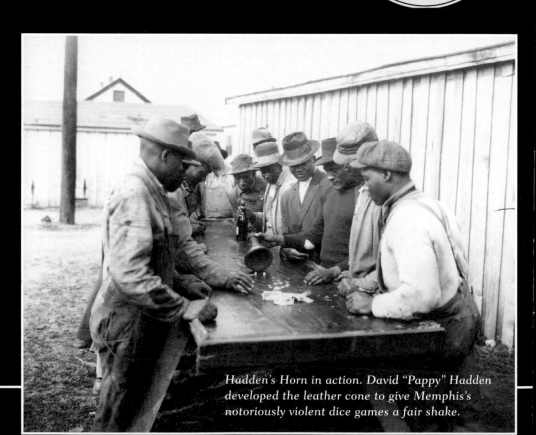

Hadden's Horn in action. David "Pappy" Hadden developed the leather cone to give Memphis's notoriously violent dice games a fair shake.

Street children, standing at the
corner of Beale and Main in 1901,
the Grand Opera House at their right.

Church's Park
Auditorium as it
appeared at its
opening in 1901.

Roustabouts unloading cotton bales on the cobblestone
Mississippi River landing at Beale, 1906.

The high-powered corner of Beale and Hernando streets, 1906, looking east towards Pee Wee's saloon.

Robert Church Sr. opened the Solvent Savings Bank at 392 Beale in 1906.

An elderly Robert Church Sr. at home on Lauderdale Street.

Robert Church Jr., the new boss of Beale Street as of his father's death in 1912, with his father's diamond pin in his tie.

Edward Hull Crump, Memphis's young mayor, in 1909.

A gathering of the Lincoln League fills Church's Park Auditorium, 1916.

W. C. Handy, fourth from left, with his Memphis band in 1918.

Bob Church (second row, second from left) and his Republican organization departs for the 1920 Republican National Convention. Lt. George W. Lee is the first man kneeling at left.

The Crump machine in the mid-1930s: from left to right, unknown, Joe Boyle, Ed Crump, Frank Rice,

Bob Church, W. C. Handy, and Lt. George W. Lee outside Church and Lee's offices, where Handy had composed "St. Louis Blues."

The Beale Street crowd, outside the One Minute Café (right)
and the Palace Theater, 1939.

Bob Church in
his Beale Street
office, late 1930s.

Chapter 18

THE FROLIC

"Mighty Beale" regained its old verve under the restored Crump machine, though a new cast of characters controlled the action.

"It wasn't a dull minute around Beale Street no matter what hour, day or night," recalled Frank Liberto. "You see, the Greeks had the restaurants, the Italians had all the vice on Beale Street, all of the gambling, bootlegging, everything, the Jewish people had the dry goods stores and the pawnshops, and the colored people was the customers."

Liberto stood right in the middle of the action. When Gayoso Street went legitimate residential in 1920, the former whorehouse delivery boy needed a new occupation and eventually found gainful employment one street over. Liberto ran the Cadillac Inn on Beale next door to the Palace Theater and the Gray Mule saloon. Show people from the Palace dined at a back table in the Cadillac, wearing smudges of burnt cork and eyeliner, or wigs askew. Liberto promoted middleweight pugilistic contests at the Cadillac, featuring his fighter Gorilla Jones. He ran a speakeasy for colored customers there and operated a daily lottery drawing, known up and down the street as "policy." Bettors picked a sequence of three numbers and bet anywhere from a nickel up, in hopes of cashing in if their number hit.

The Cadillac wasn't the only policy house on or around Beale. "Every one of them [saloons] had policy. Not only mine, every one of them," Liberto said.

Policy writers knocked on doors throughout the district. "When you got a ticket," Liberto said, "they'd tell you where the drawing was going to be and what time at what house."

Superstition heavily influenced bets. "See the colored people was funny," Liberto said. "They'd dream of blood and blood had a number. When they dreamt of somebody that was dead a long time, that had a number and that's how they played policy."[1] Musician and policy player Alex Simms said, "That's the only way I'd catch policy, have a dream and look in the dream book and see what the number was. Yeah, it worked two or three times."[2]

Houses played it cynical. They hosted open drawings to gain the public trust, making a dramatic show of pulling numbered balls out of a bag to determine the winning digits. The house operators watched the weather and the news for clues about the next heavily played numbers. Negro bettors often went on group hunches, informed by the traditional numbers played for a full moon, a heavy snow, a murder. When a heavily bet number won, "the train hit the house," in the operator's terminology. "But," as a report on the game and its crookedness explained, "the careful operator circumvents any such eventuality by either freezing 12 balls or heating them before they are placed in the sack. One may be sure that the sensitive fingers of the drawer will find these heated or frozen balls and forthwith produce them. One may also be sure that these balls will not correspond to the heavily played number combination."[3]

The hot ball trick limited payouts by eliminating the most widely played numbers, but the game still paid off and money got around. As one player explained, big winners always tipped the runner who sold them the winning numbers. Losers were only out a few cents a throw.

Policy had been played on Beale since the 1890s, but lately it had reached pandemic proportions thanks to an Italian entrepreneur. "Now Nello Grandi was one of the most lovable persons," Liberto explained. "Never was arrested in his life, never got a traffic ticket in his life. And he done all of the business for every one of these places we're talking about. All these policy businesses and games had to go through Nello Grandi."[4]

Nello Grandi and his brother Olento arrived on Beale before 1910, tall Nello becoming Big Grandi and diminutive Olento, Little Grandi. Big Grandi worked with Vigelio "Pee Wee" Maffei in one of the little legend's saloons. This joint sat practically on the banks of the Mississippi, and here Big Grandi saw strapping Negro roustabouts with their hundred-dollar pay strolling straight down a cotton steamer gangplank right into Pee Wee's, which promptly soaked them for every cent.

The business model appealed to young Nello. The attendant violence, however, struck him as wasteful. He was no dice-shooting brawler like Maffei but a capitalist in the modern sense. The insane demand for policy at Pee Wee's more famous saloon up on Beale at Hernando suggested to him an opportunity.

Unlike cards, policy required no skill. Unlike dice, policy shed no blood. It cost as little or as much as a player wished to gamble. Consequently, working people—and not just the colorful card sharks of Fatty Grimes's era—could play everyday. Rather than supervise one single game or one single saloon, Big Grandi franchised policy across Memphis, encouraging operators to get into the game while he saw to their safety from law and extracted a fee.

Through Big Grandi's guidance, policy became the visible hand on Beale Street, remaining the dominant economic force throughout the 1920s. Policy kept the street wide open in a legal sense, moving graft among police officers and packing the saloons, which carried over to the theaters, hot dog cafés, and shoe shine parlors. Steady business in the gambling saloon block meant steady business due west on pawnshop row. A raggedy urchin carrying a shiny pearl-colored Stetson down the street became a common sight. "If [a gambler] get broke in a crap game," he'd send a runner to a pawnshop for $20 to keep the game rolling,"

Thomas Pinkston explained. Professional gamblers Kid Henry, Baby England, and Poor Tom stood in good stead with the brokers. They either repaid their loans or surrendered their pearly Stetsons.[5] "That was the quality merchandise," said Leo Schwab, Beale merchant.[6]

Policy rewarded players just enough to be a legitimate factor in the day-to-day struggles of waiters, washerwomen, cooks, maids, chauffeurs, stevedores, singers, and yard men.

Policy followed the path blazed by W. C. Handy's blues. From the back room at Pee Wee's, the fever spread beyond Beale Street to the rest of Memphis. A reporter explained the phenomenon of white people getting hooked on the Negro game: "They learned from their maids, chauffeurs, and cooks who were always meeting strange negroes at the servant's entrance, mumbling three numbers, and slipping the writer a coin."[7] As policy trickled up Main Street, it all tracked back to Big Grandi, and policy trickled all the way up Main Street. A Grandi employee took bets at the police station. The Crump machine took its tithe. Judge Harry B. Anderson stood accused of receiving $10,000 from Grandi, but nevertheless President Calvin Coolidge appointed Anderson federal judge in 1925. Bob Church had personally delivered the nomination to Coolidge at the president's summer retreat.

◆　◆　◆　◆

Prohibition moved Pee Wee's longtime proprietor Lorenzo Pacini out of the saloon business, but he didn't venture far. Pacini entered into partnership with the Barrasso family, operators of several theaters for Negro customers, including the Palace, across the street from Pee Wee's at 324 Beale.

Pacini's two sons followed in his footsteps, though down different paths. Both were big jolly boys. Nello Pacini worked at the Palace. Lantern-jawed Joe Pacini became a bootlegger. And in this pursuit as well, a Pacini affiliated himself with a Barrasso, both working under the boss bootleggers Frank and Johnny Bellomini. The Pacinis, Barrassos, Bellominis, and Grandis, among them, controlled gambling, bootlegging, and the black music business around downtown Memphis throughout the 1920s and well into the 1930s.

"The bootlegging that we was doing in them days had gotten pretty rough," Frank Liberto recalled. He stayed current on his payoffs, but Beale Street beat police had grown rich off the trade and greedy. They told Frank they needed more. "I told 'em there wasn't no more," he said.

The police promptly raided the Cadillac Inn. They found his whiskey right where they knew it'd be. Next to it, they found another box of bottles, these full of embalming fluid, one of the many noxious poisons that had suddenly become fit for human consumption with the passage of Prohibition.[8] "They claimed I was putting it in the white whiskey to color it," said Liberto. He faced charges of violating the liquor law, but even worse, his reputation as a trustworthy bootlegger was at stake. Liberto claimed innocence, at least of the embalming fluid fiasco. If he were dosing his liquor with formaldehyde, he reasoned, "I'd a killed everybody I knew. My daddy would drink two and three bottles of that whiskey every day. He's the first one I'd a killed."

Liberto retained the services of underworld attorney Charles M. Bryan, who boasted strong affiliation to the Crump machine and a clientele that included Bob Church and the bootlegging Bellomini brothers.[9] Judge Clifford Davis, a good Crump man himself, dismissed the charges—corks popped that night at the Cadillac.

Next door at the Palace Theater, an unruly white crowd jostled its way indoors to witness the Midnight Frolic. Thursday nights at eleven, for seventy-five cents, the doors to black culture swung open for the white audience.

From the outside, the Palace appeared as grand as any white theater in town, three stories tall with high arched windows. The inside looked plush, with a gold-leafed balcony, gold wallpaper, and a red carpet leading to the gold velvet stage curtain. Fresh popcorn and roasting hot dogs perfumed the Palace air, and the theater orchestra, a versatile unit featuring banjo serenader Thomas Pinkston, pianist James Alston, and a cornet player named Charlie Williamson, supplied raggy blues and jazz. Trick drummer Booker T. Washington (no relation) delighted the crowd, twirling his sticks high in the air and punctuating hard, fast drum attacks by blowing the smoke off his sticks like a victorious gunslinger.

Out flew the chorus line—"they look just like creamy milk chocolate," one observer said, "beautiful girls"—most noticeably among them, the four-and-a-half-foot-tall "Little Bit" in rhinestone tights and a spangly costume, cut above the thigh in an age when bathing suits tickled the ankles. They danced smutty routines like the sister act, "two girls dancing together, just a vulgar act," Little Bit said.[10]

From here, lusty Negro dances like the Memphis Twist and the Black Bottom crossed over into polite society, from Beale Street to Main Street.

On February 24, 1927, as Frank Liberto went to court to face his booze charge, the Victor Recording Company began a recording session in Memphis that would capture the sounds of Beale Street. The Beale Street Frolic Orchestra recorded its good-time, up-tempo tunes. Charlie Williamson, leader of the Frolic Orchestra, made his greatest contribution to American culture as a talent scout for the on-location recording—he introduced Victor producer Ralph Peer to the Memphis Jug Band.[11]

They were a ragged ensemble of Beale Street corner guitar pickers and furnished-room poets. They improvised instruments, building a bass guitar from a washtub, broom handle, and string, and converting an earthenware whiskey jug into a lazy, loping rhythm instrument, not by tapping or beating the thing but by blowing into it. The band featured odd combinations of mandolin, harmonica, violin, female vocalists, male vocalists, and the occasional comb solo.

Though their style would be welcomed at the Palace Theater only on amateur night, the Memphis Jug Band became a favorite of Mr. Crump's, as well as Crump's lieutenants', performing at birthday parties at Frank Rice's house and perennially accompanying the boys on the train to Hot Springs, Arkansas, for the horse races. A blessed lyricist named Will Shade held the cacophonous conglomerate together. He wrote songs and rehearsed the group. They were all thin, wiry, dark-skinned men. They worked as mechanics, porters, and yardmen.

The Memphis Jug Band's records became some of the most enduring snippets of this history, beginning with their February 1927 session for Victor. Will Shade remembered Charlie Williamson, the Palace band-leader and Victor's talent scout, as a dapper dresser. Charlie had shown up at Victor's ad hoc studio in the middle of a Memphis Jug Band song, wearing a gray suit, gray spats, a green paisley waistcoat, and a crisp white derby. Charlie didn't realize they were recording. He removed his hat, as such an exemplary gentleman should, and loudly set it down on the piano, making an indelible clomp in the Memphis Jug Band's "Stingy Woman Blues." Fifty years from this moment, Beale Street would be lying in shambles, with Shade and most of his colleagues at rest in pauper's tombs, but the music of the Memphis Jug Band would live to tell just how this tough place and struggling life had been.

The Memphis Jug Band could sound playful, but just as skillfully, they could evoke the sinister, such as the medic fondling an injured female in "Ambulance Man"—"Can't you see I'm cut in the stomach?" she asks. The song describes a dark slice of Beale life, where the colored mortuaries operated ambulances. The morticians made their money in funerals, not in emergency medical care. Will Shade himself explained the folk belief behind the song. "If you wasn't dead, well they'd have two drivers in there and one driver take a needle and stick it in you, and you'd be dead before you reached the hospital. . . . Come feel your pulse and say 'Aw . . . he's dead, come on, let's take 'im to the morgue.' That's the end of you. You automatically dead."[12]

Will Shade's "Ambulance Man" helps himself to his patient's jellyroll as she fades out.

The Memphis Jug Band belts out the Beale classic "Cocaine Habit Blues," in 1902 coke party style, a single voice on the verse—"I love my whiskey and I love my gin, but the way I love my coke is a doggone sin"—until the chorus comes in with steam-whistle power—"Hey, hey, honey take a whiff on me!"

The Jug Band's immediate success brought Victor and other national record companies back to Memphis for numerous sessions. The second generation of Beale Street blues players—Jim Jackson, Furry Lewis, Memphis Minnie, Frank Stokes, and Cannon's Jug Stompers—sang of voodoo rituals, vulgar dance steps, toxic moonshine, and the great Mississippi flood, saving street lingo and unwritten history while spreading the Memphis legend. This Southern black bohemia emerged simultaneously, more or less, to the highbrow Harlem Renaissance and made its own significant, if underappreciated, cultural impact. Memphis Minnie and Joe McCoy singing "When the Levee Breaks," Robert Tim Wilkins performing "Rolling Stone" and "That's No Way to Get Along," and Gus Cannon's jug band doing "Walk Right In" and "Minglewood Blues" were common musical currency in Memphis during the late 1920s, songs that would return to life through Led Zeppelin, the Rolling Stones, and the Grateful Dead over forty years later. Furry Lewis, Frank Stokes, and Jim Jackson all bummed around Beale Street in the 1920s, playing guitar for coins. "Jim Jackson's Kansas City Blues," recorded in Memphis in December 1927, became a landmark hit, though the Memphis Jug Band had recorded the song first. Furry Lewis, a one-legged hobo, medicine show performer, and former employee of Jim Kinnane, got to see his picture in a *Chicago Defender* advertisement for his "Billy Lyons and Stack O' Lee" record. If you could have told this ragtag bunch of musicians that in eighty years their work would be synonymous with Beale, while the powerful and suave Bob Church would be forgotten, they would have laughed.

◆　◆　◆　◆

Around the corner from where the Memphis Jug Band rehearsed, a rail-thin Mississippi boy stayed up late reading contraband Mencken, borrowed from the library with a forged note from a white man, as he ate cold beans straight out of a can.

It was not only the despair and the insanity lurking down the district's alleys that inspired great art. Redemption too could be found there. "It was on reputedly disreputable Beale Street in Memphis," Richard Wright wrote in his memoir *Black Boy*, "that I discovered that all human beings were not mean and driving."[13]

Chapter 19

THE UNHOLY
COMBINATION

In the spring of 1927, a month after Victor Records packed up their microphones, scandal simmered the Memphis tenderloin. Word got around that federal Prohibition agents had raided the bootlegging joint of the Bellomini brothers and located a secret ledger.

Frank and Johnny Bellomini stood among the giants of Memphis's underworld, bossing the bootleg liquor trade in the Beale Street district. "I think Frank Bellomini was sort of like Nello Grandi was," recalled Frank Liberto, who had done business with both. "All the Italian people believed in him. He was a fine person. I mean he'd do anything and wasn't anybody any rougher or tougher than Frank and his brother Johnny. I mean they were people that didn't want to be bothered and they didn't bother anybody. Bellomini was next to Grandi as far as being anybody in this kind of business. He was one of the big ones."

The Bellomini ledger detailed payoffs from the bootlegging establishment to dozens of city police and county deputies. A number of entries fell under the more general heading "Government."

◆　◆　◆　◆

Mr. Crump, after leaving the county trustee position in 1924, had held no formal political office. He ran a growing insurance company, and though he was certainly known around town as a power broker, few citizens realized the full extent of his authority.

Mayor Rowlett Paine (who'd succeeded Frank Monteverde in 1919) owed his stint in office to Crump, who had lent his vote-gathering skills to the Paine effort—including Bob Church's thousands of ballots. But Paine and Crump fell out—Paine asserted more autonomy than Mr. Crump liked—and Crump and his chief strategist Frank Rice determined to find a more agreeable mayor. Paine wanted to keep his job and declare his independence from the Crump machine.

The Bellomini book arrived at a crucial moment in an election year, with the potential to expose Crump and liberate Paine.

Paine launched a brave, perhaps suicidal offensive against Crump. Understanding that the city and county law enforcement and judicial powers all belonged to the machine, Paine realized he had two options—to incite public outrage, or to cause a federal investigation. He took his story to the public. In a special address at City Hall, he declared, "There are a number of people in Memphis who shake with fear at the thought of a thorough, searching, far-reaching federal grand jury investigation.

"As long as the public is indifferent to the rotten politics that has cursed Memphis in recent years," he added, referring to the sort of relationship he'd entered with Crump to win his prior elections, "it is going to be difficult to break up the unholy combination that most people believe exists between the political gangster, the bribe-taking official, and the professional bootleggers and gamblers."

The speech and Paine's offstage maneuvers were nothing short of audacious. He let it be known that he'd requested an investigation into graft in the police department from federal circuit court judge Harry B. Anderson, Church nominee and Coolidge appointee, who had allegedly received a $10,000 bribe from Big Grandi.

Mayor Paine tried to involve the U.S. attorney's office, but federal district attorney Lindsey Phillips, another Bob Church nominee, threw the ball back to local authorities, saying that the federal government would gladly help enforce its own laws, but that since city and county officers were implicated by name, city and county authorities would have to do the work.[1] The man in charge of the federal Prohibition agents in the city stated that he had no obligation to conduct an investigation, adding that the local powers had all the resources needed to pursue the case. Federal judge Anderson happened to be off trying cases on another circuit. Uncle Sam was not coming to help Mayor Paine. All federal authorities deferred to the county—to Crump.

Even Paine's ploy of provoking public outrage backfired. Following his inspired "unholy combination" speech, a group of anonymous citizens, identifying themselves as his supporters in two previous elections, cautioned the mayor:

> We are going to watch and see if you are in earnest in closing up some of the regular joints where men, women and even boys go and buy whiskey, wine, and home brew galore. We have kin folks and members of our families who go to Grandy's [sic] joints . . . and buy anything they want. Now you can send a man in there and tell them you are Mr. Rice's friend and if you don't look too much like law, you can buy anything easy.

The voters, it seemed, did not exactly rally to the mayor's call.

Boss bootlegger John Bellomini, whose ledger provoked the uproar, eventually ate an illegal liquor charge stemming from the raid, spent time in the penitentiary, and kept his mouth shut.

◆   ◆   ◆   ◆

Richard Wright's memoir, *Black Boy*, contains rare insight into the lives, minds, and chatter of Memphis Negroes during these days. He lived in boardinghouses throughout the Beale district from 1925 to

1927, working downtown in an optical factory, moving from the despair of the black world to the discomfort of the white world. "Among the topics that Southern white men did not like to discuss with Negroes were the following," Wright wrote:

> American white women; the Ku Klux Klan; France, and how Negro soldiers fared while there; Frenchwomen; Jack Johnson; the entire northern part of the United States; the Civil War; Abraham Lincoln; U.S. Grant; General Sherman; Catholics; the Pope; Jews; the Republican party; slavery; social equality; Communism; Socialism; the 13th, 14th, and 15th Amendments to the Constitution; or any topic calling for positive knowledge or manly self-assertion on the part of the Negro.[2]

Bob Church had publicly stood for quite a few of these dangerous items. "His work is done in his Beale Street office in Memphis and in the White House in Washington," a *Commercial Appeal* editorial would note. "No federal appointment is made in Memphis and Shelby County under a Republican administration without his endorsement."[3]

Church's national reputation awed the regular guys on Beale Street. "We would read about Church's exploits and his visits to the White House and at that time it was almost unknown for Negroes to go to the White House," said Lester Lynom, a volunteer in the Church organization.[4]

The 1927 Memphis mayoral election found Church poised to have a greater impact than ever on his hometown. His goal at the time was simply to educate and invigorate Negro voting, to get as many people as possible registered to vote, knowledgeable and comfortable with the process, and active in democracy—in tandem with his ambition to help his people to become politically alive. He saw around him a poor and undereducated people who needed familiarity with the fundaments of American democracy before they could aspire to broader participation and positions of power.

"We looked at Mr. Church as our emancipator," said Lynom. "We each felt that if we were to be delivered, Mr. Church would be the one to do it."

Church explained his strategy to trusted members of his organization. The time was not yet right to challenge white Democrats for office. "It was understood that we weren't to try to elect any local," Herbert Brewster, a Church campaigner, recalled.[5] Instead, Church's black voting league would practice suffrage, registering ever more voters, and spreading the knowledge of how, where, and when to vote. Once they reached a formidable level of numerical strength and voting ability, they might be able to get their own people into office. Top-level Republicans seem to have understood this, and Church had proved his loyalty beyond doubt in national elections. Supporting the local Democrat was a necessity of Church's overall political survival.

Secondarily, Church exchanged the thousands of black votes he represented into promises from candidates for black citizens, a dicey prospect. In the previous mayoral election, Rowlett Paine had promised improved parks, schools, and streets for colored Memphis. Bob Church delivered for Paine, but Paine failed to deliver for Bob Church.

Paine's behavior in office had made it awfully hard to ensure further support from Church, particularly considering that in 1927 Paine was running against an old Church family friend, Watkins Overton.

Overton, whose grandfather had been Robert Church Sr.'s greatest white ally, entered the campaign with the full force of the Crump machine behind him, as the organization moved for complete control of the city. Overton had started his career as one of Frank Rice's protégés in the state legislature and distinguished himself as competent, loyal, and deserving of higher office.

Gone were the days of Crump throwing last-minute support behind a chosen candidate. By now the machine had mastered fund-raising and electioneering, to the point that, as operative Guy Bates would explain, "We ran full slates of candidates, legislature, judges, county officers, city, and everything out of the same kitty. In fact there are very few people who are conversant about the financial end of the organization. This is one end that Mr. Crump almost held in his hand, the money."[6]

The great challenge of political candidacy—fund-raising—ceased to be an issue, at least for those in Crump's favor. "Money was really no object," Bates said. "The only trouble you had was getting on the ticket. Once you were selected and had the laying on of hands, you didn't worry about anything."

◆　◆　◆　◆

At a Halloween-night rally, Mayor Paine thundered, "Crump is the opposition candidate for mayor and Watkins Overton is only his proxy. . . . Overton is on the Crump ticket because he is a cog in the political machine."[7]

Meanwhile, colored voters rallied at Church's Auditorium. Lt. Lee delivered an electrifying speech. After a heated debate, they unanimously endorsed Overton.

Ten days remained until the election. The move to endorse at all had provoked some controversy within the Negro bloc. As the pastor of Beale Street Baptist Church pointed out, "You are giving the opponent a whip with which to hit back and if you endorse here tonight you will be sorry before next Monday night." He'd hoped black voters would hold out and could provide the margin of victory in a close race, in exchange for a package of concessions.

In past races, the colored bloc endorsing late had absolved candidates from having to take a public stance on race issues. Black affiliation with Overton at this early stage gave Paine more than enough time to race bait his way to victory, scaring white voters out to the polls to defeat a candidate of black preference. The next day, with the colored endorsement firmly against him, Paine ran the black flag to the top of the pole. With his penchant for equating whoever opposed him with the dark forces of evil, the mayor charged that "an unholy alliance" existed between Crump and Bob Church. As a past recipient of Crump favors, Paine understood well the terms of such a deal.

"The reason for the alliance," stated the mayor, "lies in the fact that there is more than $22,000 in back taxes due on property owned by

Bob Church and some of it runs back to 1917. No wonder that Bob
Church can afford to be a friend to the machine that controls the back
tax office." Paine wielded a handful of tax bills like a preacher's Bible.
Since Church converted his brothels into Negro housing in 1920, he
had increasingly come to rely financially upon Crump and Rice in
the tax office. Without knowing it, Paine foreshadowed the fall of the
Church empire.

◆   ◆   ◆   ◆

Despite the mudslinging, a sense of great promise and a moment
of new possibility spread across Beale Street. In the South not ten years
earlier, Negroes had been lynched, and their sections of town burned,
over their attempts at voting. Now Herbert Brewster rode around town
in a car equipped with a loudspeaker, going down alleys, hitting the
factories at lunch hour, urging every Negro he could find to register and
vote for Overton. "[Church] organized and got this crowd together and
would send certain people out to certain groups," Brewster recalled,
"somebody to go out and organize the women, someone who had appeal
with the youngsters." If Church got a little help from the city tax man,
that was okay with his supporters, though probably surprising. In their
eyes, he had earned it, and he clearly worked hard on their behalf.

Lt. Lee assumed much of the responsibility for street-level tactics.
As a seasoned campaigner, he understood the importance of delivering
the right message in the proper manner. As an insurance man who'd
worked black Memphis door to door, he knew the character of each
neighborhood and who it would respond to. "Now there were some
groups that if you sent a man there with too much polish he couldn't get
away with it," Brewster said. "They wanted you to come down to earth
and talk street talk. We had some fellow who could do that and beat
the world doing it."

As the black campaign workers invaded the streets, Mayor Paine
stoked white fears with the specter of Negro policemen, Negro firemen,
and Negro access to all parks at all hours. "If the Negro vote, organized

by Bob Church, is permitted to name the mayor of Memphis, it will become necessary for every candidate hereafter who runs to get [his] permission."

Paine said, "The Overton ship started well, but became enmeshed in dark and dusky waters of Beale Street."[8]

Overton denied that any pact existed between himself and the colored voters, while Overton headquarters opened at the corner of Beale and Hernando, with Lt. Lee managing.

As the campaign wore down to its last days, Paine refined his message. "Shall candidates for office in this city run on their own merits and qualifications or shall they be compelled to obtain the endorsement of E. H. Crump, the white boss, and Bob Church, the negro boss, in order to be elected to office in the city of Memphis?"

◆ ◆ ◆ ◆

On November 8, 1927, two nights before the election, an orchestra of colored schoolboys and their teacher played the Palace Theater, and local radio broadcast the late-night show all over the city—"WMC will present the Chickasaw Syncopators in the 11 o'clock frolic program," read the announcement in the paper. "Jimmie Lunceford will lead this 12-piece negro orchestra through the various modulations and gyrations of a syncopated dance hour. The Chickasaw Syncopators are rapidly coming to the front as a dance orchestra and are taking their place in social functions."[9]

The Syncopators began life as the school band at colored Manassas High School. Jimmie Lunceford taught English and Spanish while coaching sports at the school. He started the band from scratch, with no plan or finances for music instruction in the Negro schools. They played at the Hotel Men's Improvement Club, overlooking Beale from Hernando Street. They would graduate in time to the Cotton Club in New York, shedding the old name to become the Harlem Express. Manassas students Jimmy Crawford, the drummer, and Moses Allen, bass, joined Lunceford for the entire journey. Lunceford would rise from being mocked in local gossip columns to the renown of the swing era's greatest artists. "Duke is great, Basie is remarkable, but Lunceford tops them both," Glenn Miller would say.[10]

The Syncopators' sweet swing poured from radio sets and out open windows, down the street from the Palace Theater, to Overton head-quarters and the Negro voting school on Beale. There instructors showed voters sample ballots, teaching them where to mark and where to sign. Voters could practice as many times as they wished.

At nine o'clock on election eve, the voting school was packed. A deafening boom exploded from the building's entrance. The front door splintered, windows shattered, and everyone evacuated the school. The explosion ripped through the floor, but injured no one. An investigation revealed that a bomb had been tossed into the basement.

Meanwhile Mayor Paine exhorted supporters. "Church and his aides are engaged in the most sinister political activities ever undertaken in this city," he said. "The duty of Memphians is clear. It is to stop Bob Church and his club with ballots now."[11]

In the end, Generalissimo Rice whipped Mayor Paine coming and going. Paine's race-baiting tactics were no match for the wily machine. Rice registered all the bawds and bootleggers in town. Fraudulent votes from Napoleon Bonaparte, George Washington, and Abraham Lincoln landed in the ballot box, though Paine placed poll watchers in all the battleground wards to prevent the machine's traditional shenanigans.

Rice's aide Bert Bates had to dislodge one poll watcher who, after hours of friendly chitchat, still refused to budge. Finally, Bates went to the drugstore next door and bought some chocolate and some Ex-Lax. Bates returned to the poll and started popping chocolates. "You want some chocolate candy?" he asked the poll watcher.

The poll watcher gobbled Ex-Lax as Bates waited. The pollster began shifting uncomfortably in his seat and suddenly rushed off. "Bert, would you watch this thing, I've got to go."

Bert pulled the lock off the ballot box, fattened the ballots cast with a bundle for the machine, and slammed the box shut.[12]

A brass band marched along Main Street behind Crump and Overton. The parade added marchers as it moved through the city. Fireworks streaked overhead. Crump and Overton were lifted and carried above the crowd. Down Beale Street, "where the dusky citizenry joined in the general acclaim, went Crump and his boys."[13]

The next morning's tally showed nearly 20,000 votes for Overton to fewer than 7,000 for Paine. Negroes made up an unknown but substantial portion of voters, as a reported 6,000 had paid their poll taxes.[14] The race put the Crump machine in complete, uncontested control of city politics. Bob Church had demonstrated his organization's effectiveness in local campaigning, a nice complement to his federal sway, and it brought results.

Lt. Lee would praise Mayor Overton: "I have seen parks and playgrounds spring up in densely populated Colored sections where Negro children lived in two room shanties. . . . I have seen muddy and unpassable streets that marked the section in which my people lived, beautified, paved, and made passable."[15]

Crump now took his place as the acknowledged, even celebrated boss of Memphis. In his triumph, he sat in the top-floor suite of the E. H. Crump Company, his insurance and real estate brokerage. The slender six-story building stood across the street from the Shelby County courthouse, now the Crump organization citadel, where everyone could look out and see his name in big bronze letters and know who was in charge.

He couldn't have done it without black support. The extraordinary civic vitality of Beale Street gained notice from Houston to Harlem, as colored newspapers lauded, "The example set by Bob Church and the Negroes of Memphis, Tennessee, who organized their forces, put up their own money, and waged their own campaign for the successful mayoral candidate [shows that] the race's political salvation could be worked out right in the heart of the South."[16]

Still, the promising victory wasn't enough for some colored residents. Nineteen-year-old Richard Wright left Memphis for Chicago during Beale Street's finest hour. He'd spent two years living on and near Beale, and he'd been bullied and intimidated, seen his own educational and economic opportunities stifled. He needed more than promising political developments to make a life in Memphis.

Jimmie Lunceford wasn't far behind him, departing with his unproven orchestra for the uncertainty of the road rather than life in the Bluff City.

And just as surely as 1927 showed Bob Church's power, it also exposed his Achilles' heel. Those unpaid taxes would come back to haunt him.

Chapter 20

SNITCHIN'
GAMBLER BLUES

After the Overton election, Mr. Crump offered a quiet solution to Bob Church's persistent demand for a black presence on the police force. The Crump camp knew that the general public wouldn't abide black uniformed police, so a compromise emerged: the city permitted plainclothes black police officers.

Two of Bob Church's team received the honor—pharmacist Dr. J. B. Martin and Lt. Lee.[1] They were issued badges and revolvers but no uniforms. They had the right to make arrests, but mostly Lee and Martin stood as a buffer between black citizens and police brutality—something for which Memphis cops had been widely feared since with the 1866 riot. Lee and Martin functioned as trusted go-betweens, reporting real crime and real criminals to the uniformed cops while protecting unfairly arrested black suspects.

The gain for black Memphis, although small, carried a consequence. In addition to empowering good citizens like Lt. Lee and Dr. Martin, the secret colored police program tapped deep into the underworld for Negro law enforcement agents as well. Under these auspices, a white Memphis police sergeant named Alfred O. Clark began a partnership with a man who lived on both sides of the law and both sides of the racial divide, Red Lawrence.[2]

A. O. Clark, born in 1900, started his career with the county sheriff's department in the early 1920s. During those years a county grand jury indicted a man known as King Bimbo of the gypsies, who'd gone on the lam. Clark heard a rumor that King Bimbo had bobbed up in Chicago. He went in pursuit and found King Bimbo in a pool hall. He arrested the gypsy and handcuffed him. The two got into a taxi, but as the cab sped off, the driver ran a red light. A local cop pulled it over. The local cop, issuing the driver a citation, looked in the backseat and saw Clark sitting on King Bimbo with his pistol in the gypsy's mouth. In commemoration of this event, Clark became known as Bimbo.

Bimbo Clark earned acclaim for his fearless and resourceful pursuit of criminals, with headline-grabbing flair. He once dressed in drag to break up a petting party robbery.[3] He left the county for city police work in 1928, at the beginning of the Overton administration, where his knack for finding the limelight continued. In 1933 Bimbo Clark would be among the cops and FBI men who apprehended a badly hung over and pajama-clad Machine Gun Kelly at a Memphis cottage. Bimbo heard whatever Kelly muttered that in FBI lore would become the infamous "Don't shoot, G-men, don't shoot!"

Clark gambled and fought in Negro dives and killed numerous colored citizens in and out of the line of duty. On the police force, he was known to operate a stable of Negro criminal informants, none whose exploits have ornamented Beale Street lore more than Red Lawrence.[4]

Red Lawrence belonged to a premium caste, that of the white Negroes, who held preeminent status over the more common Beale Streeters, while maintaining a certain prestige among white men in power. Lawrence was an echo of Ed McKeever, Church Senior's underworld attaché who chose to live as a Negro around Beale Street for adventure despite having descended from a respectable white family. As Rufus Thomas said, "If you were black for one Saturday night on Beale Street, you would never want to be white anymore."[5]

Red Lawrence was a Negro only according to the one-drop rule, whereby a faint rumor of colored lineage categorized someone as *black* even in the absence of visible African heritage. Red Lawrence had perfectly straight hair and white skin. He inherited these features from his mother, also nominally black but white by any noticeable standard. His father seems never to have been in the picture, and his contribution to Red's racial identity remains a mystery. He was his mother's son—she a white Negro, he a white Negro.

Red Lawrence grew up in the world that Bob Church Sr. had made, and a violent episode typical of life in the empire determined his destiny. On October 23, 1905, he was twelve years old, walking home from a show.[6] His outift at the time consisted of a white, collared shirt, suspenders holding up his cuffed trousers, and buttoned-up shoes on his feet. He wore a newsboy cap turned sideways, high on his head. He exuded an intense self-assuredness, even as a boy.

It was after ten o'clock at night. Red lived with his mother, Maude, in a nicely furnished home at the corner of Fourth and Pontotoc, a few blocks south of Beale. He arrived there as a crowd was forming around his house. He went inside and discovered his mother, dead from a single gunshot to the head. She was thirty. Oscar Taylor, her lover, lay dead beside her, also of a single gunshot. A friend had sat in the front room of the house and seen the incident transpire. Taylor had shot Maude and then turned the pistol on himself. News reports implied that Maude supervised a brothel and stated in no uncertain words that Taylor had, in jealousy, confronted her about running the streets at night. Red, standing over his mother's body—and that of her killer—vowed vengeance against no-good Negroes like Taylor: cheating gamblers, pimps, brawlers, and vagrants.

After his mother's death, Red Lawrence joined an Irish family and made friends with the politically connected ward boss for his neighborhood, Jim Mulcahy. Mulcahy had added his footnote to history by hiring bandleader W. C. Handy to perform for the Crump mayoral campaign of 1909, resulting in "Mr. Crump," better known as "Memphis Blues." Mulcahy had remained in the boss's good favor ever since.

In the wild years of Prohibition, Red worked as a rumrunner, transporting shipments of liquor from the river to the speakeasies. He serviced the finest nightclub in the city, Bob Berryman's Silver Slipper, and ran his own downscale colored place, the Bucket of Blood. Mr. Crump closely regulated vice in the time-honored fashion, keeping the business in local hands and keeping strangers out. The police handled intruders: when Al Capone's brother John showed up at the edge of the red-light district, the police locked him up overnight and kicked him out of town.[7]

One night Red picked up a shipment but had to use a Packard rather than his recognizable Cadillac. On Front Street the police tried to stop the Packard and, failing, shot it full of holes. The Packard rolled to a stop on the cobblestones at the river landing, and the police rushed to apprehend its occupant—"Oh, sorry Red, we didn't know it was you in there."

Red Lawrence also worked as a gambler, earning a violent reputation, though his methods were seen as legitimate according to underworld code. "He didn't bother decent people," said Thomas Pinkston, a musician at the Palace Theater. "It was the tramps who didn't have any respect for themselves . . . they fool around and get in Red's way, Red would just shoot 'em. That was all and I confidently think he was right for doing it. Now he was just as nice as he could be, other than don't fool with him or get out of line around him cause he would sure kill you."[8]

Bimbo Clark cultivated Red Lawrence as an informant and sometimes partner in Mr. Crump's secret police program. As a secret, perhaps even dubious, lawman, Red technically faced the same legal consequences any citizen would, his specific law enforcement status being rather too hazy to justify killing. He enjoyed a certain legal immunity that surfaced in court, where he would face four murder indictments over the years, beating two and serving brief penitentiary sentences for the two others. The local press would reflect, "Lawrence was well known to Memphis police and frequently worked with police officials in apprehending negroes."[9] A former law enforcement official in a nearby county would recall, "I knew him when I was sheriff. He sometimes sends me cotton laborers," in reference to a long-standing practice of rounding up Beale Street dice rollers to pick cotton at harvest time.[10]

Shortly after the inauguration of Crump's secret police, the Memphis Jug Band recorded "Snitchin' Gambler Blues," immortalizing the sort of Beale Street character who stayed in trouble but avoided punishment.

On May 12, 1928 (weeks after the jug band recorded "Snitchin' Gambler"), Red Lawrence became embroiled in an argument at Willie Butts's dice hall. Butts, a pimp attached to a Beale Street brothel, went for a pistol, but Red had his sleek revolver in hand quicker. He shot and killed Willie Butts and wounded Willie's friend Cut Deep through the chin.[11] Red turned himself in. He faced his charges, murder and assault to murder, in county court and got a fifteen-year penitentiary sentence. He served less than a year.

The empowerment of Red Lawrence and Bimbo Clark to rough up black citizens reflected a citywide trend of intimidation. As Mr. Crump tightened his control over Memphis in the coming years, a tough guy named John Phillips would beat and bully Crump's outspoken white critics and political opponents.[12]

Red Lawrence's presence in black Memphis showed just how precarious a position Bob Church and his constituents occupied, especially at a moment when they might have enjoyed a sense of optimism. Church had helped carry an election for the boss and negotiated a little police influence for his trouble. The Crump forces warped the program designed to reward Bob Church, using it to spy on, intimidate, and kill the very people Church tried to protect.

◆   ◆   ◆   ◆

In the sixty years since the end of slavery, black voters had identified with the Republican Party. To them, in the words of Frederick Douglass, the party of Lincoln was the ship and all else the sea. Now Bob Church felt as if he stood against an overwhelming historical tide. "In 1928," he wrote, "many questions embitter the country, and historians will come back to them as the beginning of an epoch. . . . After November 6, fifty years will be required for our Nation to balance itself. From this time on orators will enjoy a new text and writers a new theme."[13]

August 11, 1928, found him in Palo Alto, California, where he and prominent Republicans from every state had arrived to formally deliver the party's presidential nomination to Herbert Hoover at Stanford University. Church was the first person of color to serve in such a capacity.

Hoover had made a national name for himself supervising the South's recovery from the devastating 1927 Mississippi River flood. Running for the presidency, Hoover avoided making bold proclamations, or many public statements at all, delivering just seven speeches during his entire campaign. He hoped that his reputation in flood relief and the party's tradition would sufficiently attract the Negro vote. On race, he said nothing.

Even "Silent Cal" Coolidge had held forth animatedly on the subject: "There is especially due to the colored race a more general recognition of their constitutional rights." Citing colored enthusiasm for the American war effort, Coolidge added, "Surely they hold the double title of citizenship, by birth and by conquest, to be relieved from all imposition, to be defended from lynching and to be freely granted equal opportunities."[14]

Colored Republicans had grown accustomed to this sort of statement. Hoover gave them nothing. He seemed averse to offending Southern whites. Even worse, he placed leading black educators who had no political experience or clout in charge of his colored voters division, infuriating Bob Church. In 1920 Church had found a sympathetic ally in the Republican war room, Will Hays. But now a Tennessee lily-white rival named Horace Mann (not to be confused with the famous educator of the same name) assumed an important and autonomous position with the Hoover campaign. Mann had neither guidance nor restraint from Republican leadership, just a broad mandate and a blank check to win votes for Hoover down South.[15] There would be no repeat performance of Church's dazzling feats in the 1920 presidential race. "I could not in conscience associate with political parasites and pretenders," Church told the *Chicago Defender*, explaining his absence from the Hoover campaign.[16]

The Democrats meanwhile made a play for the colored vote, buying influence with leading black newspapers.[17] The *Defender*, the *Baltimore Afro-American*, and the *Harlem Star* opened their pages to Democratic ads and proclaimed support for Hoover's opponent, New York governor Al Smith.

As the election neared, more colored papers followed the *Defender* and *Afro-American* into the Democratic camp. Frustrated with both the sudden Republican indifference and the Democratic history of race-baiting, W. E. B. Du Bois counseled black voters to avoid the election altogether. As November 6 neared, the very real possibility of black voters turning Democrat or returning the GOP's apathy suddenly frightened Hoover.

"Puzzled and worried nominee Hoover summoned millionaire Church to Washington," *Time* reported.

Hoover presumably gave Church personally what he could not give black voters publicly—reassurance that they still had a place in the party. It wasn't much, but Hoover kept Church's faith alive.

Church returned to Beale Street. On October 26, 1928, in his office in the old Solvent Savings Bank building, he wrote an impassioned letter to colored voters, the thousands who looked to him for leadership. Torn and embittered, he had reasoned his way to a decision, and explaining it took up a full page in the *Defender*. "I, too, am confused in the unwarranted heartlessness of our countrymen and in the undeserved indifference of the party of our love and hope," he wrote. "With those of our household who feel inclined to desert the family altar I have neither fault to find nor criticism to bestow."

He balanced the histories of the two parties. Wherever in those histories he saw Negroes losing their power to vote, he found Democrats. He noted that a painting of Lincoln graced the Republican convention, while the Democratic convention displayed a portrait of Robert E. Lee.

As I thought of my letter to you a fact knocked ever at the door. Wherever the Republican party controls the state, you have the ballot and are permitted to cast it as you please. . . . Although you may use it to advance Mr. Smith towards the White House, remember that to countless thousands of us that same ballot is denied wherever the Democratic party controls the state.

Church addressed the fear that newly influential Republican strategists had it in for Negro voters. "I am not satisfied with some of Mr. Hoover's company," referring to Horace Mann and the lily-white element, "but clearly do I see in Mr. Smith's company the entire array of gentlemen I know who would deny me life, liberty, pursuit of happiness, and a chair car for our women to ride in."

Church reluctantly endorsed Hoover. "The Republican Party offers us little. THE DEMOCRATIC PARTY OFFERS US NOTHING."[18]

The Church letter had the desired effect for Hoover. "Toward the close of the campaign all but six of the leading Negro newspapers were calling for Smith's election," noted *Time*. "In the last week of the campaign, most of the rebellious journals, at Church's command, changed front and Hooverized vociferously."[19]

Hoover rode a landslide victory into the White House, winning the Northern black vote and six Southern states. For the moment, Church may have helped slow a black exodus to the Democratic Party that would begin anew in four years with Franklin Roosevelt's campaign.

◆ ◆ ◆ ◆

In March 1929 President Hoover sought Church's counsel and shortly thereafter issued his most forceful statement on race yet, insisting that the GOP needed to eliminate hatred from itself before it could flourish in the South. Church emerged from his presidential summit practically glowing with optimism. "Mr. Hoover will prove a shocking disappointment to . . . 'famished lilies' and 'suit-case Democrats' who expect him to put colored people back into slavery," he said.

Hoover's next moves, however, embittered Church and began a transformation of the nation's racial political identity.

Corruption charges hit longtime black Republican leaders of Mississippi and Georgia, as well as the white leader of a mixed-race South Carolina coalition. Hoover replaced colored and mixed-race state delegations down south with lily-whites. This unplugged tens of thousands of longtime loyal black voters from the national apparatus, while Hoover's leadership purge left Church as the last black Republican leader standing.

◆　◆　◆　◆

On November 6, 1929, a year after Hoover's election, Church sent a letter from his Beale Street office to the White House.[20] He told President Hoover of the extent of Negro disenchantment with their party. "Their resentment is universal," he wrote. Church warned that the continued exclusion of black participation "will leave the Republican party a wreck upon the shores of the political ocean; but a memory to those who once loved it, and a chapter in the history of governments." His forecast proved partially accurate. The GOP would lose the next five presidential elections. After being entirely affiliated with the Republican Party since emancipation, black voters defected in great numbers to the Democratic side.

Chapter 21

GOD'S
CHILLUN

In the spring of 1932 a banjo strummer sang,

> *Ashes to ashes*
> *Dust to dust*
> *If the gin don't get you, the workhouse must.*
> *I get nothing for working,*
> *Dirt for pay,*
> *Police come and get me, just any old day.*

A young reporter—a short, dark man wearing thick glasses—stood in a patch of grass and benches where the market house once stood, at Beale and Hernando, recently dedicated as W. C. Handy Park, and jotted down the words the banjo man sang.[1]

The reporter's name was Nat D. Williams. In his mid-twenties, he was teaching history at Booker T. Washington High School. In time, he'd lead the famous amateur night at the Palace Theater, where Rufus Thomas, B. B. King, and Bobby "Blue" Bland would perform in their hungry days. Williams worked the Palace crowd into a lather to begin each program with a chant of "Beale Street Blues! Beale Street Blues!"

Later, he'd go over the airwaves of radio station WDIA as purport-edly the first black disc jockey on American radio. Late in life, after he'd suffered a series of debilitating strokes that robbed much of his trademark verbal dexterity, he could still sing every word of the W. C. Handy song that made his street famous, emphasizing his own tagline, "I'd rather be there than any place I know."

Nat D. had been born on the street in 1907 into a struggling family. He grew up on Beale, and the street ran through him like blood. His mother worked as a dancer at the Palace, and Nat hung around W. C. Handy's office, singing kids' street rhymes for the composer. He left for college, finishing Tennessee A&I in Nashville in 1928 and venturing to New York. He freelanced at New York papers and took courses at Columbia. He returned home, with connections to the newspaper busi-ness, and took a job teaching at Booker T.

In 1931 Nat D. began writing a column for the *Memphis World* news-paper called "Down on Beale." He immediately became the street's con-science, black Memphis's most captivating journalist since the days of Ida Wells, and once "Down on Beale" went into syndication, he rein-forced the street's relevance to black America. He supplied a voice for the educated Negro as well as a record of the unwritten lingo among the street's unlettered inhabitants. Williams proved as fearless tackling dangerous social circumstances as he was self-deprecatingly humorous. Nat walks into a speakeasy and hears a bawdy woman announce his arrival, "Nothing but a little smoke looking for a fire." On the issue of Negro mental health in a racist city, he concluded, "Rather than spend a reasonable sum of money for psychiatric treatment for black folks' brains, the majority of the ruling class save money by paying the comparatively small cost of a forty-five slug."[2] Nat glibly referred to his people as "God's chillun" and "cullud folk" and his home street as "Chocolate Avenue." He celebrated and preserved the street's unique ways of life, and without him, there'd be no record of Josephine the street evangelist or of the fact that Thursday was All Maids' Day, as domestics let their tongues loose after holding them all week, amid the singe of the hot comb in a beauty parlor.

Nat D. lampooned the annual Cotton Carnival, a pageant the white city threw in honor of the golden crop, at which a King and Queen were selected: "the only recognition accorded the black man's part was assignment to leading the mules in parades, spinning thread in a store window for advertisement purposes, or appearing half naked and in scarlet breeches as attendants on the white man who was king."[3]

Nat D. was everywhere, making notes, listening. On a midsummer day in 1932, he saw a breadline stretching down Chocolate Avenue.

◆   ◆   ◆   ◆

After spending decades controlling politics and vice—marshaling W. C. Handy's creativity and Red Lawrence's brutality—in a little neighborhood known as Shinertown, Jim Mulcahy made his belated debut on Beale. He took over the Panama Café, corner of Fourth, in 1932.

Mulcahy restored some color to the beat-up street. The apple-faced Irishman wore silk shirts, ate oranges constantly, and consumed sweet milk by the cold quart. He brought a number of his friends to the neighborhood, including his protected bootlegger Professor Green, always tuxedo clad, and a bartender named Long Distance. And wherever Jim Mulcahy held forth, Red Lawrence was not far off. All of them lent a charitable hand, volunteering at the soup kitchen Mulcahy established in an abandoned storefront a block west of the Panama, at Beale and Hernando.[4]

The stock market had crashed during Hoover's first year in office, and neither the administration nor the economy had recovered. The Depression hit Beale Street hard. "There were people lined up and pushing and shoving to get in the garbage receptacles to eat," observed Joseph Burkley, who'd recently moved to the city from Mississippi. "The One Minute was open on Beale Street and they sold food cheaper there than any place in the city. You could go in there and put your plate down and folks would come and grab it and take your food from you. And they would say, 'I'm hungry,' and take it."[5]

Bob Church relied on working class people to pay rent in his properties, but with hunger rife, real estate became a risky business. Customarily, he had enjoyed lenience on his property tax payments thanks to his support of the Crump machine—financial help that he needed now more than ever. Nonetheless, he did a peculiar thing. As Mr. Crump sought reelection to his district's seat in the U.S. Congress and pushed a Democratic candidate for governor, Church resisted the local boss for the first time.

To counteract the surprising competition, Crump called on an old friend for help. Jim Mulcahy, like a biblical apostle, gathered the blind, elderly, and infirm to vote in his ward.[6] The Republicans cast nearly twenty thousand ballots supporting their candidate, but both Congressman Crump and his governor won.

Church may have thought it a shrewd move to oppose the boss once, showing his strength and thus the necessity for Crump to keep him happy. But Crump apparently disagreed—if Church wouldn't deliver his crucial black votes to his machine, someone else would have to. Mulcahy's appearance at the Panama harkened a return to the old divekeeper days, just in time for the 1932 presidential election. Beale Street constituents had buttered Church's bread for the past fifteen years, since the demise of old-time saloonocrats Mike Haggarty and Jim Kinnane. Now he had competition for the Beale Street vote. Nat D. noted, "Thousands of the avenue's unfortunates were fed hot nutritious soup, bread and coffee, as well as provided with benches around a warm stove on which they might sleep during the cold nights."[7]

Mulcahy's arrival on Beale signaled a change in Church and Crump's relationship. Their association went from grudging partnership to rivalry.

◆　◆　◆　◆

On February 25, 1933, at three a.m., a black woman named Fannie Henderson awoke to the sound of an argument coming from an alley off Third Street. She looked out a window. The alley was tight, ten or fifteen feet across. A tall brick hotel stood on the other side of the alley from her view.

She saw four or five policemen arresting a colored boy. He was Lavon Carlock, a nineteen-year-old. Fannie heard the police tell him "We are going to fix you tonight."

She heard Carlock say, "Officer, if I have did anything, please ride me to the police station."

A policeman replied, "We are going to give you a ride. It is going to be a damn long ride. The first ride is going to be to the undertaker and the next ride will be to the goddamn cemetery." The police handcuffed Carlock.

Fannie moved to the front door and opened it a little. She saw a white woman come out of the hotel: Ruby Morris, a sporting woman. The police asked Ruby, "Is this the one?" She looked at Carlock and said, "Yes."

The police began beating Carlock with their clubs. Fannie watched and listened from the door. "His neck shook like a chicken's neck when you break it," she would say. Carlock was still cuffed.

"You better not holler, you son-of-a-bitch," a policeman said. Carlock didn't say anything. The police threw him down the alley. Fannie saw pistols flash in the dark.

A policeman shined his flashlight on Carlock. "Why, that son-of-a-bitch ain't dead yet," said the cop, and he shot Carlock through the head.

Ruby Morris, the white sporting woman, sat in a police car and watched. The police got into the car with her and drove off.

A colored funeral home ambulance arrived ten or fifteen minutes later to take Carlock's body away.

After dawn Fannie went into the alley. She looked around and saw Carlock's blood and brains and a spent bullet. A drizzling rain came and washed the boy's blood down the gutter.[8]

The afternoon news printed the police department's summary of the case. Carlock had attacked Ruby Morris, been arrested, and escaped from police custody. Officers had gunned him down in pursuit.[9] The

Memphis World, February 28, 1933, had questions about the official
version of events. An uncredited writer whose energetic style and rigor-
ous rhetoric uncannily resembled that of Nat D. Williams asked, "Why
was Lavon Carlock, nineteen-year-old youth, shot to death by six police
officers . . . ? Did the boy assault a white woman as was alleged by the
police . . . ? Why was it necessary for six men to apprehend him? But the
biggest why in this sensational case . . . is, Why was Lavon Carlock shot
in the face and stomach if he was running from officers?"

The Carlock incident was symptomatic of an increasingly violent,
paranoid atmosphere pervading the city. The killing, conducted openly
by public employees, defied any sense of goodwill between the white
city and the black city. The war between Crump and Church was heating up.

The paranoia infected white Memphis, too. An anonymous citizen
wrote a letter to Frank Rice, addressing the Generalissimo as "Shelby
Election Thief and Gangster." The writer accused Crump and Rice of
ordering an assault on the leader of a local voters' league, Ben Kohn.
"You criminals did not give Mr. Kohn as much warning as a rattlesnake
gives its victim before striking," the letter said. "We cannot get rid of
you thru elections so the only course left is to do away with both of you
thru the same methods that you use to get rid of those who oppose you."

◆ ◆ ◆ ◆

Just over a month after Lavon Carlock's murder, Congressman
Crump and friends showed up at the White House.

President Franklin D. Roosevelt had just begun his first term and
had to thank Crump for turning out the faithful in Memphis. Their
relationship, however, had been brief and testy. Back during primary
season, with Roosevelt's nomination in doubt, FDR practically begged
for a conference with Crump prior to the Democratic National Convention. "I should much like to talk with you before you go to Chicago,"
Roosevelt wrote.[10]

Delegate Crump not only delivered Tennessee for Roosevelt, he'd supported pro-Roosevelt delegations from other states, helping Roosevelt lock up the Democratic nomination. Still, Roosevelt would make no Tennessee speech. Now president Roosevelt needed to assuage his man in Memphis.

In the White House, Roosevelt ribbed Crump for getting sore at him about skipping Memphis on the campaign trail. Crump chuckled dutifully (as he expected *his* underlings to do for his own cutting remarks) and replied, "Have you any censure for what I did for you in Chicago?"

Roosevelt smiled, shook his head, and said, "No."

They parted on good terms. Roosevelt called Crump a "good Tammany Hall Tennessean," a neat reference to the most infamous political machine in American history.

Crump's Generalissimo, Frank Rice, couldn't attend the White House summit as he ailed at home. Crump sent him a letter summarizing the highlights. "The point is . . . we have always been sincere and rendered all possible assistance," the boss wrote. "So many go through life thinking only of getting without giving."[11]

◆　◆　◆　◆

Back on the street, Nat D. Williams observed, "Now that Roosevelt is president, bois and guls, what effect has that had on your Saturday night baths? Dismiss a comparatively small number of post office jobs and two or three bones thrown in the direction of the bigger dogs and you won't be able to tell if a donkey is puling the cart or an elephant is pushing it."

But there was a difference. The Carlock murder carried a message: if Bob Church wanted to play hard with Boss Crump, Church's people would suffer. With a Democrat in the White House and a ward heeler on Beale, Church could no longer protect his people from the machine.

Chapter 22

WITHIN THE GATES
OF MEMPHIS

At least some of Bob Church's circle continued to pros-
per. Lt. George W. Lee enjoyed tremendous success in business.
An insurance executive, he owned a modern home, employed a
housekeeper, and wore a dapper suit each day of the week. He
lived well for a black man in the South. His name and face stayed
in the papers, Memphis's white dailies and the weekly colored
sheets. Despite deepening differences between Church and Mr.
Crump, Lt. Lee held on to his privileged position as a secret cop
and continued his warm friendship with Generalissimo Rice. In
1931 the two men had coordinated the naming and dedication of
W. C. Handy Park—a block west of Church's Park—thought at
the time to be the only such civic honor bestowed upon a Negro
in the South.

A bachelor, Lt. Lee traveled extensively, whether working on
national Republican campaigns or in his capacity as a prominent Elks leader, all of which fed his robust ego. He judged
Elks-sponsored bronze beauty contests and puffed expensive
cigars at Elks smokers in New York, Chicago, and Philadelphia.

He also fancied himself a writer and spent late nights in his office on the second floor of the old Solvent Savings Bank building, in the exact spot where Handy had composed "St. Louis Blues" and "Beale Street."

Lee nursed a liquor bottle and typed. Having spent the past fifteen years as a fixture on Beale, he'd become, like Nat D. Williams, wrapped up in the romance of the street.

In the block down from Lee's office, the One Minute Café, next door to the Palace, stayed open all night, slinging five-cent frankfurters to an unending line of customers. Owner Hot Dog Jimmy estimated that he sold 3,600 dogs a day. "A dash of mustard, a jet of chili, and the masterpiece is finished," he'd say.[1]

The men hanging around the One Minute modeled the height of rural-meets-urban fashion—starched new overalls, black bowler hats, shiny pointed-toe yellow shoes, bandanas around necks, and ten-inch knives for toothpicks.

On the Palace's amateur nights, a one-man band rigged his bullhorn-bell-harmonica rack to his collar and tuned up his guitar, while a tap dancer warmed up his high-speed routine with toes peeping out of his tennis shoes.[2]

Battered, boxy pickups, shiny, curved Cadillacs, and buxom Chevrolets lined the curb from Church's Park along five or so blocks to the river. Foot traffic stayed as thick as when Ida Wells had to push through the crowds to reach the *Free Speech* offices, or when W. C. Handy strolled past the Monarch. The same silty river breeze blew, thick and hot in summer and piercingly cold in winter.

The policemen kept their pistol holsters unbuttoned and grimly spun their batons. Rats nibbled at the toes of passed-out drunks.[3]

People danced along, and music drifted from every direction—a symphony of banjos and spoons in Handy Park, harmonica blaring from Jim Mulcahy's, and dance orchestras at the Hotel Men's club at Hernando and Beale.

Lee relished Beale more than Bob Church ever allowed himself to. Church was so serious and formal, he set himself off from the barbecue-rib essence of the street. Lee, after all his success, remained a self-made man from Mississippi.

He had a direct line to the street's institutional memory. His older friends and colleagues remembered Wells's fiery gaze and Mike Haggarty's coffin-plate smile. They shared the district's secrets.

In 1934 George W. Lee's *Beale Street: Where the Blues Began* was released.

Lee's *Beale Street* played the same notes as W. C. Handy's "Beale Street," safely evoking the mysterious Negro world for white people. His book gleefully celebrated raucous tradition with a sense of nostalgia for a precarious way of life. Prostitutes, madams, killers, and gamblers of yore danced once more in his pages. He refrained from activism, for the most part, but wedged in a few juicy observations of current events from down on the old avenue. "The colored sections today are policed by white men," he wrote, "with the aid of stool pigeons who creep about the dives and underworld places, gain the confidence of law violators and hunted men, coax them to talk about their exploits, and then pass the information on to the police."[4]

The book found much fanfare, garnering positive reviews and gaining notice from the influential Book-of-the-Month Club. Clifton Fadiman, reviewing it for *The New Yorker*, wrote, "I wish to pin a small but distinctive badge (with ribbons) upon the honest colored breast of George Washington Lee."[5] The sensation spread overseas—Lee's voice would go over BBC radio, talking Beale Street for Alistair Cooke's *American Half Hour*.

Like Handy's song, Lee's book foretold danger and darkness. In time, the proud author would feature in the street's climactic chapter.

◆　◆　◆　◆

Though Lt. Lee's book celebrated a safely bygone era, another writer would soon show that Memphis hadn't changed all that much.

The Crump machine's enduring success owed something to concealing Memphis's commercialized vice. While clergymen, prosecutors, and Prohibitionists harassed notorious neighborhoods like the Levee in Chicago and completely closed Storyville in New Orleans—both of which were running concurrently to Crump's stint as mayor in the 1910s—outsiders never successfully invaded the Memphis underworld, and local reform never materialized beyond political cliché. Memphis's underworld never achieved the notoriety of its sinful sister cities, and so it received less of the unwanted attention.

After twenty-five years of open vice, however, the city finally got its due when Owen P. White's "Sinners in Dixie" exposé ran in the January 26, 1935, issue of *Collier's*.

A Texan who branded himself a "durable sinner," White loved lurid tales and larger-than-life characters; his Memphis feature read like William Faulkner's Gayoso Street novel *Sanctuary*. Of Memphis prostitutes, he wrote, "They offer their services to you in the street, speak to you in hotel lobbies, call you by telephone, smile alluringly at you through their own front windows, and coo invitingly to you from automobiles parked—with police consent, I assume—along the curbs."

White needed no escort on his underworld foray—he located easily everything a durable sinner could want, and the locals spoke openly about the reason for these prevailing conditions. "[It] is upon commercialized vice that the burden of paying its overhead has been placed by Congressman Crump's political organization, which runs Shelby County," White concluded.

> Believe it or not, that's a fact. Professional sinners, therefore—that is, men and women who run gambling houses, dance halls, blind pigs, policy rackets, houses of ill fame, and all that sort of thing—being cash assets for professional politicians, are not only encouraged to operate but are actually instructed to go ahead and provide everybody, both visitors and home folks, with as much wide-open wickedness as possible. Thus no stranger within the gates of Memphis need worry about how to spend either his time or his money.[6]

Five hundred policy solicitors, he estimated, canvassed the city every day: "Another popular method whereby the citizens of Memphis contribute to the pampered upkeep of their politicians and gamblers is for them to play policy. And do they play it!" The white-run vice business alone, he said, supported seven thousand "professional sinners whose sole business it is to provide everybody with a good time."[7]

"Sinners in Dixie" embarrassed Crump. More than that, it scared him. Prohibition remained in effect in Tennessee, and gambling and prostitution violated the law. But White had revealed that these offenses received the blessing of Crump himself, a federal officeholder. Worse, White had connected this illegal activity with the Crump organization's "overhead," suggesting corruption or racketeering activities that might interest the federal government.

"Sinners in Dixie" hearkened back to the 1910 Memphis exposé that had foreshadowed Crump's disgraceful removal from the mayor's office. For a quarter-century, the boss had maintained equilibrium locally between the polite world and the underworld, but outside attention to Memphis's unusual governance upset his balance. His entry into mainstream discourse forced him to adopt a more mainstream attitude—or posture, at least—toward vice. In the article's immediate aftermath, Crump, through police commissioner Cliff Davis and Mayor Watkins Overton, put the lid on policy. Nello Grandi, the man who'd made a fortune on bringing the nickel-and-dime Negro game to the masses, marched right up to Overton's office and demanded that the police lift the lid, but to no avail.[8] Mr. Crump's Memphis would have to make some changes.

Chapter 23

A BOYLE
FESTERS

Joe Boyle had been a good soldier, having campaigned
with the Crump forces as far back as 1909. He'd impressed his
superiors and taken his rewards, working for the county as collector of licenses and as a poll tax collector. He spent most of the
1920s and 1930s, though, as courthouse custodian. It seems an
unimportant, even demeaning position in a political organization,
but one instance summarizes Boyle's value to the organization.

In 1930 Senator Gerald Nye, a powerful Republican, came to
Memphis to investigate voting fraud. He wanted to inspect the
ballots cast in a recent election. The ballots were stored in their
rightful ballot boxes, he was informed, in the courthouse basement. Nye found the ballot boxes empty. Questioned about the
location of the ballots, the courthouse custodian told Senator Nye
that he'd burned them to make room in storage. Nye asked, "Mr.
Boyle, did the ballot boxes take up any less room empty than full?"
Boyle said nothing.[1]

Boyle gained influence within the Crump machine as Frank
Rice's health declined. While Rice kept quiet on matters of pol-

itics and race, Boyle loudly disdained Negroes and newspapermen and attacked political foes. He was a born hatchet man, and his bluntness became increasingly attractive to an aging Mr. Crump. Boyle was angry, racist, and paranoid, unlike Rice, who'd remained close with Lt. Lee and the Bob Church Republicans. A big promotion to county commissioner of revenue in 1936 empowered Boyle to go after enemies real and imagined. From that point forward, he jealously protected his relationship with Crump and eliminated competing voices.

Rice spent increasing amounts of time napping on his office couch and at home in bed as he battled that foe of royalty, the gout. He surrendered his power to Boyle, who little by little assumed many of his responsibilities and much of the trust Crump had previously vested in him. After taking over as revenue commissioner, Boyle assumed Rice's duties as ward and precinct organizer for election campaigns. He became a driving force in the city of Memphis.

◆　◆　◆　◆

In late winter 1937, with Boyle's influence on the rise, the Mississippi River flooded the city.

Police descended on Beale to press both the grimy farmer and the immaculate idler into duty to stem the horrific tide. Pianos ceased, and dice stopped. Joints were deserted. What men could be found, police herded into flatbed trucks, like livestock, and dropped them off in river bottoms. There they worked at gunpoint, carrying sandbags to the water's edge as freshly shined shoes sank into the muck.[2]

As the river rose, undercover man Red Lawrence appeared before a judge, facing another charge of murder. A Negro named Eddie Walker had been shot and killed in Red's resort. Walker had drunkenly refused to leave Red's place. "I don't care if you are Red Lawrence" were Walker's last words.[3] A witness came forward to testify that though Red had shot Eddie Walker, Walker had a pistol in his hand, corroborating Red's self-defense plea. This witness was none other than Memphis police Sgt. Bimbo Clark.[4] Red Lawrence walked away free.

◆ ◆ ◆ ◆

Mr. Crump's exploits provided regular fodder for *Time* and *Collier's* politics columns, and he appeared as a feature subject in *The Saturday Evening Post*. His image beyond Memphis mattered him. He controlled every other potential source of dissent; only the national media remained beyond his grasp.

Despite his permanent closure of the policy game following the 1935 *Collier's* exposé, reporters continued to highlight the negative. "The Crump dynasty is supposed to be financed by various forms of 'protection money' from bootleggers, gamblers, *et al.*," wrote *Time*. "Be that as it may, Boss Crump keeps taxes low, picks good competent men for public office and—unusual in the South—cultivates and delivers a solid block of Negro votes. Result of this system is that in 30 years of bossdom, Edward Crump has had a record of 60 electoral victories, no defeats in Memphis and Shelby County."[5]

Regardless of what anyone had to say about him, Crump stood at the peak of his power—his mayor and four councilman had run unopposed in the latest municipal election, while his choice for governor had won the Democratic primary, carrying Memphis 60,208 to 881.

Seeing the futility of directly engaging Crump at home, Bob Church turned his attention to national Republican politics. He worked out of his Washington, D.C., office, conferring with leading Yankee Republicans like the Pews and Du Ponts in Pennsylvania on national party strategy. He led black voting drives in Indiana, Ohio, and Pennsylvania that helped return Republicans to the Senate during 1938 midterms.[6]

Church's departure left Lt. George W. Lee alone in Memphis, in a vulnerable position. But he also remained close to the machine, even without Church to fall back on. And brutality hung thick around him—Red Lawrence killing for free, the police ignoring Negro rights, and more beatings, even of white political opponents. Unlike Church, Lee couldn't escape to a Washington, D.C., office. He had to make the best for himself at home. So he curried favor with the Crump overlords. To Lee, appeasing, and not angering, the machine meant survival.

Lt. Lee remained a Republican. He also remained Crump's steadfast ally and soon surpassed Church as black Memphis's most visible leader. The city administration placed him on every committee that required symbolic colored participation. He ran the colored unemployment and relief committee and helped steer the city's Negro slum clearance efforts while the black population grew by nearly 30,000 to 121,536 between 1930 and the end of the decade.[7]

In the fall of 1935 Mayor Overton and Tennessee's U.S. senator Kenneth McKellar announced that thousands of dollars from WPA funds would go to improve the now publicly owned and segregated Church's Park and two colored schools. When city officials cut the ribbon on a new modern hospital for the colored population in June 1936, Lt. Lee stood with them, holding the giant scissors.[8] These advancements contributed to Lee's status as reigning Beale Street dignitary: Handy Park, his successful book, and his efforts to build a better black community.

Upon Lee's shoulders fell the duty of representing the ordinary Negro, although he was anything but ordinary. His successful Elks charity drives and civic victories contented him but did little to cure the poverty, squalor, and danger around his beloved Beale Street. Life for most of his growing constituency continued to be rough. The black population made up between 30 and 36 percent of the city's jobless in the 1930s, and three-fourths of government job applicants.[9] A 1940 WPA study would find 77 percent of black-owned housing substandard.[10] Petty gambling disputes so routinely turned to murder that the police commissioner suggested legalized, city-supervised gambling: "I honestly believe that murders and a great many other crimes would be more effectively curtailed," remarked Cliff Davis to Mayor Watkins Overton.[11]

◆　◆　◆　◆

With Lee on the rise, Mr. Crump moved against Bob Church. Church's daughter Roberta, born in 1914, had spent most of her life in the family home that her grandfather had built; she attended college locally and aspired to follow in her father's footsteps. Roberta recalled, "Mr. Crump commenced to try to actively harass my father in a more overt fashion through the city offices . . . constantly finding different types of flaws in the real estate my father owned, some of which was residential, he owned quite a few houses." She explained:

> If you put in a fire escape after the fire inspectors had been to the property, then they'd find some trouble with the electrical wiring, after you got the wiring repaired, there'd be some trouble with the exits, when you had the exits repaired like they wanted them, they'd find some trouble with the roof, if the roof was at fault and you got that repaired, then they'd find some trouble with the sprinkler system—all these types of things.

Church's stiffest trouble, Roberta said, came from the tax office.

> Also during this period of time, there was a continuing increase in the assessment of my father's property far above what it was actually worth. . . . I remember his telling that he had this terrible session with some assessors in the tax office about the value of certain property. And he was telling them, "Well if you tax it that high, I'd be willing to sell it to you for that value." It would have been impossible for him to get a buyer at the price they were saying it was worth as far as taxes were concerned.

Truthfully, Church hadn't paid his city and county property taxes in years, thanks to his support of the Crump machine. Roberta claimed that her father allowed his tenants to skip rent payments during the Depression; if true, his generosity too came back to haunt him. On March 24, 1937, commissioner of finance Joe Boyle issued distress warrants, allowing the city to collect the rent directly from Church's tenants until he paid his property taxes. Three months later Boyle announced his drive to collect $4 million in unpaid city and county property taxes, and his intention to sue anyone who hadn't paid. Bob Church's free ride was over.

◆ ◆ ◆ ◆

January 3, 1938, was a cold, bright night. At about eight-thirty, a colored postal worker named George Brooks pulled his car up along the curb toward the corner of Main Street and Iowa Avenue. There a white woman stood. Brooks opened the passenger door to let her in. As she sat down, Memphis police ran toward the car, shouting, "This is the police!" The woman jumped out, and Sgt. Bimbo Clark jumped in. Clark fired his weapon repeatedly, hitting Brooks in the chest, face, and head. Brooks died before arriving at the hospital.[12]

In the aftermath, Clark explained that Brooks had pulled a .32 revolver and fired a bullet between Clark's legs—and missed, fortunately for Bimbo. The white woman, he said, had complained to police that Brooks regularly harassed her, so police set a trap for him. They asked the woman to agree to meet Brooks for a date and planned, supposedly, to ambush Brooks and question him about harassing the lady. Things went awry when Brooks shot at Clark.[13]

Because Brooks had allegedly shot first and didn't live to say otherwise, police brass immediately exonerated Bimbo Clark.

Brooks, twenty-eight years old, was a Bob Church Republican, a postal carrier since 1929, for whom Church had found federal employment. Bimbo Clark was Crump's chief officer of dark operations. With the Brooks killing, the machine carried its assault on Church from the tax office and the city courts into the street.

In the summer of 1938, Mr. Crump threw his weight behind a Tennessee gubernatorial candidate; the race was essentially to be decided in the statewide Democratic primary in August. For Bob Church, under severe pressure, his fortune and his people in danger, the primary offered a last chance to rejoin the Crump flock. But Church quietly told his people to stay away from the polls.[14]

The next spring the city seized Church's real estate, a dozen properties in all, including his father's historic headquarters at Second and Gayoso, the former brothels on Gayoso, the Solvent Savings Bank building (holding Church's current office), several storefronts on Beale Street, and the family home. Church owed a total of $89,000 in city, county, and state fees, some of which had gone unpaid since 1919, the year after Church first supported the Crump ticket in a local election. Now Crump turned this old reward for Church's help into a trap.[15]

On March 15, 1939, on the courthouse steps, in the shadow of the E. H. Crump Company building, the city of Memphis auctioned off Bob Church's property. "They completely stripped him financially of his real estate which, of course, was his income, and that left him in a state of financial disaster," Roberta Church said.

Church's inability to provide for his daughter left him devastated. "And of course it meant quite a curtailment of his living habits," she said, "but I must say he was a very strong person with a very forceful personality and a very disciplined man, and I never recall him complaining during all the years up to his death, when he must have suffered greatly."[16]

The strain on Church's life became visible. The formidable, six-foot-tall, two-hundred-pounder withered into a gray wisp of a man. He moved to an apartment on Champlain Avenue in Chicago. He would now try to manage his Memphis Republicans from exile.

Church's opponent didn't look too well himself. Mr. Crump had lately become careless of his appearance. He wore a black overcoat everywhere and quit visiting the barbershop. His tangle of white hair grew down his back. As Church's world crumbled, chaos swirled around Crump. Frank Rice, machine Generalissimo since 1905, died on Christmas Day 1938. Rice had stood beside the boss during Crump's humiliating ouster in 1916 and had helped orchestrate his comeback. Sharing the Boss's grand aspirations, Rice had steadily guided the machine, working in numerous capacities, implementing campaign strategy, filling the war chest, and rigging beneficial legislation in the state's General Assembly.

As Crump coped with the loss of his trusted partner, he suddenly lost his heir apparent, the machine's future. Five months after Rice died, Crump's twenty-nine-year-old son John perished in a plane crash in Mississippi.

◆　◆　◆　◆

Crump reacted to this chaos in perhaps the only way he knew how: he closed ranks in the machine and tightened his control.

He sent a note to Frank Rice's protégé, Bert Bates, a popular, relatively young man with a bright political future. Bates organized charity drives and American Legion activities, nonpolitical stuff with real political value. Bates also maintained a close friendship with Lt. George W. Lee.

"Dear Bert," Crump's letter read, "I am well aware now that you want to be king of the underworld in Memphis." Bates thought the old man had completely slipped his cogs. Bates had made no move to become "king of the underworld." The accusation made sense only as a ploy to get rid of him.

The letter went on to sever Bates's connection with the organization. The whole thing reeked of Boyle. Bates and Boyle had never gotten along. Bates suspected that Boyle resented him. Bates, as Rice's protégé, might have stood to gain Rice's old position of influence in the machine, next to Crump. Boyle wasn't letting anyone else get in the way.

"In your position in a political organization, you're always envied by the people that are under you and disliked by the people that are ahead of you," explained Bates's son.[17]

With Rice dead, Church out, and Bates exiled, the Crump machine had but one connection to black Memphis: Lt. Lee.[18]

Chapter 24

THIS IS A
WHITE MAN'S
COUNTRY

"It's been going on since the time of Adam and Eve," a Memphis prostitute mused as the news of the latest vice crackdown got around. "Well, this is no Garden of Eden. But at that, I'll be lonesome for my room here."[1]

It was April 1940. Joe Boyle had a new job and a new nickname. Having taken over as police and fire commissioner, he had ordered the underworld closure and acquired the moniker "Holy Joe."

The madams and their inmates were outraged. They'd just paid their poll taxes. They'd just voted down the line for the organization men, including the one who'd now deprived them of their livelihood. Theories abounded among the damsels about what had provoked Crump to put on the lid. Some speculated that the old man had gotten religion after his son died, while others thought he'd caught a venereal disease and lost his mind.

Asked about the sudden crackdown, Holy Joe grinned. "When

I was finance commissioner, didn't I make people pay back taxes who never paid before?"[2]

He laid down a May 7 deadline, and they abided. The twenty-one known places of prostitution went vacant.

Holy Joe whispered to Red Lawrence that he'd better spread the word over Beale Street that the town wouldn't be run wide open any longer. He revoked Red's unwritten license to kill, asking the undercover man to turn in his pistol to Mr. Crump. Red said that if Mr. Crump wanted the pistol, he could come get it himself. The pistol stayed with Red.

The lid aftermath made the right kind of national news for the boss. "Gone from hotel lobbies were the expectant blondes," *Time* reported. "Brothels were closed; their staffs had fled. Bookies had shut up shop. Even bingo was outlawed. Tourist camp proprietors conspicuously took the numbers of incoming automobiles, thus discouraging nocturnal disorder."

◆　◆　◆　◆

Meanwhile Crump's political friend Franklin Roosevelt was seeking a third term in office. As Hitler conquered Europe, war fears and antifascist, antidictator rhetoric spread across the country. Wendell Willkie emerged as the Republican contender to Roosevelt. Campaigning, Willkie connected the headlines—a three-term president was a dictator in training. In his stump speeches, he tied Roosevelt to notorious Democratic municipal dictators: Pendergast in Kansas City, Hague in New Jersey—and Boss Crump, thanks perhaps to Bob Church's involvement in Willkie's campaign strategy.

Willkie also rode an explicitly pro-civil rights platform. While recent Republican candidates had scarcely verified the existence of Negroes, Willkie called for the integration of Washington, D.C., antilynching legislation, and protection of Negro suffrage. Quite naturally, the Willkie candidacy energized black Republicans in Memphis.

Bob Church still ran Memphis Republican strategy from exile and had to name a manager for the local Willkie campaign. Though Lt. Lee had led every campaign and run every Beale Street election headquarters since 1927, Church picked Dr. J. B. Martin to head the Willkie drive.

Martin had ridden with Church in every political battle dating back to the founding of the Lincoln League in 1916. Martin was financially independent, owning a share of the Memphis Red Sox of the American Negro Baseball Association and the stadium the team played in, as well as a drugstore in South Memphis that housed a post office. He was not free from compromise with respect to the city administration. He had been a special officer of the Memphis police department for over ten years, carrying a badge and revolver like Lt. Lee and Red Lawrence. The city permitted him to work as a bondsman without a license. He allegedly had the power to get people out of jail or to otherwise mediate in their legal difficulty. He performed this service in exchange for payment, which he would then divide with the arresting officers to drop or reduce charges.[3]

Dr. Martin opened Republican headquarters on Beale Street on October 1, 1940, with seventy-five campaign volunteers on hand.[4] He scheduled rallies for successive Mondays, October 14 and 21.

While Dr. Martin readied his troops, Crump probed for weaknesses. Martin's special privileges, if revealed to the public, would reflect just as poorly on the Crump administration as on Martin—nothing to hold over him there. Crump obtained a credit report on Martin and his business. The report showed that Martin owned outright several pieces of real estate, and it valued Martin's South Memphis Drug Co. at $101,000, concluding that Martin ran "a well managed business, affairs are in good condition."[5]

Martin was rock solid. The machine had no recourse but to spy, threaten, and intimidate—the sort of job made for Holy Joe Boyle.

The Republican meetings went off October 14 and 21 at black churches, Beale Street Baptist and Centenary Methodist. Hundreds attended. Dr. Martin later recalled, "At that second meeting, we set another meeting for the next Monday night."

The next day, while at work in his drugstore, Martin received a message from Lt. Lee: "They said for you not to have that meeting next Monday night. If you do have it, they'll police your drugstore." Lee,

Martin later explained, "said that the organization was very much upset about the meeting we had."

Martin asked Lee what this "policing" would entail, and Lee said he didn't know and that the boss gave Martin until the end of the week, Friday at 3:45, to call off the next Republican rally.

At 3:30 that Friday, October 25, Lt. Lee showed up at Republican headquarters. He asked Martin, "Well, what have you decided?"

Martin said, "People have been notified and it has been advertised and it has been in the papers, and I am not going to call it off." He asked Lee once more what was meant by "policing" the drugstore. What exactly did Crump plan to do?

Lee told him the police would patrol his business around the clock and pat down every customer going into the place.

Martin said he didn't believe Crump would stoop so low.

Lee said, "They would stoop to do anything, and I would advise you to call it off." He walked out of headquarters onto Beale Street.

Martin's home phone rang at six that evening. It was Lee. As promised, two policemen were searching everyone entering Martin's drugstore.

The next day's *Press-Scimitar* quoted "Holy Joe" Boyle and Dr. Martin. Boyle had concocted a law-enforcement justification for the pat-downs. "We are trying to break up Negro dope peddling," he said.

Martin countered that Boyle's motive was political. "I was told that if I did not call off the rally Monday night," he said, "that my business would be policed."

To create cover for the drug accusation against squeaky-clean Martin, the police also targeted the business of Elmer Atkinson, another longtime Republican booster who ran a poolroom, restaurant, and cabstand on Beale known as the Stag. Atkinson, unlike Martin, had been in trouble—a narcotics arrest some years past. "His place was just about a block from the Republican headquarters," Martin said. "It is about the most prominent place on Beale Street, more people go in there, and he was helping me out in the campaign at all the meetings."

Over the next six weeks, two officers remained outside Martin's drugstore during its sixteen-hour business day. Elmer Atkinson couldn't endure it and closed the Stag after a couple of weeks. As news of the crackdown circulated, local Negroes organized a counteroperation and swarmed Martin's drugstore, making the pat-down line run down the street, in hopes of overwhelming the police. A teacher brought her kindergarten class for ice cream, and the police dutifully patted down every little child.

The police stepped up their tactics in response, frisking customers who were leaving the store and destroying merchandise in the ostensible search for narcotics. One patron unwrapped a new, sealed package of cigarettes and handed it over to an officer, who broke every stick in the pack and dumped the mess into the customer's hat. People who picked up their mail at the post office substation in the store were forced to open their packages for the police, who then read the mail. "They held one person as long as fifteen minutes reading his letters," Martin said.

The police guards prevented a prominent white citizen from entering and told him to move on. "I thought the streets were free," he said. "We'll show you how free they are," the police said, and threw him in a patrol car.

Dr. Martin went to see county attorney general Will Gerber, a Crump machine stalwart.

"Well, I was surprised that you had taken the attitude that you did," the attorney general told Martin. "The old man is awfully sore about you having those meetings."

Now merely canceling the next meeting wouldn't be enough to save Martin. "The thing for you to do," Gerber advised, "is to call a mass meeting and tell them that you are through, that you are closing up your headquarters. Discharge the people that you have employed, resign as chairman, and if you do that, everything will be all right."

Martin told him it was too late. The election was now a matter of days away.

As election day approached, an anonymous letter reached several prominent Negroes, including Dr. Martin and the Negro newspaperman Nat D. Williams. The letter read:

When any man, white or colored, gets too big for the town, the town don't want him and won't have him. You are one of those fresh, impudent kind talking social equality.

This city won't stand for . . . any Negro stirring up racial hatred. . . . Many states and many cities have had bloodshed. There has been none here. BUT IF THE BALL STARTS ROLL-ING THERE IT GOES.[6]

Holy Joe Boyle publicly declared that the police were watching nine-teen black citizens "who have been fanning race hatred," to share a phrase from the anonymous letter. He repeated his mantra of the times: "I will say again, this is a white man's country, and always will be, and any negro who doesn't agree to this had better move on."[7]

Boyle's words clattered around Beale Street, echoing what another policeman had said as black Memphis burned in 1866: "This is white man's day!"

The Republican campaign in Memphis raised only about $800 to finance its ward activities. Franklin Roosevelt rode a landslide into his third term on November 5, 1940. The election brought Dr. Martin no relief.

Holy Joe's police had discovered no evidence to connect Dr. Mar-tin or any customer of the store to illegal drugs. Still the pat-downs continued, every customer entering Martin's drugstore, and every cus-tomer leaving the place, sixteen hours a day, seven days a week. "Not even a ten-year-old child will believe that this public searching has law enforcement as its object," wrote *Press-Scimitar* editor Edward Meeman in the November 25 edition. "It is political persecution because Dr. Martin supported the Republican Party."

The sense of persecution extended beyond politics as black Mem-phis history came under assault. The city changed the name of Church Park and Auditorium to Beale Avenue Park and Auditorium. A reporter asked the mayor, "Is this intended as a slap at Bob Church?" The mayor replied, "It isn't intended as a slap at anyone. As a matter of fact, I don't know how the park and auditorium were named."[8]

A few days later police closed Pee Wee's. They patrolled the remaining nightclubs. The lid was on tight.

In December a group of colored local Democrats visited Crump to protest the treatment of Dr. Martin. In response, Crump reportedly "declared that Bob Church had been spending most of his time in Philadelphia and up North and that he had been staying in white hotels up there and had come back to Memphis, 'spreading ideas of social equality' and that Martin had abetted him in it."[9]

After six weeks and no narcotics arrests, Holy Joe Boyle called off the policing of Martin's drugstore. Dr. Martin, in fear, had fled to Chicago, where Bob Church lived.

◆   ◆   ◆   ◆

A *few days later* an envelope arrived on the desk of President Roosevelt's secretary. Inside were a handwritten note from Edgar McWilliams addressed to Mr. Roosevelt and a newspaper clipping. In the clipping, one underlined phrase stood out. Holy Joe Boyle's mantra—"I say again, this is a white man's country, and always will be, and any negro who doesn't agree to this had better move on."

McWilliams's letter said, "I don't think it is such a nice remark."[10]

Holy Joe's remark made national news, featured in *Time* on December 9, 1940. Subsequently, the Southern Conference for Human Welfare and the NAACP pressured Attorney General Robert Jackson to investigate what had happened in Memphis.[11]

Roosevelt's secretary received letters addressed to the president from the Southern Negro Youth Congress in Birmingham and the American Student Union in New York.[12] Both letters singled out a familiar name to Roosevelt, "Boss" Ed Crump. One captured the tenor of Negro life in the dictatorship:

> There is a concerted drive . . . to force Negro leaders out of business and out of town and to intimidate the entire Negro population by wholesale arrests every day and by placing heavy police

guards in peaceful Negro neighborhoods. Memphis residents suffering under the Crump machine domination cannot protest for
they know that speaking out would mean the end of their economic security and possibly the bloodshed that has been threatened in the press and in letters received by leading citizens.[13]

Would the president move to destroy an old Tammany Hall Tennessean, a man who had delivered his state three times to the Roosevelt
cause and guided other Southern boss delegations into the Roosevelt
camp? The alleged civil rights violations under Crump echoed other
current events—the president was already under fire from civil rights
activist A. Philip Randolph, who proposed a mass Negro march on
Washington to protest discrimination in hiring for war industry jobs.

Pressure in Washington to look into the Crump machine mounted—
letters and clippings from Memphis circulated to the Department of
Justice, where the story got the attention of Henry Schweinhaut, head
of the department's civil liberties division. Schweinhaut took up Martin's case enthusiastically, even though to proceed with it would be
a politically delicate matter. Schweinhaut needed Attorney General
Jackson's authorization. The best the attorney general's office could
do was to send attorney Amos Woodcock down to Memphis for an
inquiry.

Woodcock landed in Memphis on January 1, 1941. He reportedly
spoke only to Holy Joe Boyle and to none of the Negro principals in
the case. Details of Woodcock's visit leaked to the press, and black
newspapers were outraged. The director of the Associated Negro Press
contacted Attorney General Jackson to request a copy of the report
Woodcock had filed. In his reply, acting assistant attorney general Wendell Berge relayed the opinion that "evidence is not available in this case
to establish a conspiracy to injure or oppress citizens in the free exercise
of a right secured to them by the Constitution."[14]

Though the Woodcock inquiry effectively closed the case, it wouldn't
stay shut. Thurgood Marshall, special counsel to the NAACP, wrote
the attorney general, "The report of Mr. Woodcock, based solely on his

investigation with . . . the chief of Police without any discussion with the Negroes affected by these activities of the local police, is one-sided to say the least. We therefore urge that an investigation be made of both sides of this question to the end that the Civil Rights of Negroes in Memphis be protected."[15]

Marshall's note fell to acting assistant attorney general Berge, who replied, "The federal government has no jurisdiction over the behavior of the police toward Negroes or anyone else."[16]

At the Department of Justice, Henry Schweinhaut would not give up. He pushed Woodcock to directly answer Thurgood Marshall and the Associated Negro Press request for more information about the Memphis inquiry. Schweinhaut pushed Berge, his superior, challenging Holy Joe Boyle's justification for the policing of Martin's drugstore. "It is obvious that an open, notorious, public, and continuing search of all the patrons of a business establishment would not constitute an honest attempt to ferret out an illicit drug business," Schweinhaut wrote. "The traffic in narcotics is highly secretive. The use of uniformed policemen who publicly search everyone . . . is just the procedure that is likely to turn up nothing in the way of illegal drugs."[17]

Schweinhaut concluded that sufficient justification existed for the Department of Justice to investigate violations of federal civil rights laws by the Memphis police.[18]

As of early 1941, the Crump machine crackdown had deprived black Memphis of its top two leaders. Black citizens lived in an oppressed state—afraid of both police brutality and financial ruin at the hands of the boss. But this surge of power for the Crump machine also left it vulnerable.

A federal indictment against the Crump machine hinged on the one charge that would have to be proven in court as a violation of constitutional rights: that the crackdown on Dr. Martin had truly been political in nature, not part of a narcotics investigation, as Holy Joe had publicly claimed.

Only one man could contradict Holy Joe and cinch the indictment—Lt. Lee.

Lee had delivered the message to Martin that the Republican rallies had to stop or else Martin would be "policed"—a violation of Martin's right to free speech and the Negro Republicans' right to peaceably demonstrate. Lee must have gotten his orders from someone. Revealing that information could deliver the Crump machine a devastating, possibly lethal blow.

◆   ◆   ◆   ◆

On March 12, 1941, Bob Church and Dr. J. B. Martin came to the Department of Justice in Washington. Their issue could not have been timelier. Chapters of the March on Washington Movement were adding membership throughout the country, building toward a mass demonstration against the government, planned for summer. The movement for Negro rights seized on the paradox of our nation readying for war against fascist oppressors abroad while supporting a racial caste system at home.

Church and Martin entered the vast new Justice Department building and met civil liberties department head Henry Schweinhaut, who'd taken the most interest in the Memphis case so far. Schweinhaut and two other officials interviewed Martin, with Church adding a few points and interjecting questions. Martin told the story of how and why his store had come to be policed, the real reason for the action, as he had been told, and how he had been told. Martin's story impressed Schweinhaut, who thought out loud about indicting Holy Joe, Shelby County attorney general Will Gerber, Lt. Lee, and possibly even the boss himself.

Martin and Church left the Department of Justice confident that an investigation would result. The plan hinged on scaring Lee into exposing the Crump machine's violation of Martin's constitutional rights. As the interview concluded, Church told Schweinhaut, "I want Lee not to know anything about this before it happens because he will say only what . . . Boyle will let him say unless he thinks he is going to [the federal penitentiary in] Atlanta because he is just a creature of circumstances."[19]

◆ ◆ ◆ ◆

Lt. Lee's account of the 1940 events, given years later to historians, would corroborate Dr. Martin's story entirely: the police harassment of Dr. Martin's business had been politically motivated.[20] Lee's testimony might have been enough evidence to secure indictments and perhaps even convictions.

But Lt. Lee stayed quiet in 1941. Lacking key testimony, Attorney General Jackson refused to authorize an investigation.

Though Roosevelt had appointed all of the Department of Justice officials who knew about the Memphis incident, Jackson and the president were particularly close. He didn't need Roosevelt to tell him not to pursue indictments against a FDR-friendly organization in Memphis. Crump had been good to Roosevelt, and a scandalized Crump could only harm the president.

Roosevelt ameliorated civil rights agitation when he signed Executive Order 8802 on June 25, 1941, banning racially discriminatory practices in the U.S. defense industry. A. Philip Randolph called off the march on Washington, and Roosevelt cemented his reputation as a racially progressive president.

Within a few years, most of the Justice officials involved with the abortive Crump inquiry were promoted and dispersed. Attorney General Robert Jackson became associate justice of the U.S. Supreme Court in July 1941. Henry Schweinhaut, the man who had pressed hardest for an investigation, received Roosevelt's nomination as federal judge for the District of Columbia in 1944. Holy Joe nailed it—This is a white man's country.

◆ ◆ ◆ ◆

Dr. J. B. Martin lived in Chicago for the rest of his life. Pee Wee's never opened its doors to Beale Street again. The lid stuck on tight, for years this time. The brothels, saloons, and gambling joints stayed dark. Bob Church returned to Beale Street to shore up his political base but never made Memphis his home again. He and his former protégé Lt. Lee never reconciled.

Lee and Church's political rivalry intensified as they struggled for control of Republican power in Memphis. In 1952 Republican presidential prospects brightened after twenty years of defeats. Church came to Memphis in mid-April to campaign for a seat at the Republican National Convention.

But Church's triumphant return to power would not materialize. Staying at a hotel around the corner from his old family home, he sat in a plain room one evening, talking strategy on the phone with Matthew Thornton, the man who'd brought W. C. Handy to Memphis nearly a half-century before. Thornton heard Church gasp. The phone dropped—and Thornton got the hotel operator on the line. A Negro undertaker's ambulance took Church to the hospital, where he was pronounced dead.[21]

Robert Church Jr.'s funeral procession went past the family home, operating as a boardinghouse at the moment, on its way to Elmwood Cemetery. Church was laid to rest beside his father, in the family crypt.

Church's daughter Roberta ran against Lt. Lee for a seat in the Tennessee Republican delegation and won, becoming the first black female from the city to do so.

Church's supporters believed, until they went to their own graves, that he had been the victim of jealousy among the very people he had committed his life to help. "He not only bore a cross, but he bore a double-cross," Herbert Brewster said. "I think if black people had understood what he meant when he tried to explain the power of a vote instead of a bullet, Beale Street would have ended up with a better name."

Roberta Church believed that her father could have kept his wealth and local status had he curtailed his political efforts against the Crump organization. "I would not have my father have taken any other course," she said, "because although it has meant great deprivation for me, I think that unless you have your honor and integrity intact and can call your soul your own, there's no point in living. Money is transient. Honor is more permanent."[22]

Of course, Church might never have displayed his honor had Crump let him slide on his taxes forever.

Less than a year after Robert Church Jr. died, a public safety convention met in Memphis. It showcased the latest in fire extinguishing technology, featuring vendors from across the country. The organizers wanted someplace to show off their equipment. The city generously obliged—a vast old empty house was available. The place stood three stories tall and had turrets and gables—with plenty to burn, it'd be an ideal place for a demonstration. City fire personnel stood at the ready as the Church home was set ablaze.[23]

Not fifty years before, the house had been the pride of the city, a monument to what a black man could accomplish in Memphis. Frederick Douglass and Booker T. Washington had graced its foyer. The firemen torched the rooms that NAACP officials had used as their secret headquarters for an undercover investigation of tenant farming in Mississippi.

At the end of the demonstration, charred ruins stood where the house had been. A colored family had lived here, side by side with prominent and wealthy white citizens. Other successful colored families had lived on the block in the 1880s. Soon a housing project for poor blacks, with all the architectural splendor of a medium-security correctional facility, would be built over this symbol of black prosperity and racial integration.

"When we were children we would ride down Lauderdale Street, the Church house was always pointed out," said L. Raymond Lynom. "We didn't have many three-story houses then. It wasn't just the house, it was what the house represented. To me [it] was almost a lynching of the Negroes of Memphis. They burned his house to the ground."[24]

EPILOGUE

With the home went the Church family's importance. In Memphis today nothing much remains of the world that Robert Church Sr. made, though the city is still known, for tourism marketing purposes, as the home of the blues. The old saloons are gone, except the Monarch building. Gayoso Street scarcely exists at all, and not a brass railing from its red-light heyday still stands. Though the family name has been restored to Church Park, its splendor will likely never return.

Beale Street enjoyed a tremendous comeback beginning in the late 1940s. Its nightclubs and entertainers, Little Junior Parker, B. B. King, Johnny Ace, and Booker T. Jones, to name just a few, played as vital a part in the birth of rock 'n' roll and the flowering of soul music as Jim Turner, Benny French, Son Wright, and W. C. Handy had played in the birth of the blues.

The late-1940s Beale Street music comeback, however, had no political counterpart comparable to the organization that Robert Church Jr. had assembled thirty years earlier. The lines of communication between black leadership and white leadership had been open, and productive, mutually beneficial progress had resulted. The destruction of the Crump-Church coalition, the bipartisan, biracial cooperation during the 1920s, had lingering and brutal effects. Turmoil between black citizens and white leaders would characterize Memphis life in the decades after Church's departure, and it long outlived Boss Crump, who died in 1954.

This ongoing conflict culminated in tragic consequences, on April 4, 1968, when an assassin killed Martin Luther King Jr. on the balcony of a Memphis hotel. King had come to protest a purely local dispute between the city's white leadership and the largely black sanitation workforce. King fell about a hundred yards from the initial shots that had sparked the Memphis Riot of 1866.

Just as the street's musical spirit refused to die with its old haunts, the black power philosophy proved resilient on Beale. After the King assassination, a group of young black men and women calling themselves the Invaders showed some of what Ida B. Wells had called "The True Spark of Manhood." In the early 1970s, the Invaders patrolled the Beale district streets in the footsteps of the Black Caps, the group who had fought to protect black women from white men nearly a century before. The Invaders published broadsheets, from an office just a whisper away from where Wells had written her *Free Speech* columns, urging armed resistance to racist rule. The FBI spied on the Invaders, the police infiltrated and arrested them, and the Invaders went the way of the Black Caps, broken up and silenced.

By the late 1970s the scene of thriving black commerce and revolutionary black culture, improbable black political triumph and crucial black protest, looked postapocalyptic. A crumpled chain-link fence encircled Beale Street, and weeds cracked the sidewalks. Windows busted out or boarded, collapsed roofs, charred bricks, and threadbare bums abounded.

Nostalgia for Robert Church's world persisted. Beale Street lay almost abandoned until it made another comeback in 1983, this time as a tourist attraction like Bourbon Street in New Orleans. In 2014 the Memphis mayor expressed his hope that the street could return to its roots, and that black attorneys and dentists would open offices on Beale, even though a Hard Rock Café stands over Pee Wee's old spot, the Monarch has become a police substation, and steel girders support old gutted buildings, leaving an elaborate facade.

ACKNOWLEDGMENTS

WHILE WRITING THIS BOOK, it has been my good fortune to work with a splendid variety of talented people.

G. Wayne Dowdy and the Memphis Public Library history department staff—Sarah Frierson, Gina Cordell, Verjeana Hunt, and Laura Cunningham—are all good friends and fine historians. Wayne in particular provided tremendous inspiration and information.

At the University of Memphis Special Collections, Ed Frank, Brigitte Billeaudeaux, and Chris Ratliff have terrific resources and go above and beyond the call of duty, providing outstanding archival service. Chris contributed his own superb research skills, and I am doubly grateful to him. Ernestine Jenkins provided help in locating an important image.

Memphis has a hardworking and accomplished group of digital historians. At the Shelby County archives, Vincent Clark and his staff, especially Frank Stewart, always responded promptly and thoroughly to my e-mail requests for old wills and deeds. Shelby County register Tom Leatherwood has digitized Memphis history and provided an open online archive of local city directories, property records, and death certificates.

Finally, one gentleman historian deserves thanks not only from me but from every student of Memphis's history yet to come. Charles Crawford is responsible for saving many of the most intriguing and important details of the fabled city's unwritten history. In coordinating the oral history department at the University of Memphis, he has interviewed members of the Crump machine, the Robert Church family, and the Church political organization, plus other significant and insightful figures, many of whom have died and would never have left a record of their important knowledge without Charles.

My special thanks as well go to Margaret McKee and the late Fred Chisenhall, though I've never met them. These Memphis journalists conducted hours of interviews with Beale Street old-timers in the early 1970s, preserving the street's history at a time when the street itself was being destroyed.

Thanks to Perry Walker and the late Nathan "Pedro" Lewis for some deep, illuminating discussions of Memphis history.

Gene Gilmore has opened a portal to the city's past at www.historic-memphis.com, where I found plenty of inspiration and guidance.

Thanks to Charles Hughes and Molly Whitehorn for help on the ground.

I thank Robert and Dorothy Pugh for their love and hospitality, their daughter, and the occasional dig into the Memphis phonebook.

Robert Riesman, author of the fine biography of Big Bill Broonzy, *Feel So Good*, kindly provided material regarding the Joe Turner/Turney blues.

Dr. Christina Jones at the National Archives located previously unresearched documents from an abortive Department of Justice investigation into E. H. Crump's 1940 attack on black Republicans.

Historians Ted Frantz, of the University of Indianapolis, and Don Lisio, professor emeritus at Coe College, provided helpful references and perspective on the Republican Party during its transformative years of the 1920s and 1930s.

I enjoyed corresponding with Bob Eagle and Robert Ford, preeminent blues music researchers. They provided files of primary source material from their digging into census data and newspaper archives. The great researcher Jim O'Neal has shined light on all sorts of new angles of W. C. Handy's story. Andy Horowitz tracked down a manuscript of Handy's autobiography that contained some different details from the published *Father of the Blues*.

Agent Paul Bresnick and editor Tom Mayer are blessings, and assistant editor Ryan Harrington brought creative perspective to this project. Janet Biehl made it look right.

I'm constantly grateful for my children and, most of all, for my wife Elise who brought me to Memphis, told me that this book needed to be written, and helped it get done. She is that lovely woman who'll feel honored to have a book about race, violence, gambling, liquor trafficking, prostitution, and political chicanery dedicated to her.

NOTES

PROLOGUE

1. Mary Church Terrell. *A Colored Woman in a White World* (Washington, D.C.: Ransdell, 1940), p. 6

2. That the *Victoria* was on the water that day is borne out in *The Official Record of the War of the Rebellion*. She was taken at anchor with crew, then refitted and relaunched in service of the Union as the *Abraham*. A slave named Robert Church was not among the property seized from her—at least providing a small opening in the historical record through which he might indeed have jumped. But the question of whether he needed to escape was rendered academic by an order from Col. Charles Ellett to a Lt. Crandell: "You will set these men on shore in Memphis and not again receive . . . any runaway negroes or any pursuer."

3. Charles Farley, *Soul of the Man: Bobby "Blue" Bland* (Jackson: University Press of Mississippi, 2011), p. 13.

4. Quoted in Peter Guralnick, *Last Train to Memphis: The Rise of Elvis Presley* (Boston: Little, Brown, 1994), p. 7.

Chapter 1
THERE IS NO YANKEE DOODLE IN MEMPHIS

1. Mary Grady, testimony published in *Memphis Riots and Massacres: Report of the House Select Committee* (Washington, D.C., 1866), p. 188.

2. *Daily Memphis Avalanche*, April 15, 1866.

3. Much of this news appeared in the papers as untitled, unsigned brevities, and so only the publication name, date, and page number can be provided. *Memphis Daily Appeal*, July 16, 1859, p. 3; October 20, 1858, p. 3; September 11, 1860, p. 3.

4. *Memphis Daily Appeal*, July 21, 1858, p. 2.

5. *Memphis Daily Appeal*, August 4, 1858, p. 2; June 25, 1859, p. 3.

6. Statistics from *Fort Pillow Massacre: Report of the Committee on the Conduct of the War* (Washington, D.C.: House of Representatives, 1864), pp. 97–98; quote from W. Ferguson testimony, p. 100.

7. The bureau was located on Second Street between Beale and Gayoso, while the entrance to Gayoso House was at Front and Gayoso.

8. *Memphis Riots and Massacres*, p. 244.

9. Eric Foner, *Reconstruction: America's Unfinished Revolution, 1863–1877* (New York: Harper & Row, 1988), p. 244.

10. "The Triumph of the Radicals," *Public Ledger* (Memphis), April 16, 1866, p. 4.

Chapter 2
A Promiscuous Running Fight

1. "The Civil Rights Bill—Miscegenation—," *Memphis Daily Commercial*, April 18, 1866, p. 3.

2. Ibid.

3. "Legal Intelligence," *Daily Memphis Avalanche*, April 17, 1866, p. 3.

4. "The Civil Rights Bill in Memphis," *Charleston Daily News*, April 23, 1866, p. 2.

5. *Daily Memphis Avalanche*, April 18, 1866.

6. Capt. Allyn in *Memphis Riots and Massacres*, p. 245.

7. Ellen Dilts, ibid., p. 64.

8. Primus Lane, ibid., p. 97.

9. Ben Garrett, ibid., p. 327.

10. Ellen Dilts, ibid., p. 65.

11. C. M. Cooley, ibid., p. 73.

12. Lavinia Goodell, ibid., p. 77.

13. Lucy Tibbs, ibid., p. 161.

14. Cynthia Townsend, ibid., p. 163.

15. J. S. Chapin, ibid., p. 193.

16. According to the Rev. Ewing O. Tade, an Iowan who was in Memphis to preach the gospel and teach Negroes at the Lincoln Chapel, in *Memphis Riots and Massacres*, pp. 91, 115, 121.

17. S. J. Quimby, ibid., p. 107.

18. Ibid.

19. John Oldridge, ibid., p. 122.

20. "Shooting and Burning of Rachel Hatcher," *Memphis Riots and Massacres*, p. 16.

21. Harriet Armour, ibid., p. 176.

22. C. M. Cooley, ibid., p. 73.

23. Ibid., p. 264.

24. Mary Jordan, ibid., p. 235.

25. Adam Lock, ibid., p. 116.

26. Ibid., p. 117.

27. Sophia Garey, ibid., p. 114.

28. Guy Thomas, ibid., p. 236.

29. "The Memphis Mob," *Highland Weekly News*, June 14, 1866, p. 1.

30. *Memphis Riots and Massacres*, p. 264.

31. Circular dated May 6, 1866, reprinted ibid., p. 22.

32. Mary Wardlaw, ibid., p. 233.

33. Margaret Gardner, ibid., p. 98.

34. Austin Cotton, ibid., p. 102.

35. Robert Church, ibid., p. 227.

Chapter 3
A FRIGHTFUL STATE OF MORAL DARKNESS

1. Mary Church Terrell, *A Colored Woman in a White World* (Washington, D.C.: Ransdell, 1940), p. 6.

2. "Colored Sport—A Policeman Shot At," *Public Ledger*, February 4, 1867, p. 3.

3. "From Memphis," *Milwaukee Sentinel*, February 5, 1867, n.p.

4. "Negro Shooting Affray," *Public Ledger*, October 5, 1866, p. 3.

5. "The City," *Public Ledger*, February 4, 1870, p. 3.

6. Terrell, *Colored Woman*, p. 2.

7. Ibid.

8. Ibid., pp. 7–8.

9. "A Curious Story," *Memphis Daily Appeal*, August 14, 1868, p. 2.

10. "Police Items," *Memphis Daily Appeal*, August 15, 1868, p. 2.

11. "Voudooism," *Memphis Daily Appeal*, December 3, 1869, p. 2.

12. "Voudooism, African Fetich Worship Among the Memphis Negroes," *Memphis Daily Appeal*, date and author unknown, reprinted in Paschal Randolph's *Seership!* (1870), excerpted online at www.southern-spirits.com.

13. "Miscegenation," *Memphis Daily Appeal*, June 10, 1870, p. 3.

14. "City Affairs: Adjourned Meeting of the Board of Aldermen and Council," *Memphis Daily Avalanche*, March 4, 1870, p. 3.

15. "Billiard and Oyster Saloon," *Little Rock Sun*, November 8, 1870, p. ??.

16. "Billiards," *Memphis Daily Appeal*, September 2, 1870, p. 4.

Chapter 4
BIRTH OF A KINGPIN

1. "An Interview with Gen. Forrest: A Talk About the Negro and Railroads," *Memphis Daily Appeal*, March 12, 1869, p. 4.

2. The earliest documented black musician to live in the district was Wesley Simmons, about whom nothing more than his address is known: corner of Gayoso and

De Soto, where Bob Church kept a saloon. Simmons's city directory listing has him there in 1870.

3. "Local Paragraphs," *Memphis Daily Appeal*, September 20, 1869, p. 4.

4. "Local Paragraphs," *Memphis Daily Appeal*, September 30, 1872, p. 4.

5. "Blood. A Radical Negro Barber and Gambler Kills a Colored Brother. The Mary Burton Rioters Determined to Wade in Blood—The Headquarters of the Infamous Gang," *Public Ledger*, August 3, 1876, p. 3.

6. "To the Public," *Memphis Daily Avalanche*, August 4, 1876, p. 4. Overton and Church would complete the sale of Second and Gayoso on June 1, 1877, for $7,000.

7. Mary Church Terrell, *A Colored Woman in a White World* (Washington, D.C.: Ransdell, 1940), pp. 36–37.

8. John E. Harkins, *Metropolis of the American Nile* (Woodland Hills, CA: Windsor Publications, 1982), pp. 88–89. Harkin's brevity is suited to my purpose, but there are two full, excellent accounts of the Memphis yellow fever epidemic. Molly Caldwell Crosby follows the fever from its outbreak in Memphis to its cure in *The American Plague* (New York: Berkley Books, 2006). Jeanette Keith keeps the story local, chronicling the epidemic's transformative power over Memphis in *Fever Season* (New York: Bloomsbury, 2012).

9. John Preston Young and A. R. James, *Standard History of Memphis, Tennessee, From a Study of the Original Sources* (Knoxville, Tenn.: H. W. Crew, 1912), p. 174.

10. Harkins, *Metropolis of the American Nile*, pp. 90–91.

11. John M. Keating, *History of the City of Memphis Tennessee* (Syracuse, N.Y.: D. Mason & Co., 1888), p. 141. Forrest's death is recorded in *Register of Deaths in the City of Memphis*, record 17114 A. The place of death is listed as 395 Union.

12. John Overton to Robert R. Church, Warranty Deed, *Shelby County Register of Deeds*, bk. 128, p. 147; James E. Warner to Robert R. Church, Warranty Deed, *Shelby County Register of Deeds*, bk. 128, p. 196.

13. That Church's purchase had been Bond No. 1 may be an exaggeration. Moreover the price of the bond, $1,000, equaled a decent annual salary in 1880 and is more repeated legend than documented fact. The earliest documentation of Church's bond purchase extant, a scrap of newspaper from 1882, says, "he purchased one of the first bonds issued when money was sorely needed to clear off the debt."

14. "Independent Ticket," *Public Ledger*, January 3, 1882, p. 1.

15. *Shelby County Register of Deeds*, bk. 145, p. 4.

Chapter 5
DIVIDING THE WAGES OF SIN

1. "David Is Down on Dives," *Public Ledger*, May 7, 1888, p. 4.

2. "Charles Gallina Is Gone to His Reward," *Commercial Appeal*, August 3, 1914, p. 7.

3. "Independent Ticket," *Public Ledger*, January 3, 1882, p. 1.

4. *Memphis Daily Avalanche*, January 6, 1882, p. 4.

5. Miriam DeCosta-Willis, ed., *The Memphis Diary of Ida B. Wells* (Boston: Beacon Press, 1995), p. 80.

6. "A Darky Damsel," *Memphis Daily Appeal*, December 25, 1884, p. 4.

7. Paula J. Giddings, *Ida: A Sword Among Lions* (New York: HarperCollins, 2008), p. 67.

8. *Living Way*, edited by the Rev. R. N. Countee of Beale Street Baptist Church and the Rev. W. A. Brinkley, billed itself "Organ of the West Tennessee Baptist Convention" in an ad on page seven of the 1885 *Sholes Memphis City Directory*.

9. Alfreda Duster, ed., *Crusade For Justice: The Autobiography of Ida B. Wells* (Chicago: University of Chicago Press, 1970), pp. 23–24.

10. Giddings, *Ida*, p. 69.

11. Wells quoted in Linda O. McMurry, *To Keep the Waters Troubled: The Life of Ida B. Wells* (New York: Oxford University Press, 1998), p. 95. Exemplary of the spotty trail of Wells's early writing, this piece first ran in the *Living Way* in September 1885, and an excerpt was reprinted in the *New York Freeman*. Only the *Freeman* excerpt survives.

12. Giddings, *Ida*, p. 81.

13. "Local Brevities," *Memphis Daily Appeal*, September 24, 1886, p. 4.

14. "A Big Blaze" *Daily Memphis Avalanche*, July 30, 1885, p. 5. "Big Blaze" *Memphis Daily Appeal*, July 30, 1885, p. 4.

15. Bob Church's trail of property deeds corresponds to city directories, which listed brothel proprietors with the capitalized prefix *Mad.* and also to fire insurance maps, which designated brothels as *F.B.* for "female boarding" and subcategorized them by race. The newspapers provided night-to-night descriptions of the characters boarding at his addresses and their activities. The national census, though providing a sample only every decade, further fleshes out red-light demographics.

16. Arthur Webb, "Memphis Icon Robert Reed Church Sr.: Saint or Sinner?" *Tri-State Defender*, April 26, 2003, pp. A-1, 3.

17. W. C. Handy to Annette Church, December 19, 1956, Roberta Church Collection, Memphis Public Library.

18. John E. Harkins, *Metropolis of the American Nile* (Woodland Hills, CA: Windsor Publications, 1982), pp. 94–103.

19. Bessie Blanden, "Our Colored Society," *Appeal-Avalanche*, April 5, 1890, n.p., clipping, Robert R. Church Collection, University of Memphis Special Collections.

20. Mary Church Terrell, *A Colored Woman in a White World* (Washington, D.C.: Ransdell, 1940), p. 57.

21. Annette Church, interview by Charles W. Crawford, January 4, 1973, Mississippi Valley Collection, University of Memphis Library.

22. McMurry, *To Keep the Waters Troubled*, p. 92.

23. Ronald A. Walter, "Achievers Led Memphis Black High Society," *Commercial Appeal*, October 5, 1995, p. CE2.

24. Willis, *Memphis Diary of Wells*, p. 59.

25. Duster, *Crusade for Justice*, p. 25.

26. Willis, *Memphis Diary of Wells*, p. 100.

27. Duster, *Crusade For Justice*, p. 25.

28. Ibid., p. 31.

Chapter 6
CONTRIBUTIONS FROM MALEFACTORS

1. "Police Court," *Public Ledger*, August 19, 1889, p. 1.

2. "Saturday's Matinee," *Public Ledger*, July 20, 1889, p. 1.

3. "Culprits Corralled," *Public Ledger*, October 3, 1886, p. 4.

4. "Getting Good," *Public Ledger*, October 21, 1886, p. 4.

5. "The Police Department," *Public Ledger*, September 1, 1888, p. 4.

6. "St. Louis Loafers," *Public Ledger*, October 29, 1886, p. 4.

7. "The 'Living Way' Wrecked," *Public Ledger*, September 9, 1886, p. 4.

8. Quoted in Paula J. Giddings, *Ida: A Sword Among Lions* (New York: Harper-Collins, 2008), p. 133.

9. Ibid., p. 150.

10. George W. Lee, *Beale Street: Where the Blues Began* (New York: Ballou, 1934), pp. 121–25.

11. Ibid., pp. 126–27.

12. "Hadden the Happy," *Public Ledger*, January 16, 1888, p. 4.

13. "The Tycoon's Tribunal," *Public Ledger*, April 7, 1888, p. 4.

14. "A Pickpocket Pinched," *Public Ledger*, April 18, 1888, p. 4.

15. "Hadden the Happy," *Public Ledger*, January 16, 1888, p. 4.

16. "David Downs Davis," *Public Ledger*, April 24, 1888, p. 4.

17. "Last Licks," *Public Ledger*, January 4, 1888, p. 4.

18. Ibid.

19. "A Blow Below the Belt," *Public Ledger*, May 3, 1888, p. 4.

20. "David Down on Dives," *Public Ledger*, May 7, 1888, p. 4.

Chapter 7
FREE SPEECH, HIGH REVELRY, AND LOW SONG

1. Respectively, *Daily Memphis Avalanche*, July 12, 1889, p. 2; and *Memphis Daily Appeal*, July 11, 1889, p. 4.

2. "The Black Cap Brigade," *Daily Memphis Avalanche*, June 25, 1889, p. 1.

3. "Grand Union Fraternity," *Memphis Daily Appeal*, June 26, 1889, p. 4.

4. "Shaw et al. to Judge Du Bose," *Public Ledger*, June 27, 1889, p. 1.

5. "The Police Court," *Public Ledger*, June 27, 1889, p. 1.

6. "Local Brevities," *Daily Memphis Avalanche*, June 26, 1889, p. 2.

7. "Letters from the People," *Public Ledger*, July 12, 1889, p. 4. The writer was C. D. Greene.

8. "White Caps vs. Black Caps," *Public Ledger*, July 15, 1889, p. 4.

9. "The Black Caps," *Public Ledger*, July 15, 1889, p. 4.

10. "Police Victims," *Public Ledger*, July 16, 1889, p. 1.

11. "The Police Court," *Public Ledger*, July 21, 1889, p. 1.

12. "The Police Court," *Public Ledger*, August 7, 1889, p. 4.

13. "Local Brevities," *Public Ledger*, August 9, 1889, p. 4.

Chapter 8
THE TRUE SPARK OF MANHOOD

1. "Now, Isn't This Nice?" *Memphis Daily Appeal*, August 16, 1890, p. 4.

2. Alfreda Duster, ed., *Crusade for Justice: The Autobiography of Ida B. Wells* (Chicago: University of Chicago Press, 1970), p. 41.

3. "Live Oak Club Banquet," *Memphis Watchman*, February 9, 1889, p. 1. This edition of the *Watchman*,, one of the few extant, is in the Robert R. Church Collection, Special Collections, University of Memphis.

4. "A Little Plain Talk," *Memphis Daily Appeal-Avalanche*, September 6, 1891, p. 4.

5. Ibid.

6. *Memphis Daily Appeal*, October 17, 1891, p. 2.

7. "Working Out a Destiny," *New York Age*, March 9, 1889, n.p.

8. "A Bloody Riot," *Memphis Daily Appeal-Avalanche*, March 6, 1892, p. 1.

9. "The Affair at the Curve," *Memphis Daily Appeal-Avalanche*, March 7, 1892, p. 4.

10. Fred L. Hutchins, *What Happened in Memphis* (Kingsport, TN: Kingsport Press, 1965; copyright David A. Less, 1979), p. 40.

11. "Negroes Lynched by a Mob," *New York Times*, March 10, 1892, p. 1.

12. "The Ring Leader's Story," *Memphis Daily Appeal-Avalanche*, March 6, 1892, p. 1.

13. "Frank Schumann Jugged," *Memphis Daily Appeal-Avalanche*, March 10, 1892, p. 4.

14. "The Triple Funeral," *Memphis Daily Appeal-Avalanche*, March 11, 1892, p. 3.

15. Duster, *Crusade for Justice*, p. 52.

16. Wells address at the Tremont Temple in Boston, Mass., February 13, 1893.

17. "To Punish the Lynchers," *New York Times*, March 11, 1892, p. 5.

18. Duster, *Crusade for Justice*, p. 58.

19. Ibid., p. 66.

20. Duster, *Crusade for Justice*, p. 66.

Chapter 9
Red, Gray, and Blue

1. "An Ex-Slave's Gift," *Commercial Appeal*, January 30, 1901, p. 3.
2. "Indictments by the Wholesale," *Memphis Daily Appeal-Avalanche*, March 4, 1893, p. 5. On the Brinkley donation, see William D. Miller, *Memphis During the Progressive Era, 1900–1917* (Memphis: Memphis State University Press, 1957), p. 112.
3. "Related to a Senator," *Commercial Appeal*, June 3, 1895, p. 5.
4. Ibid.
5. "R. L. Roane Has Kinsmen Here," *Commercial Appeal*, October 25, 1895, p. 3; "Rescued by His Relatives," *Commercial Appeal*, November 2, 1895, p. 3.
6. "Bob Church Explains," *Commercial Appeal*, October 17, 1895, p. 3.
7. The best indicators of Gayoso's growth in the late nineteenth century are the 1888 and 1898 Sanborn Fire Insurance maps of Memphis, showing just the changes described here.
8. George W. Lee, *Beale Street: Where the Blues Began* (New York: Ballou, 1934), pp. 104–5.
9. "Stories of the Streets," *Commercial Appeal*, December 22, 1895, p. 11.
10. "Stories of the Streets," *Commercial Appeal*, October 13, 1895, p. 16.
11. "A Fight in the First," *Memphis Evening Scimitar*, July 21, 1894, p. 3.
12. "An Ex-Slave's Gift," *Commercial Appeal*, January 30, 1901, p. 3.
13. Annette Church, interview by Charles W. Crawford, January 4, 1973, Mississippi Valley Collection, University of Memphis Library.
14. Robert Hooks Sr., interview by Margaret McKee and Fred Chisenhall, Everett Cook Oral History Collection, Memphis Public Library.
15. "Church-Wright," *Memphis Daily Avalanche*, January 2, 1885, n.p., Robert R. Church Family Papers, University of Memphis Special Collections.
16. *Memphis Evening Scimitar*, Souvenir Edition, October 1891.
17. "Robert R. Church," special supplement to *Memphis Evening Scimitar*, April 1899.
18. "Out of the Depths," *Colored American*, March 24, 1900, p. 14.
19. "Robert R. Church," *Colored American*, February 16, 1901, p. 9.

Chapter 10
Doctor Said It'd Kill Me, but He Didn't Say When

1. "'Coke' Center," *Commercial Appeal*, July 27, 1903, p. 7.
2. Ibid.
3. "The Use of Cocaine," *Memphis Evening Scimitar*, January 10, 1899, p. 8.
4. "The Cocaine Demon," *Commercial Appeal*, June 7, 1900, p. 6.
5. "Anti-Cocaine Bill," *Commercial Appeal*, January 31, 1901, p. 7.

6. These extracts are both from Fred L. Hutchins, interview with Ronald Walter, 1976, Memphis Public Library.

7. "The Coon Song Craze," *Memphis Evening Scimitar*, January 14, 1899, p. 4.

8. George W. Lee, *Beale Street: Where the Blues Began* (New York: Ballou, 1934), p. 76.

9. Ibid., p. 75.

10. "Williams the Winner," *Commercial Appeal*, January 7, 1898, p. 4.

11. David W. Maurer, *The Big Con: The Story of the Confidence Man* (New York: Anchor Books, 1999), p. 151.

12. Ibid., p. 25.

13. "Alibi for Angy Arata," *Commercial Appeal*, April 27, 1902, p. 4.

14. Ibid.; "Acquittals for Shanley and Honan in Election Riot Case," *Memphis Evening Scimitar*, May 19, 1904, p. 1.

15. "NOTICE. OFFICERS OF ELECTION," *Commercial Appeal*, December 3, 1903, p. 5.

16. "Clapp on Social Evils," *Appeal-Avalanche*, January 20, 1893, p. 5.

17. "Grand Jury and the Gamblers," *Commercial Appeal*, June 22, 1902, p. 3.

18. "John Persica Meets Death in Joy Ride," *Commercial Appeal*, November 11, 1913, p. 1; "Family of Persica Get Condolences of Many Sports," *Memphis Evening Scimitar*, November 11, 1913, p. 1.

19. "More Guests For the County," *Commercial Appeal*, May 28, 1895, p. 3.

20. Church's Park and Auditorium program, "Engagement Extraordinary! Black Patti Troubadors," April 15–16, 1902, Robert R. Church Collection, University of Memphis Special Collections.

21. Anna Wright Church and Robert Church to Annette Church, November 20, 1902, and "Reception at Church's Auditorium" (program), November 19, 1902, both in Robert R. Church Papers, University of Memphis Special Collections; "Vice-Governor Luke E. Wright and President Theo. Roosevelt," *Nashville Clarion*, November 29, 1902, p. 1.

22. "The New Southland," *Colored American*, June 13, 1903, p. 2.

23. "A King of Commerce," *Colored American*, October 18, 1902, p. 1.

24. "The New Southland," *Colored American*, June 13, 1903, p. 1.

Chapter 11
PURIFYING THE MORAL ATMOSPHERE

1. "Hear True Bills," *Commercial Appeal*, July 13, 1904, p. 5.

2. "Two Officers Dead From Raid; Five Men Have Surrendered," *Memphis Evening Scimitar*, July 12, 1904, p. 1.

3. "Hear True Bills," *Memphis Evening Scimitar*, July 13, 1904, p. 1.

4. "Character Study of Honan," *Memphis Evening Scimitar*, August 25, 1904, p. 1.

5. *Commercial Appeal*, August 20, 1904, p. 5.

6. "Argument of Honan Case Will Begin Today," *Commercial Appeal*, August 21, 1904, p. 5.

7. "Defendant Takes Stand," *Memphis Evening Scimitar*, August 17, 1904, p. 1.

8. Ibid., p. 4.

9. "Kinnane on the Stand," *Commercial Appeal*, August 20, 1904, p. 5.

10. "Argument of Honan Case Will Begin Today," *Commercial Appeal*, August 21, 1904, p. 5.

11. Ibid., and *Memphis Evening Scimitar*, August 18, 1904, p. 6.

12. "R. H. Elkins," *Commercial Appeal*, August 21, 1904, p. 5.

13. "Justice Davis Says the Mayor Is Most to Blame," *Memphis Evening Scimitar*, July 13, 1904, p. 1.

14. "Monuments for Honan," *Memphis Evening Scimitar*, August 22, 1904, p. 1.

15. "Trouble over Dead Negro," *Commercial Appeal*, September 22, 1905, p. 5.

16. "Police Now Want Hammitt Ashford," *Memphis News-Scimitar*, September 24, 1905, p. 7.

17. "Senator Carmack's Opinion of Some 'Reform' Leaders," *Commercial Appeal*, October 28, 1905, p. 9.

18. "Mystic Seven Hit the Pipe," *Commercial Appeal*, September 25, 1905, p. 4.

19. "Grand Jury's Work," *Commercial Appeal*, September 27, 1905, p. 5.

20. "Tick Houston Saloon Again," *Commercial Appeal*, October 15, 1905, p. 5.

21. "Chicago Crooks Arrive in Time for Election," *Commercial Appeal*, November 6, 1905, p. 4.

22. "Verdict Not Guilty," *Commercial Appeal*, November 22, 1905, p. 4.

Chapter 12
THE GIG

1. W. C. Handy, *Father of the Blues: An Autobiography* (Boston: Da Capo Press, 1991), p. 77.

2. All Thomas Pinkston quotes are from an interview by Margaret McKee and Fred Chisenhall, October 31, 1973, Everett Cook Oral History Collection, Memphis Public Library.

3. Handy, *Father of the Blues*, p. 91.

4. George W. Lee, *Beale Street: Where the Blues Began* (New York: Ballou, 1934), p. 128.

5. Frank C. Taylor with Gerald Cook, *Alberta Hunter: A Celebration in Blues* (New York: McGraw-Hill, 1988), p. 9.

6. *Moon Illustrated Weekly*, March 2, 1906, p. 13, Robert R. Church Family Papers, University of Memphis Special Collections.

7. Though Handy recalled that Turner and Bynum fronted a band together that carried both their names, advertisements for dances at Church's Park between 1906, when Handy had moved to the city, and 1908 when Handy became a bandleader, show either Turner's Orchestra or Bynum's, never both.

8. Dance card from 1906 Iroquois Club Dance, Roberta Church Collection, Memphis Public Library.

9. Beale acquisitions in *Shelby County Register of Deeds*: Arnold heirs to Robert R. Church, April 18, 1901, bk. 289, p. 261; Arnold heirs to Robert R. Church, November 13, 1903, bk. 333, p. 565; and Philomena Cuneo to Robert R. Church, March 6, 1906, bk. 369, p. 579. Gayoso acquisitions in *Shelby County Register of Deeds*: Maggie Britton to Robert R. Church, bk. 243, p. 337; Ella Ennis to Robert R. Church, June 20, 1899, bk. 267, p. 523; Massey to Church, December 17, 1902, bk. 312, p. 509; 1905, bk. 367, p. 357; and Petty to R. R. Church, August 6, 1910, bk. 492, p. 515.

10. *Memphis News-Scimitar*, June 19, 1906, p. 5.

11. "What Memphis Needs," *Commercial Appeal*, May 7, 1907, p. 6.

12. "Crump Never Elected," *Commercial Appeal*, November 2, 1907, p. 6.

13. "Why Walsh Is for Crump," *Commercial Appeal*, November 5, 1907, p. 6.

14. "The Crump Lid Lifted Again," *Commercial Appeal*, January 17, 1908, p. 5.

15. "Mr. Crump Gets Busy," *Commercial Appeal*, January 19, 1908, p. 10.

16. "No Session of Council," *Commercial Appeal*, January 21, 1908, p. 4.

17. "Gaming Charges Are Sustained," *Commercial Appeal*, January 22, 1908, p. 5.

18. Alex Simms, interview by Margaret McKee and Fred Chisenhall, November 11, 1973, the Everett Cook Oral History Collection, Memphis Public Library.

19. Jelly Roll Morton, *The Complete Library of Congress Recordings*, disc 4, tracks 10, 11, and 12.

Chapter 13
WE GONNA BARRELHOUSE ANYHOW

1. J. J. Williams, "Public Sentiment Recoils Against Crump," *Commercial Appeal*, October 31, 1909, p. 8.

2. W. C. Handy to Annette Church, December 19, 1956.

3. W. C. Handy, *Father of the Blues: An Autobiography* (Boston: Da Capo Press, 1991), p. 96.

4. G. P. Hamilton, *The Bright Side of Memphis* (Memphis: G.P. Hamilton, 1908), p. 95.

5. Lt. George W. Lee, interview by Jack Hurley, February 6, 1967, University of Memphis Special Collections.

6. Handy, *Father of the Blues*, p. 98.

7. Ibid., p. 93.

8. Ibid., p. 100.

9. Ibid., p. 99.

10. "Official Ballot Was Circulated, Officers Claim," *Memphis News-Scimitar*, November 4, 1909, p. 1.

11. Poston Cox, interview by Charles Crawford, April 7, 1986, University of Memphis Special Collections.

12. Dr. Daniel H. Williams to R. R. Church, December 10, 1910, Robert R. Church Family Papers, University of Memphis Special Collections.

13. Mary Church Terrell, "What It Means to Be Colored in the Capital of the U.S.," speech to United Women's Club, Washington D.C., October 10, 1906.

14. Handy, *Father of the Blues*, p. 126.

Chapter 14
Like a Stone Cast into the Sea

1. Mary Church Terrell to S. M. Neely, July 18, 1913, Robert R. Church Family Papers, University of Memphis Special Collections.

2. Letter dated February 24, 1890, Robert R. Church Family Papers, box 1, folder 26, University of Memphis Special Collections.

3. "Memphis . . . Millionaire," *Chicago Defender*, September 7, 1912, p. 8.

4. "Robert R. Church's Will Broken," *Chicago Defender*, December 6, 1913, p. 1.

5. Robert R. Church obituary, *Commercial Appeal*, August 30, 1912, p. 5.

6. "From Slave to Millionaire, Is Story of Church," *Memphis News-Scimitar*, August 30, 1912, p. 1.

7. Booker T. Washington to Robert R. Church Jr., September 9, 1912, Robert R. Church Family Papers, University of Memphis Special Collections.

8. William Christopher Handy, interview by Capt. Ed Langford and Paul Flowers, December 1, 1954, at the 30 Club, Memphis, Everett R. Cook Oral History Collection, box 24, cassette 1, Memphis Public Library.

9. "Agent Joe Turney, of the penitentiary, departed last Sunday night for Nashville." *Memphis Daily Appeal*, July 14, 1885, p. 4. "Agent Joe Turney carried the following convicts to the penitentiary this morning." *Public Ledger*, July 31, 1889, p. 2.

10. Scholars and folk musicians, independently of one another, reached the same conclusion about the Joe Turney blues, better known by the title "Joe Turner." In the introduction to *Blues: An Anthology*, published in 1926, Abbe Niles wrote, "I have been referring frequently to *Joe Turner*, and it is quite likely that this folk song was the grandfather of all blues. All early blues may have been merely conscientious renditions of *Joe Turner*, to the best of the singers' memories. . . . The framework and harmonic scheme of *Joe Turner* were familiar everywhere." The familiar framework and harmonic scheme are closely related to the ubiquitous "Make Me a Pallet on Your Floor," one of Jelly Roll Morton's nominees for real first blues. Lucius Smith, a banjo player born in 1885 in rural northern Mississippi, said, "All these blues come from 'Joe Turner' more or less." Carl Sandburg, in *The American Songbook*, published in 1927, quoted the song's verses and noted, "W. C. Handy refers to Joe Turner as a granddaddy of the blues."

Black musicians in far-flung, isolated locations around the South heard the Joe Turner blues before sheet music, recordings, or any other musical mass media delivered it. The folklorist Howard Odum transcribed one version of the song, containing the key image of Turney's forty links of chain, in an article published in 1911, the year before Handy published "Memphis Blues." Fiddler Henry "Son" Sims, born south of Memphis in the Mississippi Delta in 1890, recorded a version for folklorist Alan Lomax in 1942. Brothers Bob and Miles Pratcher, born in 1893 and 1895, lived in Panola County, Mississippi, not far south of Memphis. They knew the song, and Bob Pratcher played fiddle, like *Jim* Turner. They would record the song for Lomax in 1959. Bill Broonzy, born in 1903, learned the song from his uncle in Arkansas. The folklorist Dorothy Scarborough transcribed a version, published in a 1925 article without identifying her source or the location, containing the lines:

> *They tell me Joe Turner's come to town*
> *He's brought along one thousand links of chain*
> *He's going to have one nigger for each link.*

The lyrics had not been recorded in time to influence any of these instances, and aside from publication in Odum's and Scarborough's academic articles and Niles's and Sandburg's excerpts, they hadn't been printed. The only thing absent from the case for Joe Turner Blues as the original is any acknowledgment of the man who disseminated the song.

11. City of Memphis Burial Permit 21302. Turner was interred at Zion Cemetery.

12. Silas Bent, "Prohibition in the City of Memphis," *Mixer and Server* 19, no. 11 (October 1, 1910), p. 28.

13. "One Policeman Dropped," *Commercial Appeal*, July 6, 1913, p. 4.

14. "Woman Sleuth to Get on Trail of Street 'Mashers'," *Memphis News-Scimitar*, July 7, 1913, p. 1.

15. "Charge Pair in Intimidating Witnesses," *Memphis News-Scimitar*, July 17, 1913, p. 1.

16. E. H. Crump to Hon. K. D. McKellar, July 26, 1913, E. H. Crump Papers, Memphis Public Library.

17. *Shelby County Register of Deeds*, bk. 1489, p. 337. The original document of this sale, a warranty deed recorded in book 525 on p. 599, does not exist, but it is referred to in a 1935 indenture, the aforementioned 1489-337, that shows Crump and Rice furnished the purchase money for the property, which was to be held in trust only in Rice's name but for both Rice and Crump, their heirs and assigns.

18. "After Idle Negroes," *Commercial Appeal*, November 9, 1913, p. 6.

19. E. H. Crump to R. A. Utley, November 18, 1913, E. H. Crump Papers, Memphis Public Library.

20. "John Persica Meets Death in Joy Ride," *Commercial Appeal*, November 11, 1913, p. 1.

21. Handy, *Father of the Blues*, pp. 110 and 126. The Blanks sisters properly spelled their names Arsceola and Birleanna.

22. David Robertson, *W. C. Handy: The Life and Times of the Man Who Made the Blues* (New York: Alfred A. Knopf, 2009), pp. 131–36.

23. Handy, *Father of the Blues*, pp. 107–9.

24. "Negroes Taught to Write 'Riechman,'" *Commercial Appeal*, August 2, 1914, p. 10.

25. Blair T. Hunt, interview by Margaret McKee and Fred Chisenhall, February 6, 1973, Everett Cook Oral History Collection, Memphis Public Library.

Chapter 15
I'D RATHER BE THERE THAN ANY PLACE I KNOW

1. "Slayer of Honan Released on Bond," *Commercial Appeal*, January 12, 1915, p. 1.

2. See Handy's notes to "At the Monarch" in *Father of the Blues*, p. 152. "The following style of piano playing, by Benny French and Sonny Butts at the Monarch on Beale Street, was my source of inspiration for . . . *Beale Street Blues*, *Yellow Dog Blues*, and a few others."

3. *Freeman*, April 24, 1915, p. 5. With a tip of the cap to Lynn Abbott and Doug Seroff.

4. William D. Miller, *Memphis During the Progressive Era: 1900–1917* (Memphis: Memphis State University Press, 1957), p. 173–76.

5. "Some Ouster Charges in Substance," *Commercial Appeal*, February 23, 1916, p. 1.

6. "Up Jumps Mr. Crump; Off Flies the Lid," *Commercial Appeal*, February 13, 1916, p. 4.

7. "R. R. Church to Be Tennessee's Leader," *Chicago Defender* (Big Weekend Edition), February 12, 1916, p. 7.

8. From two newspaper clippings in the Robert R. Church Family Papers, University of Memphis Special Collections. One is hand-dated August 11, 1916, while the other is datelined August 9. No publication name or page numbers are available.

9. "Memphis Negroes Go to Voting Schools," *Commercial Appeal*, October 21, 1916, p. 6.

10. "Down in Tennessee," *Chicago Defender* (Big Weekend Edition). October 14, 1916, p. 3.

11. All Brewster quotes from an interview by Charles Crawford, July 6, 1983, University of Memphis Special Collections.

12. William Grant Still, "Horizons Unlimited" (1957), in Leo Treitler and W. Oliver Strunk, eds., *Source Readings in Music History* (New York: W. W. Norton, 1998), p. 1421.

13. W. C. Handy, *Father of the Blues: An Autobiography* (Boston: Da Capo Press, 1991), p. xi. Years later Handy's friend George W. Lee hired Henry "Son" Wright for work in the insurance business and helped publicize Wright's forgotten role as the inspiration for the blues beat. "Honor Founder of Blues Beat," *Tri-State Defender*. July 2, 1955, p. 1; "Henry Wright to be Honored: 'Grandfather of the Blues,'" *Commercial Appeal*, June 26, 1955, sec. 3, p. 12.

14. William Grant Still, "Horizons Unlimited," p. 1421.

15. Handy, *Father of the Blues*, p. 179.

16. "Lincoln League," article datelined July 2, 1917, from unknown publication, reproduction from the Library of Congress in the Robert R. Church Family Papers, University of Memphis Special Collections.

17. "Fines Bartender; Owner Goes Free," *Commercial Appeal*, July 14, 1917, p. 4.

18. "Margerum Held for Grand Jury Action," *Commercial Appeal*, July 24, 1917, p. 4.

19. "City's Underworld Wiped Out for Good," *Commercial Appeal*, July 15, 1917, p. 1.

20. Handy, *Father of the Blues*, p. 178.

Chapter 16
ALL THE PRETTY GIRLS LIVED GOOD

1. Elizabeth Gritter, *Black Politics in the Age of Jim Crow: Memphis, Tennessee, 1865 to 1954*, Ph.D. dissertation, University of North Carolina, 2010, p. 60.

2. All Bates quotes are from an interview by Charles Crawford, February 15, 1977, University of Memphis Special Collections.

3. "National Affairs, Tennessee: Crimp in Crump," *Time*, November 1, 1937, p. 22.

4. Poston Cox, interview by Charles Crawford, April 7, 1986, University of Memphis Special Collections.

5. Ibid.

6. Frances Rice, interview by Charles Crawford, September 13 and 21, 1989, University of Memphis Special Collections.

7. "No Session of Council," *Commercial Appeal*, January 21, 1908, p. 4.

8. Poston Cox, Crawford interview.

9. "Senator Kenneth McKellar," *Commercial Appeal*, December 30, 1938, p. 8.

10. House Journal of the Seventy-first General Assembly of the State of Tennessee, January 2, 1939, p. 23.

11. George W. Lee oral history, April 17, 1966, University of Memphis Special Collections, Mississippi Valley Collection, Politics Project.

12. David Tucker, *Lieutenant Lee of Beale Street* (Vanderbilt University Press, 1971), pp. 100–1.

13. Bates explained the tax forgiveness–political donor fund-raising scheme. His knowledge of the Crump machine's inner workings dated back to at least 1927, when his father Bert became Rice's right-hand man. Before 1927, Bert Bates worked with Rice in the local branch of the state revenue office. It's my own conclusion, based on Rice and Crump both being prominent county finance officials, that the practice began during this time.

14. Thomas Pinkston, interview by Margaret McKee and Fred Chisenhall, October 31, 1973, Everett Cook Oral History Collection, Memphis Public Library.

15. "Whisky and Immoral Women Are Plentiful," *Commercial Appeal*, July 14, 1918, p. 14.

16. Frank Liberto, interview by Margaret McKee and Fred Chisenhall, September 5, 1973, Everett Cook Oral History Collection, Memphis Public Library.

17. Frank C. Taylor with Gerald Cook, *Alberta Hunter: A Celebration in Blues* (New York: McGraw-Hill, 1988), p. 11.

18. Handy owned the copyright to but did not compose "A Good Man Is Hard to Find."

19. "I stand indebted to your brother for a piece of advice which I followed, it looks simple but I was copyrighting my compositions under the name of Pace and Handy Music Co., and he told me to copyright my composition in my name which I did with St. Louis Blues and it paid off." W. C. Handy to Annette Church, December 19, 1956, Memphis Public Library.

20. *Survey of Commercialized Prostitution Conditions in Memphis, Tennessee, undertaken by the American Social Hygiene Association, November 1938*, Memphis Public Library.

21. "Masked Man Kills Woman of Underworld," *Commercial Appeal*, October 9, 1916, p. 10.

22. Joseph Blotner, *Faulkner: A Biography* (Jackson: University Press of Mississippi, 2005), pp. 100–1. Blotner places these visits, roughly, between fall 1920 and fall 1921.

Chapter 17
IN A CLASS BY HIMSELF

1. *Crisis* 12, no. 6 (April 1919), p. 285.

2. Walter Adkins, *Beale Street Goes to the Polls*, master's thesis, Ohio State University, 1935, pp. 80, 88.

3. Herbert Brewster, interview by Charles Crawford, July 6, 1983, University of Memphis Special Collections.

4. *Official Proceedings of the Seventeenth Republican National Convention* (New York: Tenny Press, 1920), p. 44.

5. George W. Lee, *Beale Street: Where the Blues Began* (New York: Ballou, 1934), p. 118.

6. Elizabeth Gritter, *Black Politics in the Age of Jim Crow, Memphis, Tennessee, 1865 to 1954*, Ph.D. dissertation, University of North Carolina, 2010, p. 91.

7. Associated Negro Press, "Negro Women Allowed to Vote in Only One Ward in Atlanta," *Western World Reporter*, November 12, 1920, p. 2.

8. *Wilmington Advocate*, March 26, 1921, via Annette E. Church and Roberta Church, *The Robert R. Churches of Memphis* (Memphis: A. E. Church, 1974), p. 111.

9. Will Hays to Warren G. Harding, April 27, 1921, Roberta Church Collection, box 6, folder 9, Memphis Public Library.

10. R.R. Church to Lt. George W. Lee, May 12, 1921, Lt. George W. Lee Collection, Memphis Public Library.

Chapter 18
THE FROLIC

1. Frank Liberto, interview by Margaret McKee and Fred Chisenhall, September 5, 1973, Everett Cook Oral History Collection, Memphis Public Library.
2. Alex Simms, interview by Margaret McKee and Fred Chisenhall, November 11, 1973, Everett Cook Oral History Collection, Memphis Public Library.
3. "Police Clamp Lid on Policy Houses," *Commercial Appeal*, March 3, 1935, p. 2.
4. Liberto interview.
5. Thomas Pinkston, interview by Margaret McKee and Fred Chisenhall, October 31, 1973, Everett Cook Oral History Collection, Memphis Public Library.
6. Leo Schwab, interview by Margaret McKee and Fred Chisenhall, October 11, 1973, Everett Cook Oral History Collection, Memphis Public Library.
7. "Police Clamp Lid on Policy Houses," *Commercial Appeal*, March 3, 1935, p. 2.
8. "In City Court," *Commercial Appeal*, February 25, 1927, p. 14.
9. Bryan was "kind of a stoolie for Mr. Crump," recalled Guy Bates in an interview with Charles Crawford, February 15, 1977, University of Memphis Special Collections. Bryan was also Bob Church's attorney in 1927: "Paine Again Charges Deal with Negroes," *Commercial Appeal*, November 3, 1928, p. 1.
10. Laura Dukes, interview by Margaret McKee and Fred Chisenhall, September 6, 1973, Everett Cook Oral History Collection, Memphis Public Library.
11. Samuel Charters, *The Country Blues* (Boston: Da Capo Press, 1975), p. 106; Bengt Olsson, *Memphis Blues and Jug Bands* (London: Studio Vista, 1970).
12. Paul Oliver, *Conversation with the Blues* (Cambridge, MA: Cambridge University Press, 1997), pp. 96–97.
13. Richard Wright, *Black Boy (American Hunger)* (New York: Library of America, 1991), p. 201.

Chapter 19
THE UNHOLY COMBINATION

1. "U.S. Pay-Off Probe Has Died A-Borning," *Commercial Appeal*, July 1, 1927, p. 15.
2. Richard Wright, *Black Boy (American Hunger)* (New York: Library of America, 1991), p. 220.
3. "The Ludicrous Attempt to Create a Jim Crow Republican Party," *Commercial Appeal*, October 6, 1928, p. 6.
4. Lester Lynom, interview by Charles Crawford, July 6, 1983, University of Memphis Special Collections.

5. Herbert Brewster, interview by Charles Crawford, July 6, 1983, University of Memphis Special Collections.

6. Guy Bates, interview by Charles Crawford, February 15, 1977, University of Memphis Special Collections.

7. "Bossism to Remain Issue, Says Mayor," *Commercial Appeal*, November 1, 1927, p. 11.

8. "Paine Again Charges Deal with Negroes," *Commercial Appeal*, November 3, 1927, p. 1.

9. "Great Assortment of Radio Entertainment," *Commercial Appeal*, November 8, 1927, p. 15.

10. Lunceford gossip from "Who's Who in Memphis, edited by 'The Tattler,'" *Memphis Triangle*, August 13, 1927, n.p., clipping, Robert R. Church Family Papers, University of Memphis Special Collections.

11. "Paine Cites Record to Close Campaign," *Commercial Appeal*, November 10, 1927, p. 4.

12. Guy Bates, interview by Charles Crawford, February 15, 1977, University of Memphis Special Collections.

13. Ernest Vaccaro, "Crump and His 'Boys' Take Over the Town," *Commercial Appeal*, November 11, 1927, pp. 1, 4.

14. Walter Adkins, *Beale Street Goes to the Polls*, master's thesis, Ohio State University, 1935, p. 42.

15. Lt. George W. Lee to Watkins Overton, November 2, 1931, Overton Papers, box 7, folder 31, Memphis Public Library.

16. Elizabeth Gritter, *Black Politics in the Age of Jim Crow, Memphis, Tennessee, 1865 to 1954*, Ph.D. dissertation, University of North Carolina, 2010, p. 135.

Chapter 20
SNITCHIN' GAMBLER BLUES

1. Information about the secret black police powers comes from Dr. J. B. Martin's statement at the U.S. Department of Justice, March 12, 1941, National Archives, 144-72-1.

2. Clark was widely noted for his use of Negro informants, and Red Lawrence would become infamous as a police informant. Members of Red Lawrence's family called the working relationship of the two men a partnership, referring to Clark as Red Lawrence's partner.

3. "Veteran Sleuth 'Bimbo' Clark Is Dead," *Memphis Press-Scimitar*, August 19, 1950, p. 1.

4. "'Bimbo' Clark and Stool Pigeons," *Memphis World*. August 29, 1950, p. 6.

5. Charles Farley, *Soul of the Man: Bobby "Blue" Bland* (Jackson: University Press of Mississippi, 2011), p. 13.

6. "Shot the Woman," *Commercial Appeal*, October 24, 1905, p. 10.

7. "Al Capone's Brother Told to Leave Town," *Evening Appeal*, February 6, 1928, p. 16.

8. Thomas Pinkston, interview by Margaret McKee and Fred Chisenhall, October 31, 1973, Everett Cook Oral History Collection, Memphis Public Library.

9. "'Red Lawrence' Out on Parole," *Memphis Press-Scimitar*, February 3, 1949.

10. Ibid.

11. "Negro Killed in Row," *Memphis Press-Scimitar*, May 12, 1928, p. 7.

12. These circumstances are best illustrated in the story surrounding the death of Crump enforcer John Phillips. "Plea of Not Guilty Filed by Berryman," *Commercial Appeal*, May 31, 1940, p. 4. Philips was also named in a 1933 anonymous threat letter to Frank Rice that noted the beating of an anti-Crump political organizer.

13. R. R. Church, "Why I Am for Hoover," *Chicago Defender* (national edition), November 3, 1928, p. 3. Written October 26, 1928, according to the signature line.

14. Coolidge quoted in *New York Times*, July 28, 1920, p. 6.

15. Donald J. Lisio, *Hoover, Blacks and Lily-Whites* (Chapel Hill: University of North Carolina Press, 1985), p. 116.

16. Church quoted in *Defender*, September 15, 1928, via Annette E. Church and Roberta Church, *The Robert R. Churches of Memphis* (Memphis: A. E. Church, 1974), p. 135.

17. Kelly Miller, "Negro Weeklies Independent in Politics at Last," *Afro-American*, October 22, 1932, p. 6.

18. Church, "Why I Am for Hoover."

19. *Time*, February 18, 1929, quoted in Church and Church, *Robert R. Churches Of Memphis*, p. 135.

20. R. R. Church to Herbert Hoover, November 6, 1929, University of Memphis Special Collections.

Chapter 21
GOD'S CHILLUN

1. Nat D. Williams, "Down on Beale," *Memphis World*, May 31, 1932, p. 8.

2. Nat D. Williams, "Down on Beale," *Memphis World*, September 16, 1932, p. 6.

3. Nat D. Williams, "Down on Beale," *Memphis World*, May 17, 1932, p. 8.

4. "Beale Street Mourns As 'Mr. Jim' Mulcahy Is Summoned," *Atlanta Daily World*, September 11, 1940, p. 6.

5. Rev. Joseph Burkley, interview by Charles Crawford, March 17, 1979, University of Memphis Special Collections.

6. "White Register Cripple, Blind, and Mentally Defective to Offset Vote," *Norfolk Journal and Guide*, September 5, 1931, p. A-14.

7. "Beale Street Mourns As 'Mr. Jim' Mulcahy Is Summoned," *Atlanta Daily World*, September 11, 1940, p. 6.

8. Fannie Henderson, deposition to an unknown interviewer, Robert R. Church Family Papers, University of Memphis Special Collections.

9. "Negro Killed by Six Officers," *Memphis Press-Scimitar*, February 25, 1933, p. 10.

10. Franklin D. Roosevelt to E. H. Crump, March 22, 1932, quoted in G. Wayne Dowdy, *Mayor Crump Don't Like It* (Jackson: University Press of Mississippi, 2006).

11. E. H. Crump to Frank Rice, April 10, 1933, E. H. Crump Papers, series 3, box 92, folder 7, Memphis Public Library.

Chapter 22
WITHIN THE GATES OF MEMPHIS

1. Walter Stewart, "Memphis After Midnight: Beale Street," *Memphis Press-Scimitar*, March 2, 1935, p. 5.

2. Virgil Fulling, "Amateur Night on Beale Street," *Scribner's*, May 1937, pp. 58–60.

3. Stewart, "Memphis After Midnight: Beale Street."

4. George W. Lee, *Beale Street: Where the Blues Began* (New York: Ballou, 1934), p. 242.

5. Clifton Fadiman, *New Yorker*, July 1934, pp. 61–62.

6. Owen P. White, "Sinners in Dixie," *Collier's*, January 26, 1935, p. 43.

7. Ibid., p. 44.

8. "Policy Racket Dead; Lid to Be Permanent," *Commercial Appeal*, March 4, 1935, p. 1.

Chapter 23
A BOYLE FESTERS

1. Van Pritchartt Jr., "Today Ends Boyle's 43 Yrs. In Politics," *Memphis Press-Scimitar*, December 30, 1955. The Memphis historian G. Wayne Dowdy covered the Nye investigation in *Mayor Crump Don't Like It: Machine Politics in Memphis* (Jackson: University Press of Mississippi, 2006), pp. 62–63.

2. Dan Burley, "Dan Burley, Roving 'Back Door Man,' Misses Beale Street Blues," *Chicago Defender* (national edition), February 20, 1937, p. 5.

3. "Red Warren Is Arraigned on Killing Charge," *Chicago Defender* (national edition), February 20, 1937, p. 18.

4. "Charged with Murder," *Memphis Press-Scimitar*, February 11, 1937, p. 4.

5. "Tennessee: City & County Crowd," *Time*, August 17, 1936, p. 14.

6. James H. Purdy Jr., "$100,000 Campaign Fund Sought by Bob Church," *Chicago Defender* (national edition), March 2, 1940, p. 11. To wit: "Mr. Church . . . has been an influential factor in Indiana, Ohio, and Pennsylvania, where Republicans have made a substantial gain in both state and senatorial elections."

7. Roger Biles, *Memphis: In the Great Depression* (Knoxville: University of Tennessee Press, 1986), p. 90.

8. "Tennessee State News," *Chicago Defender* (national edition), October 5, 1935, p. 20.

9. Biles, *Memphis: In the Depression*, pp. 92–93.

10. Ibid., p. 122.

11. Clifford Davis to Watkins Overton, May 2, 1936, in Watkins Overton Papers, Memphis Public Library.

12. "Negro Mail Carrier Slain by Detective," *Commercial Appeal*, January 4, 1938, p. 11; "Officer Slays Negro Postman," *Memphis Press-Scimitar*, January 4, 1938, p. 1.

13. "Plan Protest Over Shooting," *Memphis Press-Scimitar*, January 12, 1938, p. 14.

14. Ralph J. Bunche, *The Political Status of the Negro in the Age of F.D.R.* (Chicago: University of Chicago Press, 1973), p. 499. Bunche sent a research assistant to conduct fieldwork in Memphis, uncovering this interesting fact, otherwise only hinted at in the press, as well as several other important insights. The assistant reportedly ran afoul of the Crump forces and got a sunset order, which he obeyed.

15. "Bob Church Property Will Be Auctioned," *Commercial Appeal*, February 14, 1939, p. 11.

16. All Roberta Church quotes are from Roberta Church, interview by Charles Crawford, January 4 and July 10, 1973, University of Memphis Special Collections.

17. Guy Bates, interview by Charles Crawford, February 15, 1977, University of Memphis Special Collections.

18. Lee was acknowledged within the Crump organization as early as 1935 as an informant from the Church political camp. Picard to Crump, February 12, 1935, E. H. Crump Papers, Memphis Public Library.

Chapter 24
THIS IS A WHITE MAN'S COUNTRY

1. Clark Porteous, "Underworld Bitter; Packs Up to Leave," *Memphis Press-Scimitar*, April 27, 1940, p. 2.

2. Clark Porteous, "Memphis Has Smashed Red Lights Before, But Not Like Boyle Does It," *Memphis Press-Scimitar*, May 7, 1940, p. 2.

3. Dr. J. B. Martin, interview at Department of Justice, Washington D.C., March 12, 1941, Robert R. Church Family Papers, box 7, folder 1, pp. 15–16, University of Memphis Special Collections.

4. Dr. J. B. Martin, interview at Department of Justice, Washington D.C., March 12, 1941, Robert R. Church Family Papers, box 7, folder 1, University of Memphis Special Collections.

5. E. H. Crump Papers, series 4, box 179, folder "Negroes Election Data 1940," 2/2, Memphis Public Library.

6. "Memphis Leaders Ask Officials to Probe Source of Letter Threats," *Chicago Defender* (national edition), November 2, 1940, p. 1.

7. "Boyle Keeps His Eyes on 19 Negroes" *Memphis Press-Scimitar*, December 5, 1940, p. 10.

8. "Church Park and Church Auditorium are no More," *Memphis Press-Scimitar*, November 16, 1940, clipping, Memphis Room, "Beale Avenue Park" file, Memphis Public Library.

9. *Nashville Globe*, December 20, 1940, excerpted in Department of Justice Memorandum stamped March 26, 1941, National Archives, 144-72-1.

10. Edgar McWilliams to Franklin D. Roosevelt, December 14, 1940, National Archives, 144-72-1.

11. Howard Lee to Robert Jackson, January 12, 1941. Thurgood Marshall to Jackson, January 20, 1941, references a December 27, 1940, telegram. Both are in National Archives, 144-72-1.

12. Edward E. Strong to Franklin D. Roosevelt, December 28, 1940; Mabel Houk King to Roosevelt, January 7, 1940, both in National Archives, 144-72-1.

13. Strong to Roosevelt, National Archives, 144-72-1.

14. Wendell Berge to Claude Barnett, January 30, 1941, National Archives, 144-72-1.

15. Marshall to Jackson, National Archives, 144-72-1.

16. Wendell Berge to Thurgood Marshall, February 4, 1941, National Archives, 144-72-1.

17. Memorandum for Mr. Wendell Berge (prepared by Henry Schweinhaut), February 12, 1941, National Archives, 144-72-1.

18. To be exact, Section 51, Title 18 and Section 52, Title 18.

19. Martin interview.

20. Lt. George W. Lee, interview by Jack Hurley, April 17, 1966, University of Memphis Special Collections: Lee interview by David Tucker, October 6, 1966, University of Memphis Special Collections; and David Tucker, *Lieutenant Lee of Beale Street* (Vanderbilt University Press, 1971), pp. 127–28.

21. "Bob Church, Political Leader, Dies Here," *Commercial Appeal*, April 18, 1952, p. 1.

22. Roberta Church, interview by Charles Crawford, January 4 and July 10, 1973, University of Memphis Special Collections.

23. "Fog Nozzle Spray Shows Speed," *Commercial Appeal*, February 27, 1953, p. 1.

24. L. Raymond Lynom, interview by Charles Crawford, July 6, 1983, University of Memphis Special Collections.

INDEX

Page numbers beginning with 315 refer to endnotes.